adStreet Publishing Group, LLC.
age, Minnesota, USA
adstreetpublishing.com

e Greatest Hymns Devotional

1424567058
424567065 (eBook)

otional entries composed by Sara Perry.

ting and design by Garborg Design Works | garborgdesign.com
l services by Michelle Winger | literallyprecise.com and Sarah Eral.

Printed in China.

23 24 25 26 27 28 29 7 6 5 4 3 2 1

I0817579

365 DAILY DEVOTIONS

The Greatest Hymn

DEVOTIO

Br
Sa
Br

©

97
97

De

All
any
me
quo
cop

Scri
Cop
righ
trad
quo
2004
Caro
the E
publ
quota
Bible
trade
Amer
rights
Copy
quota
Nelso
The P
Used

Typese
Editor

Let the word of Christ dwell in you richly in all wisdom, teaching and admonishing one another in psalms and hymns and spiritual songs, singing with grace in your hearts to the Lord.

Colossians 3:16 NKJV

Introduction

Traditional hymns are compelling expositions that proclaim biblical truths in profound ways. Poetic verse and evocative music beautifully intertwine, connecting our emotions with the heart of our glorious Creator. Hope soars in moments of doubt, fear, and tragedy; gratitude and joy erupt in a chorus of praise.

Hymns connect us to the saints of old who struggled with and celebrated their faith, encouraging unity among the body of Christ in a way that crosses into eternity.

The Greatest Hymns is a daily devotional that reflects on one hymn each day, providing an interesting fact, thoughtful meditation, relevant Scripture, and inspiring prayer provoked by that hymn. As you spend time contemplating each entry, be reminded of God's faithfulness, goodness, and grace. His very character is apparent in the powerful rhetoric that has stood the test of time.

January

Amazing grace, how sweet the sound
That saved a wretch like me.
I once was lost but now am found
Was blind but now I see.

At the Portal

"Be strong and of good courage, do not fear nor be afraid of them; for the LORD your God, He is the One who goes with you. He will not leave you nor forsake you."

DEUTERONOMY 31:6 NKJV

Standing at the portal
Of the opening year,
Words of comfort meet us,
Hushing every fear;
Spoken through the silence
By our Father's voice,
Tender, strong and faithful,
Making us rejoice.

He will never fail us,
He will not forsake;
His eternal cov'nant
He will never break.
Resting on his promise,
What have we to fear?
God is all-sufficient
For the coming year.

As you stand on the precipice of this New Year, perhaps you feel anxiety or questions. Maybe you feel excitement and fresh resolve. Whatever emotions you experience today, there is comfort, peace, and hope in the Spirit of God who dwells with you. God is with you every step of the path that lies ahead. He is with you now.

Frances Havergal (1836-1879), the creator of today's hymn, was the daughter of a reverend and the author of many hymns. After committing her life to Christ, she noted that everything seemed brighter. The Lord is a light, and all who walk in him are in his light. May you see the brightness of hope as you draw near to Christ.

Lord Jesus, thank you for the gift of a new year. As I look to you, I give you my worries and cares. Flood every fear with the power of your perfect love.

Great Is Thy Faithfulness

Because of the LORD's great love we are not consumed,
for his compassions never fail.
They are new every morning;
great is your faithfulness.
LAMENTATIONS 3:22-23 NIV

Great is thy faithfulness, O God my Father,
There is no shadow of turning with thee.
Thou changest not, thy compassions,
they fail not;
As thou hast been, thou forever wilt be.

Great is thy faithfulness!
Great is thy faithfulness!
Morning by morning new mercies I see;
All I have needed thy hand hath provided.
Great is thy faithfulness, Lord, unto me!

Summer and winter and springtime and harvest,
Sun, moon, and stars in their courses above
Join with all nature in manifold witness
To thy great faithfulness, mercy, and love.

Pardon for sin and a peace that endureth,
Thine own dear presence to cheer and to
guide,
Strength for today and bright hope for
tomorrow,
Blessings all mine, with ten thousand beside!

Thomas Chisholm (1866-1960) wrote this text as a poem and sent it to his musician friend, William Runyan, who composed the music. It was used often at Moody Bible Institute in chapels. Most of us know it from well-known singers and choirs like those at Billy Graham crusades. Its widespread use makes it familiar to many.

As you reflect on the great faithfulness of God your Father, may you see the new mercies he offers you today. There is grace in his presence, and provision for every need is in his hand.

Faithful One, thank you for the fresh mercies I find each new morning. You are faithful through every season and every circumstance.

God Our Help

"My God, do not take me in the middle of my life!
Your years continue through all generations.
But you are the same,
and your years will never end."

Psalm 102:24, 27 CSB

O God, our help in ages past,
Our hope for years to come,
Our shelter from the stormy blast,
And our eternal home:

Under the shadow of your throne
Your saints have dwelt secure;
Sufficient is your arm alone,
And our defense is sure.

Before the hills in order stood,
Or earth received its frame,
From everlasting you are God,
To endless years the same.

A thousand ages in your sight
Are like an evening gone,
Short as the watch that ends the night
Before the rising sun.

Isaac Watts (1674-1748) wrote this hymn when the future leadership of England was uncertain. There was a lot of fear in the protestant community because persecution could be reinstated based on who the next monarch would be. Not knowing what was to come, Watts wrote a hymn of grounding courage and peace.

If you are facing uncertainty, you can find peace and comfort in the faithfulness of your God. He is the same from age to age; he is always dependable and triumphant. He is your great hope, so put your hope in him.

O God, you have helped those who call on you throughout history, and I believe you will help me today. I stand on the foundation of your faithfulness.

Like a Shepherd

The LORD is my shepherd;
I shall not want.
PSALM 23:1 ESV

Savior, like a shepherd lead us,
Much we need thy tender care;
In thy pleasant pastures feed us,
For our use thy folds prepare:
Blessed Jesus, blessed Jesus,
Thou hast bought us, thine we are;
Blessed Jesus, blessed Jesus,
Thou hast bought us, thine we are.

We are thine, do thou befriend us,
Be the guardian of our way;
Keep thy flock, from sin defend us,
Seek us when we go astray:
Blessed Jesus, blessed Jesus,
Hear, O hear us when we pray;
Blessed Jesus, blessed Jesus,
Hear, O hear us when we pray.

This hymn was originally written for children in 1836. It reads as a prayer to the Good Shepherd of our souls. Though this style of worship song is popular in our day, it was not common for the time. Though not as heavy on theological suggestion, it is poetic and clear and perfect a child's understanding. Knowing Christ welcomes the childlike, this text is encouraging to all of us.

Whether you delight in the heft of theological hymns or in the simplicity of a sung prayer, may you draw near to the Lord as this hymn encourages. Use it as a springboard for connecting to Christ through prayer today. He loves you, and he leads you as a loyal shepherd leads his flock.

Shepherd of my soul, I look to you today. I find comfort in your leadership and your presence. Draw near even as I draw near to you.

Sweeter

I am convinced that neither death, nor life, nor angels,
nor principalities, nor things present, nor things to come...
nor any other created thing will be able to separate us
from the love of God that is in Christ Jesus our Lord.

ROMANS 8:38-39 NASB

Of Jesus' love that sought me
When I was lost in sin,
Of wondrous grace that brought me
Back to his fold again,
Of heights and depths of mercy
Far deeper than the sea
And higher than the heavens,
My theme shall ever be.

Sweeter as the years go by,
Sweeter as the years go by;
Richer, fuller, deeper,
Jesus' love is sweeter,
Sweeter as the years go by.

As we follow the Lord, our relationship with him grows deeper as we learn to trust him more. We will find his love meets us in the depths of our despair as well as in the joy of our celebration.

Lelia Morris (1862-1929) was known to write hymns as she did her housework. In the mundane tasks of every day life, she poured out her heart to the Lord in song. She went blind at an early age, but it didn't stop her from writing hymns. She found the sweetness of knowing Jesus only grew with time. Reflect on how your heart has grown in love toward your Savior and offer him praise as you go about your day.

Savior, thank you for the love you freely offer me every moment of every day. My heart grows in loving response every time I think of you.

Be Thou My Vision

Teach me your ways, O Lord,
that I may live according to your truth!
Grant me purity of heart,
so that I may honor you.

Psalm 86:11 NLT

Be thou my vision, O Lord of my heart;
Naught be all else to me, save that thou art.
Thou my best thought, by day or by night,
Waking or sleeping, thy presence my light.

Riches I heed not, nor vain empty praise;
Thou mine inheritance, now and always.
Thou and thou only, first in my heart,
Ruler of heaven, my treasure thou art.

High King of heaven, when vict'ry is won
May I reach heaven's joys, O bright heav'n's sun!
Heart of my heart, whatever befall,
Still be my vision, O ruler of all.

Beginning as an Irish hymn, this text was translated by Mary Byrne into English in 1905. It is a centuries-old poem written to honor the faith of St. Patrick who reportedly defied pagan rituals decreed by the king. The story says the king was so impressed by his devotion to Christ that he allowed him to continue his missionary work rather than execute him.

As St. Patrick did, may we find courage in making Jesus the vision of our lives. When we keep our hearts and minds fixed on him, he will guide us in truth. Nothing compares to the riches we find in having peace with God. He is worthy of our lives and devotion.

Great God, I choose to follow you and fix my heart, mind, and life on your ways. Thank you for leading me in love and for filling me with the courage I need to face whatever comes my way today.

JANUARY 7

Blessed Trinity

"Worthy is the Lamb who was slain
To receive power and riches and wisdom,
And strength and honor and glory and blessing!"

REVELATION 5:12 NKJV

Holy, holy, holy! Lord God Almighty!
Early in the morning our song shall rise to thee.
Holy, holy, holy, merciful and mighty!
God in three persons, blessed Trinity!

Holy, holy, holy! Though the darkness hide thee,
Though the eye of sinful man
  thy glory may not see,
Only thou art holy; there is none beside thee,
Perfect in pow'r, in love, and purity.

Holy, holy, holy! Lord God Almighty!
All thy works shall praise thy name in earth,
  and sky and sea.
Holy, holy, holy! Merciful and mighty!
God in three persons, blessed Trinity!

Reginald Heber (1783-1826) was inspired by the Nicene Creed to write this well-known hymn of praise. Focused on the majestic, triune nature of God, our awe is awakened by the lyrics of this song.

When we declare the majesty of God, his incomparable mercy, glory, and goodness, we join with those who have gone before in offering him the praise he is due. Spend some time either reading through the Nicene Creed or singing today's hymn to dive deeper into awe-filled worship.

Majestic One, you are Creator, Father, Son, and Spirit. You are the one who was from the beginning, who remains today, and who will continue to reign into eternity. I worship you for your greatness and for your wonderful love toward me.

Turn Your Eyes

"I am light to the world,
and those who embrace me will experience life-giving light,
and they will never walk in darkness."

John 8:12 TPT

O soul, are you weary and troubled?
No light in the darkness you see?
There's light for a look at the Savior,
And life more abundant and free!

Turn your eyes upon Jesus,
Look full in his wonderful face,
And the things of earth will grow strangely dim,
In the light of his glory and grace.

Thro' death into life everlasting,
He passed, and we follow him there;
O'er us sin no more hath dominion—
For more than conqu'rors we are!

His Word shall not fail you—he promised;
Believe him, and all will be well:
Then go to a world that is dying,
His perfect salvation to tell!

When all is dark and you can't make sense of what is going on in your life and in the world, one being shines bright and stands true. When you look to Jesus, you look to the light of the world. When you walk with him, you walk in his light.

The composer of this hymn, Helen Howarth Lemmel (1863-1961), traveled as a singer and musician. Her invitation to look to the Lord in weariness and trouble echoes both King David and Jesus. If your soul needs respite from chaos, you can find peace in the presence of Christ. Turn your eyes to the Savior and find rest in him.

Lord Jesus, I turn my attention to you today. As I do, I release the worries and anxieties I have been carrying. May every care dim in the glorious light of your presence.

JANUARY 9

Friend in Jesus

Humble yourselves, therefore, under God's mighty hand,
that he may lift you up in due time.
Cast all your anxiety on him because he cares for you.

1 Peter 5:6-7 NIV

What a friend we have in Jesus,
All our sins and griefs to bear!
What a privilege to carry
Everything to God in prayer!
O what peace we often forfeit,
O what needless pain we bear,
All because we do not carry
Everything to God in prayer!

Have we trials and temptations?
Is there trouble anywhere?
We should never be discouraged;
Take it to the Lord in prayer!
Can we find a friend so faithful
Who will all our sorrows share?
Jesus knows our every weakness;
Take it to the Lord in prayer!

Friends are a gift from God. Proverbs says, "One who has unreliable friends soon comes to ruin, but there is a friend who sticks closer than a brother" (18:24). Even in seasons of isolation, we have a faithful friend in Jesus. He never leaves or forsakes us.

Joseph Scriven (1819-1886), today's hymn writer, knew the challenges of loss. He tragically lost his fiancée in a drowning accident the night before his wedding. Later, he lost another fiancée to a sudden illness. He sought to live a faithful life to the Lord amidst hardship and loneliness. Just as he found a friend in Jesus, so can we.

Faithful Lord, I am grateful I am never alone. You are with me, and you are the best friend I could ever have.

Fount of Every Blessing

You will teach me how to live a holy life.
Being with you will fill me with joy;
at your right hand I will find pleasure forever.

PSALM 16:11 NCV

Come, thou fount of every blessing;
Tune my heart to sing thy grace;
Streams of mercy, never ceasing,
Call for songs of loudest praise.
Teach me some melodious sonnet,
Sung by flaming tongues above;
Praise the mount! I'm fixed upon it,
Mount of God's unchanging love!

O to grace how great a debtor
Daily I'm constrained to be!
Let that grace now, like a fetter,
Bind my wandering heart to thee.
Prone to wander, Lord, I feel it,
Prone to leave the God I love;
Here's my heart; O take and seal it;
Seal it for thy courts above.

The grace of God is plentiful. Its endlessness is echoed in the imagery of Christ as the giver of living water and the shepherd who gathers his sheep. He faithfully finds us wherever we are and offers us the power of his mercy. We are never too far gone. How could we not cry out to the Father of every blessing and ask him to come?

The second verse begins, "Here I raise my Ebenezer." An ebenezer refers to a stone of remembrance (1 Samuel 7:12). It stands to remind us of the power of what God has done as well as our gratitude to him. What stone of remembrance can you raise to him today?

Powerful One, come and meet me with the power of your presence today. I worship you.

JANUARY 11

Spiritual and Temporal Mercies

My soul, bless the LORD,
and all that is within me,
bless his holy name.
PSALM 103:1 CSB

O bless the Lord, my soul!
Let all within me join
And aid my tongue to bless his name
Whose favors are divine.

O bless the Lord, my soul,
Nor let his mercies lie
Forgotten in unthankfulness
And without praises die.

He fills the poor with good;
He gives the suff'rers rest.
The Lord has judgments for the proud
And justice for th'oppressed.

His wondrous works and ways
He made by Moses known
But sent the world his truth and grace
By his beloved Son.

Based on Psalm 103, this hymn is a directive to our souls to worship the faithful and true Lord. Everything we are looking for is found in the person of Christ. He forgives our sins, relieves our pain, and heals our bodies. He offers rest to the weary and justice for the oppressed.

Where do you need mercy? Is it a spiritual or temporal need? Take some time to search your heart today and ask for his mercy.

Majestic One, you are the Creator of all things, divine in all your ways, and accessible to each heart who calls on you. I praise you for all you are, all you have done, and all you have yet to do.

Blessed Assurance

He put a new song in my mouth,
a song of praise to our God.
Many will see and fear,
and put their trust in the LORD.

PSALM 40:3 ESV

Blessed assurance, Jesus is mine!
Oh, what a foretaste of glory divine!
Heir of salvation, purchase of God,
Born of his Spirit, washed in his blood.

This is my story, this is my song,
Praising my Savior all the day long.
This is my story, this is my song,
Praising my Savior all the day long.

Perfect communion, perfect delight,
Visions of rapture now burst on my sight.
Angels descending bring from above
Echoes of mercy, whispers of love.

Perfect submission, all is at rest.
I in my Savior am happy and bless'd,
Watching and waiting, looking above,
Filled with his goodness, lost in his love.

Each of us has a personal story to tell; in fact, we have many. As we journey through life, trusting the Lord, every breakthrough and comfort is a testimony of his goodness toward us. Even in the face of trials, we can find comfort and hope in the presence of Christ with us. He is our peace in the chaos. He is our safe shelter in every storm.

Though she was blind from a young age, that did not stop Fanny Crosby (1820-1915) from pursuing teaching. She wrote many Sunday school songs and many hymns we still sing today. No matter what obstacles we face, there is peace to cover us and give us courage to continue to reach our dreams. Be encouraged by Fanny's story and share yours with others today.

Savior, you are the hope of my heart and the comfort I need in every trial. Thank you for your mercy toward me and the power of your transformative love.

All Creatures

The life of every creature
and the breath of all people
are in God's hand.

JOB 12:10 NCV

All creatures of our God and King,
Lift up your voices, let us sing:
Alleluia! Alleluia!
Bright burning sun with golden beams,
Soft silver moon that gently gleams,
O praise him! O praise him!
Alleluia, alleluia, alleluia!

And even you, most gentle death,
Waiting to hush our final breath,
O praise him! Alleluia!
You lead back home the child of God,
For Christ our Lord that way has trod:
O praise him! O praise him!
Alleluia, alleluia, alleluia!

This hymn encourages us to join with all creation to offer praise to the Creator of all things. The invitation is ours, here and now, no matter where we are or what mood we are in, to offer praise to the King of kings and Lord of lords. He is worthy!

Francis of Assisi (circa 1181-1226) wrote a text that was the basis of this hymn, translated and paraphrased by William Draper (1855-1933) centuries later. Assisi wrote this as a meditation on Psalm 145, and he was known for urging the birds to praise God. All creation reflects the hand of God, and it offers praise to him. How can we also join with creation and offer the Creator the praise he is due?

Great God, you are the Creator of all things and the source of life itself. I am yours; everything I am, I offer back to you. Be glorified in my life. I praise you!

Abide with Me

"Behold, I am with you always,
to the end of the age."
MATTHEW 28:20 NASB

Abide with me: fast falls the eventide;
The darkness deepens; Lord, with me abide.
When other helpers fail and comforts flee,
Help of the helpless, O abide with me.

I need thy presence every passing hour.
What but thy grace can foil the tempter's power?
Who like thyself my guide and strength can be?
Through cloud and sunshine, O abide with me.

I fear no foe with thee at hand to bless,
Ills have no weight, and tears no bitterness.
Where is death's sting? Where, grave, thy
victory?
I triumph still, if thou abide with me.

In the face of change, one being remains constant and immovable. When the winds of change stir up our lives, we can always come to the Lord. He is our friend and Savior in every shift and transition, even death.

Henry Lyte (1793-1847) wrote this text near the end of his life. He saw the evening of his life approaching, and he chose to invite the Lord to abide with him. He was inspired by Luke 24:29, where travelers urged Jesus, "Stay with us, for it is getting toward evening, and the day is now nearly over." Wherever you are on your journey, you too can invite Jesus to abide with you.

Jesus, as change approaches, I look to you even more. I need the comfort of your presence and the power of your love in my life. Abide with me, Lord. Be near.

The Wondrous Cross

I have been crucified with Christ;
it is no longer I who live, but Christ lives in me;
and the life which I now live in the flesh
I live by faith in the Son of God,
who loved me and gave Himself for me.

GALATIANS 2:20 NKJV

When I survey the wondrous cross
On which the Prince of Glory died,
My richest gain I count but loss,
And pour contempt on all my pride.

Forbid it, Lord, that I should boast
Save in the death of Christ, my God!
All the vain things that charm me most,
I sacrifice them through his blood.

See, from his head, his hands, his feet,
Sorrow and love flow mingled down.
Did e'er such love and sorrow meet,
Or thorns compose so rich a crown?

Were the whole realm of nature mine,
That were a present far too small.
Love so amazing, so divine,
Demands my soul, my life, my all.

When we fix our hearts on the beautiful sacrifice of Christ, we have the opportunity to respond in humble surrender. Read through the text, meditate on each stanza, and reflect on their meaning.

Isaac Watts wrote this hymn in 1707 and placed it in a collection of hymns used during the Lord's Supper. Perhaps you can practice Communion in your home today by playing or singing this song in reflection and taking the bread and cup with what you have on hand. God is with you in the everyday, and he meets you where you are. His presence makes you a living temple as holy as any sacred space you will find on this earth.

Christ, thank you for the sacrifice of your life and the freedom you offer to everyone who comes to you. As I remember your sacrifice—the blood you shed, and the body broken for me—I offer you my humble life. May your will be done.

My Father's World

God's splendor is a tale that is told, written in the stars.
Space itself speaks his story through the marvels of the heavens.
His truth is on tour in the starry vault of the sky,
showing his skill in creation's craftsmanship.

Psalm 19:1 TPT

This is my Father's world,
And to my listening ears
All nature sings, and round me rings
The music of the spheres.
This is my Father's world:
I rest me in the thought
Of rocks and trees, of skies and seas—
His hand the wonders wrought.

This is my Father's world:
O let me ne'er forget
That though the wrong seems oft so strong,
God is the ruler yet.
This is my Father's world:
Why should my heart be sad?
The Lord is King: let the heavens ring!
God reigns; let earth be glad!

In creation, we see evidence of a thoughtful creator. This artist orchestrates the seasons, sets planets into motion, and breathes life into humanity. Spend time in nature today even if only for a few minutes. Turn your attention to the trees, the wind, the stars: anything around you. Let go of your worries and tune in to the present moment.

"Though the wrong seems oft so strong, God is the Ruler yet." No matter what is going on in the world, God is still God. He is still good. He is still moving in mercy. As all creation offers praise to God, we can join in. Let's garner our hope in our Creator and in his lordship over our lives and this world.

Creator, I join with nature and offer you my heart, hope, and praise.

Everlasting Arms

The people of Benjamin are loved by the LORD and live in safety beside him. He surrounds them continuously and preserves them from every harm.

DEUTERONOMY 33:12 NLT

What a fellowship, what a joy divine,
Leaning on the everlasting arms;
What a blessedness, what a peace is mine,
Leaning on the everlasting arms.

Leaning, leaning,
Safe and secure from all alarms;
Leaning, leaning,
Leaning on the everlasting arms.

What have I to dread, what have I to fear,
Leaning on the everlasting arms?
I have blessed peace with my Lord so near,
Leaning on the everlasting arms.

Anthony Showalter wrote the refrain of "Leaning on the Everlasting Arms" based on Deuteronomy 33:27: "The eternal God is your refuge, and his everlasting arms are under you." Two of Showalter's former students had lost their wives and contacted their teacher, and he offered them his sympathy along with this comforting verse.

If you are facing grief of any kind, here is an invitation to lean on the arms of your heavenly Father. He surrounds you and holds you up. Keep leaning into him and trust him to hold you when your strength fails.

Heavenly Father, thank you for the promise of your peace. Your presence is my comfort and strength, and you are my holy hope. I lean on you today.

My Jesus

This is how God showed his love among us:
He sent his one and only Son into the world
that we might live through him.

1 John 4:9 NIV

My Jesus, I love thee, I know thou art mine;
For thee all the follies of sin I resign;
My gracious Redeemer, my Savior art thou;
If ever I loved thee, my Jesus, 'tis now.

I love thee because thou hast first loved me
And purchased my pardon on Calvary's tree;
I love thee for wearing the thorns on thy brow;
If ever I loved thee, my Jesus, 'tis now.

I'll love thee in life, I will love thee in death,
And praise thee as long as thou lendest me
breath,
And say when the deathdew lies cold on
my brow:
If ever I loved thee, my Jesus, 'tis now.

In mansions of glory and endless delight,
I'll ever adore thee in heaven so bright;
I'll sing with the glittering crown on my brow:
If ever I loved thee, my Jesus, 'tis now.

Originally written as a poem by the young William Featherston mid-19th century, "My Jesus I Love Thee" persists as a beloved and well-known hymn to this day. A confession of faith and love to the Lord, this hymn is a response to the wonderful love our Savior offers us through his powerful sacrifice and resurrection.

As you meditate on this hymn, allow your heart to open in adoration before your Creator and Savior. He loves you more than you can fathom. He has already done everything necessary to break down every barrier between you and God. His love will empower you to love others, so fill up in his presence today.

Savior, thank you for the power of your love that led you to the earth and the cross. I'm grateful your mercy is more powerful than the grave. You are my Savior, and I love you because you first loved me.

A Thousand Tongues

One generation will declare your works to the next
and will proclaim your mighty acts.

Psalm 145:4 CSB

O for a thousand tongues to sing
My great Redeemer's praise,
The glories of my God and King,
The triumphs of his grace!

Jesus! The name that charms our fears,
That bids our sorrows cease,
'Tis music in the sinner's ears,
'Tis life and health and peace.

He breaks the power of cancelled sin,
He sets the prisoner free;
His blood can make the foulest clean;
His blood availed for me.

To God all glory, praise, and love
Be now and ever given
By saints below and saints above,
The Church in earth and heaven.

In 1739 on the first anniversary of his conversion, Charles Wesley wrote an eighteen-stanza poem declaring the power and victory of Christ in his life. The modernized versions of the hymn begin with the seventh original stanza, which was adapted from a quote he had heard from a friend: "Had I a thousand tongues, I would praise him with them all."

What an honor to use our voices to praise our Redeemer and sing of his goodness toward us. Consider writing your own offering to God reflective of his work in your life. You can use Wesley's hymn as a starting point and personalize your praise to your Savior today.

Great God, you are worthy of my personal praise, for you have been wonderful to me. I will give you the honor deserve as I recognize your hand of mercy resting on me now.

Nearer to Thee

"I am the LORD, the God of Abraham your father and the God of Isaac.
The land on which you lie I will give to you and to your offspring."
Then Jacob awoke from his sleep and said,
"Surely the LORD is in this place, and I did not know it."

GENESIS 28:13, 16 ESV

Nearer, my God, to thee, nearer to thee!
E'en though it be a cross that raiseth me,
Still all my song shall be,
Nearer, my God, to thee;
Nearer, my God, to thee, nearer to thee!

Then, with my waking thoughts bright with
thy praise,
Out of my stony griefs Bethel I'll raise;
So by my woes to be
Nearer, my God, to thee;
Nearer, my God, to thee, nearer to thee!

Or if, on joyful wing cleaving the sky,
Sun, moon, and stars forgot, upward I fly,
Still all my song shall be,
Nearer, my God, to thee;
Nearer, my God, to thee, nearer to thee!

Written to coincide with a sermon on Genesis 28, Sarah Adams (1805-1848) meditated on the Scripture passage where Jacob slept with a stone as a pillow while he dreamed of a ladder reaching to heaven. While we may not see a ladder reaching to heaven, we do have a direct connection to the Lord.

The Lord is with you just as he was with those in Scripture. His Spirit has already been poured out; you can fellowship with him anywhere, anytime through Christ. No matter what you need today, God has it in abundance. Find your comfort, peace, and hope in his nearness.

Glorious God, I want to know you more than I do now. I want to know the nearness of your presence in deeper ways. Be near even as I draw near to you.

JANUARY 21

Firm Foundation

The foundation that has already been laid is Jesus Christ,
and no one can lay down any other foundation.

1 Corinthians 3:11 NCV

How firm a foundation, ye saints of the Lord,
Is laid for your faith in God's excellent Word!
What more can be said than to you God
hath said,
To you who for refuge to Jesus have fled?

Fear not, I am with thee, O be not dismayed,
For I am thy God, and will still give thee aid;
I'll strengthen thee, help thee, and cause
thee to stand,
Upheld by my righteous, omnipotent hand.

When through the deep waters I call thee to go,
The rivers of sorrow shall not overflow;
For I will be near thee, thy troubles to bless,
And sanctify to thee thy deepest distress.

When through fiery trials thy pathway shall lie,
My grace, all sufficient, shall be thy supply;
The flame shall not hurt thee; I only design
Thy dross to consume, and thy gold to refine.

Though the author of this hymn is unknown, the power of its words rings true. Each verse is based on a biblical promise. In fact, the original title was "Exceedingly Great and Precious Promises." No matter where we go or what we face, God is our firm foundation and our help in times of trouble.

Which promise do you need to cling to today? Pick a stanza, memorize it, and come back to it throughout the day. As you declare God's promise through song, may you know the encouragement of his hope alive in your heart and the confidence of his hand on your life.

Father, I'm grateful for the promises you give me in your Word. I stand on the truth you have spoken and remind my soul to trust in you. Be near and encourage my heart in hope. You are my courage.

Rock of Ages

The Lord has been my refuge,
And my God the rock of my refuge.

Psalm 94:22 NASB

Rock of Ages, cleft for me,
Let me hide myself in thee;
Let the water and the blood,
From thy wounded side which flowed,
Be of sin the double cure;
Save from wrath and make me pure.

Not the labors of my hands
Can fulfill thy law's demands;
Could my zeal no respite know,
Could my tears forever flow,
All for sin could not atone;
Thou must save, and thou alone.

Augustus Toplady wrote this hymn as a poem and included it at the the conclusion of an article he wrote on God's forgiveness in 1776. It uses imagery often found in Scripture: the Lord as a safe place in a storm. Christ's redemptive work on the cross is like a cleft we can hide in from the onslaught of sin's power.

Christ is a resting place. We not only find peace and shelter in him but also restoration for our souls. Christ is the power of our salvation, and we don't have to strive for it. We come to him, hiding ourselves in his mercy, and he covers us with the power of his love and removes our sins as far as the east is from the west.

Savior, you are my safe place. I hide myself in your mercy. Liberate me from the power of shame, fear, and sin so I may walk in the freedom of your love.

He Leadeth Me

He makes me to lie down in green pastures;
He leads me beside the still waters.
He restores my soul;
He leads me in the paths of righteousness
For His name's sake.

Psalm 23:2-3 NKJV

He leadeth me: O blessed thought!
O words with heavenly comfort fraught!
Whate'er I do, where'er I be,
Still 'tis God's hand that leadeth me.

He leadeth me, he leadeth me;
By his own hand he leadeth me:
His faithful follower I would be,
For by his hand he leadeth me.

Sometimes mid scenes of deepest gloom,
Sometimes where Eden's flowers bloom,
By waters calm, o'er troubled sea,
Still 'tis God's hand that leadeth me.

Lord, I would clasp thy hand in mine,
Nor ever murmur nor repine;
Content, whatever lot I see,
Since 'tis my God that leadeth me.

In a mid-week service in 1862, Joseph Henry set out to give a message out of Psalm 23. He wrote later that he got no further than the words "He leadeth me." They struck him with such significance, he wrote the whole hymn on the back of his sermon notes.

Jesus leads us through this life. He is a careful and trustworthy guide through every circumstance. Take the hand of your Savior today by giving him the trust of your heart and obeying his Word. He will not fail you.

Faithful Lord, I open my heart and life to you today. Every morning is new, and every moment is a fresh opportunity to trust you. Lead me beside still waters and restore my soul.

Amazing Grace

Our faith in Jesus transfers God's righteousness to us
and he now declares us flawless in his eyes.
This means we can now enjoy true and lasting peace with God,
all because of what our Lord Jesus, the Anointed One, has done for us.

ROMANS 5:1 TPT

Amazing grace how sweet the sound
That saved a wretch like me!
I once was lost, but now am found,
Was blind, but now I see.

'Twas grace that taught my heart to fear,
And grace my fears relieved;
How precious did that grace appear
The hour I first believed!

Yes, when this flesh and heart shall fail,
And mortal life shall cease:
I shall possess, within the veil,
A life of joy and peace.

The earth shall soon dissolve like snow,
The sun forbear to shine;
But God, who called me here below,
Will be forever mine.

Written as a sort of spiritual autobiography, John Newton penned one of the most well-known and best-loved hymns in 1779. Once a slave ship captain, Newton turned to Christ and eventually became an abolitionist. His was an unlikely and powerful conversion.

No matter what we come from, we also can change the trajectory of our lives in submission to Christ. What we have been need not define who we will be; we can change course and change our minds just as John Newton did. Christ's amazing grace saves us and transforms our hearts, minds, and lives.

Merciful Jesus, thank you for the power of your love. It touches my heart and life and completely transforms me from the inside out. I am yours, and I want to be more like you each passing day. I am humbled by your grace and overwhelmed by your mercy.

JANUARY 25

Jesus Is Calling

"Give ear and come to me; listen, that you may live.
I will make an everlasting covenant with you,
my faithful love promised to David."

ISAIAH 55:3 NIV

Softly and tenderly Jesus is calling,
Calling for you and for me;
See, on the portals he's waiting and watching,
Watching for you and for me.

Come home, come home;
You who are weary come home;
Earnestly, tenderly, Jesus is calling,
Calling, O sinner, come home!

Time is now fleeting, the moments are
passing,
Passing from you and from me;
Shadows are gathering, deathbeds are
coming,
Coming for you and for me.

O for the wonderful love he has promised,
Promised for you and for me!
Though we have sinned, he has mercy and
pardon,
Pardon for you and for me.

Reminiscent of the parable of the prodigal son, this hymn illustrates God as one who is watching, waiting, and longing for us to turn (and return) to him. He is a loving father who celebrates our homecoming. He is a patient savior who welcomes us with open arms. No matter where we go, we can never escape the love of God.

Will Thompson (1847-1909) was a successful songwriter. While he could have used his means to live a self-indulgent life, he instead focused on ministering to others and honoring the Lord by writing only Christian songs. This particular hymn feels as gentle as a lullaby. If you find yourself overwhelmed by life today, allow the softness of this song to draw you to Jesus and settle his peace over your heart and mind.

Jesus, I hear your soft beckoning, and I answer by coming to you. Breathe life, peace, joy, and hope into my soul as I draw near.

We Gather Together

"I am in them and you are in me.
May they experience such perfect unity
that the world will know that you sent me
and that you love them as much as you love me."
John 17:23 NLT

We gather together to ask the Lord's blessing;
He chastens and hastens his will to make known;
The wicked oppressing now cease from
distressing:
Sing praises to his name; he forgets not his own.

Beside us to guide us, our God with us joining,
Whose kingdom calls all to the love which
endures.
So from the beginning the fight we were
winning:
You, Lord, were at our side; all glory be yours!

We all do extol you, our leader triumphant,
And pray that you still our defender will be.
Let your congregation escape tribulation:
Your name be ever praised! O Lord, make
us free!

Gathering is not reserved for holidays or special occasions. We were created for community year-round, in all circumstances, and through every trial and triumph. As we gather with other believers, asking for the Lord to be with us and to make himself known to and among us, we practice the power of communal invitation and connection.

Though the author of this hymn is anonymous, it was written around 1600 as a Dutch patriotic song to celebrate the freedom of their nation from Spanish rule. We can thank God for his ever-present help as we gather too. What victory can you celebrate with the body of believers?

Faithful Father, thank you for being the refuge and strength of your people through every age. I commit myself to you and your family. Thank you for responding to us in kindness, justice, and love.

Fairest Lord Jesus

My love is fit and strong,
notable among ten thousand.
SONG OF SONGS 5:10 CSB

Fairest Lord Jesus,
Ruler of all nature,
O thou of God and man the Son,
Thee will I cherish,
Thee will I honor,
Thou, my soul's glory, joy, and crown.

Fair is the sunshine,
Fairer still the moonlight,
And all the twinkling starry host:
Jesus shines brighter,
Jesus shines purer
Than all the angels heaven can boast.

Beautiful Savior!
Lord of all the nations!
Son of God and Son of Man!
Glory and honor,
Praise, adoration,
Now and forevermore be thine.

The original version of this hymn dates back well into the 1600s from a group of Jesuits in Germany. While the original author is unknown, the fourth verse was added in 1873 by Joseph Seiss. No matter who first penned it, this hymn's focus is one thing: the beauty of Christ.

Jesus stands as the Creator, ruler, and "fairest of ten thousand." He is our beautiful Savior, and his love is purer than any other. He does not have ulterior motives or seek to manipulate us to do his bidding. He loves us wholly, purely, and completely, and in this love, we truly come alive.

Jesus, as I sing this hymn of pure adoration, I invite you to move in my life. Shine on me, glorious one, and I will come alive. Let hope spring up as I praise you.

Open My Eyes

These things God has revealed to us through the Spirit. For the Spirit searches everything, even the depths of God.

1 Corinthians 2:10 ESV

Open my eyes that I may see
Glimpses of truth thou hast for me.
Place in my hands the wonderful key
That shall unclasp and set me free.
Silently now I wait for thee,
Ready, my God, thy will to see.
Open my eyes, illumine me,
Spirit divine!

Open my ears that I may hear
Voices of truth thou sendest clear,
And while the wave notes fall on my ear,
Ev'rything false will disappear.
Silently now I wait for thee,
Ready, my God, thy will to see.
Open my ears, illumine me,
Spirit divine!

Clara Scott was a wife, mother, music teacher, composer, hymn writer, and publisher. Being a wife and mother was not extraordinary in the late 1800s, but being a composer and publisher was. In fact, she was the first woman to publish a book of anthems, "The Royal Anthem Book," in 1882. "Open My Eyes That I May See" was published in 1895, and it became her most well-known hymn.

As we spend time in the Lord's presence and in his Word, we can pray for open eyes and ears. When we receive from the Lord, we can offer to others what he has given to us. What a beautiful relationship we have with the Lord; it is living, active, and wonderful.

Spirit, open my eyes, my ears, and my heart in your presence. I am listening and waiting. How I love you!

JANUARY 29

Immortal and Invisible

To the King that rules forever, who will never die, who cannot be seen, the only God, be honor and glory forever and ever. Amen.

1 Timothy 1:17 NCV

Immortal, invisible, God only wise,
In light inaccessible hid from our eyes,
Most blessed, most glorious, the Ancient
of Days,
Almighty, victorious, thy great name we praise.

Unresting, unhasting, and silent as light,
Nor wanting, nor wasting, thou rulest in might;
Thy justice like mountains high soaring above
Thy clouds, which are fountains of goodness
and love.

To all life thou givest, to both great and small;
In all life thou livest, the true life of all;
We blossom and flourish as leaves on the tree,
And wither and perish but naught
changeth thee.

Great Father of glory, pure Father of light,
Thine angels adore thee, all veiling their sight;
All praise we would render, O help us to see
'Tis only the splendor of light hideth thee.

Scottish pastor Walter Smith based the text of this hymn on 1 Timothy 1:17. The hymn of praise speaks of the inimitable glory, power, and mystery of God. In Smith's words, we can find our perspectives put right in light of who God is.

It is not bad to feel the smallness and limited nature of our lives. We cannot control the wind, and we cannot predict how the future will unfold. We can, however, trust the one who does. When you feel overwhelmed today, go to a physical or internal place where you can remember that, though you are small, you are part of a larger whole. The Creator of all things will not overlook you or your cries to him. Reach out; he is near.

Creator, thank you for the power of your presence and perspective. No matter how small I feel, set my heart straight in light of who you are. I trust you to see me, know me, and take care of me. You are always good.

Waiting Savior

"Everything that the Father gives Me will come to Me,
and the one who comes to Me I certainly will not cast out."

John 6:37 NASB

The Savior is waiting and calling,
He bids us come in to the feast;
O come, all ye hungry and sad ones,
There's room for the worst and the least.

Once they all made light of the story,
And turned to their pleasure and sin;
The proud and the careless despised him,
But the humble and poor entered in.

He spread all his bounties before them,
He sought them where'er they might roam;
With love trembling sweet in his message,
He tenderly bade them come home.

Have you ever thought of his mercy?
He graciously calls you today;
The feast of his love still is waiting;
O turn not, O turn not away.

After retiring from ministry, Reverend William Cushing (1823-1903) discovered a talenet for writing and authored around 300 hymn lyrics. He recognized the need to keep busy, and he asked the Lord to give him something to do. Cushing wasn't too old to start something new, and neither are any of us. No matter our age, we can develop new skills.

Jesus is a safe place for the humble and vulnerable. He was in his own ministry when he walked the earth, and he remains a safe place today by his Spirit. Let us throw aside our pride and stubborness and come to the one who loves us as we are. He will offer us provision for today and fresh vision for tomorrow.

Loving Lord, no one else loves the rejected just as fiercely as those who seem easy to love. I want to be more like you. Refresh my heart in hope, vision, and compassion.

JANUARY 31

Name of Jesus

At the name of Jesus every knee should bow, of those in heaven, and of those on earth, and of those under the earth.

PHILIPPIANS 2:10 NKJV

At the name of Jesus ev'ry knee shall bow,
Ev'ry tongue confess him King of glory now;
'Tis the Father's pleasure we should call
him Lord,
Who from the beginning was the
mighty Word.

At his voice creation sprang at once to sight,
All the angel faces, all the hosts of light,
Cherubim in heaven, stars upon their way,
All the heav'nly orders in their great array.

In your hearts enthrone him;
There let him subdue
All that is not holy, all that is not true;
Crown him as your captain in
temptation's hour;
Let his will enfold you in its light and pow'r.

Christians, this Lord Jesus shall return again
In his Father's glory, with his angel train;
For all wreaths of empire meet upon his brow,
And our hearts confess him King of glory now.

It is worth it to search for and read all eight original stanzas of today's hymn from 1870. We are often pressed for time, but there are moments when it is worthwhile to dig for deeper understanding and reflection. This hymn is one of those occasions. Though space does not allow us to print it in its entirety, Caroline Noel's take on Paul's confession of faith in Philippians 2 is beautiful and powerful work.

Every knee shall one day bow, and every tongue will confess that Jesus Christ is Lord. We don't have to wait another moment to do so. May we honor him with our hearts, choices, lives, and work. He is worthy of it all.

Savior, you are worthy of my love, life, and submission. Thank you for your redeeming grace.

February

O Lord my God, when I in awesome wonder,
Consider all the worlds thy hands have made;
I see the stars, I hear the rolling thunder,
Thy power throughout the universe displayed.

FEBRUARY 1

To God Be the Glory

"I am the Way, I am the Truth, and I am the Life.
No one comes next to the Father except through union with me.
To know me is to know my Father too."

JON 14:6 TPT

To God be the glory, great things he has done!
So loved he the world that he gave us his Son,
Who yielded his life an atonement for sin,
And opened the life-gate that all may go in.

Praise the Lord! Praise the Lord,
Let the earth hear his voice!
Praise the Lord! Praise the Lord!
Let the people rejoice!
O come to the Father through Jesus the Son
And give him the glory, great things he
has done!

Great things he has taught us, great things
he has done,
And great our rejoicing through Jesus the Son,
But purer and higher and greater will be
Our joy and our wonder, when Jesus we see.

Fanny Crosby (1820-1915) was a prolific hymn writer and wrote at least eight thousand of them. They were widely distributed, and this specific hymn became popular later when it was used in Billy Graham crusades. It directs our focus away from personal experiences and toward the grandeur and glory of God.

We can set aside disappointments and still praise the Lord. Even in the midst of hardship and sorrow, we can worship the Lord for his truth, glory, and power. He is merciful in every moment and situation. As the psalmists found solace in the presence of God, so can we. He is worthy of our praise, so let's fix our eyes on him and offer him the worship of our hearts.

Lord God, I believe you are not finished working out your faithfulness in the world or in my life. You are worthy of all the honor I can offer and more.

Trust and Obey

"Take my yoke upon you and learn from me,
for I am gentle and humble in heart,
and you will find rest for your souls."

MATTHEW 11:29 NIV

When we walk with the Lord
In the light of his Word,
What a glory he sheds on our way!
While we do his good will,
He abides with us still,
And with all who will trust and obey.

Trust and obey, for there's no other way
To be happy in Jesus, but to trust and obey.

But we never can prove
The delights of his love
Until all on the altar we lay;
For the favor he shows,
For the joy he bestows,
Are for them who will trust and obey.

Daniel Towner, together with John Sammis, wrote this hymn after being inspired by the testimony of a young man in a revival meeting led by Dwight L. Moody. The young man was recorded by Towner as saying, "I am not quite sure—but I am going to trust, and I am going to obey."

Whatever we do, whether temporarily or in the long-run, may we say the same. Our hearts can rest in trust of the Lord, for he is faithful. When we obey his Word and follow the leading of his Spirit, we walk in the light of his presence. He will not fail us.

Trustworthy One, even when I do not understand what is going on in the world or in my life, I choose to trust you. I choose to follow you. I choose to obey your Word and your law of love. I am yours.

FEBRUARY 3

A Mighty Fortress

God is our refuge and strength,
always ready to help in times of trouble.

Psalm 46:1 NLT

A mighty fortress is our God,
A bulwark never failing;
Our helper he, amid the flood
Of mortal ills prevailing.
For still our ancient foe
Does seek to work us woe;
His craft and power are great,
And armed with cruel hate,
On earth is not his equal.

And though this world, with devils filled,
Should threaten to undo us,
We will not fear, for God has willed
His truth to triumph through us.
The prince of darkness grim,
We tremble not for him;
His rage we can endure,
For lo! His doom is sure;
One little word shall fell him.

Written somewhere between 1527 and 1529, Martin Luther penned this hymn as a paraphrase of Psalm 46. It became a battle hymn used in the Reformation often sung before battles commenced. Though we are not in a physical fight for our faith, there is a spiritual battle going on around us. When darkness feels heavy, our God is a mighty fortress of strength to run to.

We need not rely on our strength to give us victory in this life. We can rely on the power of God whose might cannot be matched. As we lean on his strength, we have courage to overcome our fears.

Lord, thank you for the power you alone have. You are a faithful help in times of trouble, and I trust in you. Your truth can't be conquered, for you are the way, the truth, and the life.

Jesus Loves Me

The LORD appeared to him from far away.
"I have loved you with an everlasting love;
therefore, I have continued to extend faithful love to you."

JEREMIAH 31:3 CSB

Jesus loves me, this I know,
For the Bible tells me so.
Little ones to him belong;
They are weak, but he is strong.

Yes, Jesus loves me!
Yes, Jesus loves me!
Yes, Jesus loves me!
The Bible tells me so.

Jesus loves me he who died
Heaven's gate to open wide.
He will wash away my sin,
Let his little child come in.

Jesus loves me, this I know,
As he loved so long ago,
Taking children on his knee,
Saying, "Let them come to me."

The chorus of this song was written by Anna Warner (1824-1915) in a novel she wrote in collaboration with her sister, Susan. The simple chorus was used to comfort a dying boy in the story. Readers were captivated by this touching chorus, and one reader was hymnist William Bradbury. He created the simple melody that remains one of the most well-known children's songs in history.

When we need comfort, we can find it in the loving arms of Jesus Christ. His Word illuminates our hearts to his everlasting love that cannot be shaken or taken from us. His love is not reserved for those who can understand it; it is available to even the youngest child who will receive it. Let us come like children.

Jesus, I come to you as a child, no matter my age, for a piece of me will always be young, hopeful, and in need of you. Comfort me with your loving presence.

I Surrender All

I appeal to you therefore, brothers, by the mercies of God,
to present your bodies as a living sacrifice,
holy and acceptable to God,
which is your spiritual worship.

ROMANS 12:1 ESV

All to Jesus I surrender,
All to him I freely give;
I will ever love and trust him,
In his presence daily live.

I surrender all, I surrender all;
All to thee, my blessed Savior,
I surrender all.

All to Jesus I surrender,
Make me, Savior, wholly thine;
Let me feel thy Holy Spirit,
Truly know that thou art mine.

All to Jesus I surrender,
Lord, I give myself to thee;
Fill me with thy love and power,
Let thy blessing fall on me.

Judson Van De Venter wrote "I Surrender All" in 1896 in memory of when he chose to finally dedicate his life to ministry after struggling with the decision over several years. Though it may have taken him some time to surrender to the Lord's invitation over his life, he took that step and became an evangelist and hymnist.

Is there something you have felt the Lord leading you toward? Have you taken that step and surrendered to him in the process? It is never too late to say to Jesus, "I surrender all." He is with you every step of the way, and his love is close to empower you in trust and grace.

Faithful Jesus, I trust your plans for me are good. You are with me in leaps of faith and small steps of faithfulness. I surrender to you, my beautiful Jesus, for you are better to me than I am to myself. You are endlessly wise, and I trust you.

Nothing Less

"Everyone who hears my words and obeys them
is like a wise man who built his house on rock."

Matthew 7:24 NCV

My hope is built on nothing less
Than Jesus' blood and righteousness;
I dare not trust the sweetest frame,
But wholly lean on Jesus' name.

On Christ, the solid rock, I stand:
All other ground is sinking sand;
All other ground is sinking sand.

His oath, his covenant, his blood,
Support me in the whelming flood;
When all around my soul gives way,
He then is all my hope and stay.

When he shall come with trumpet sound,
O may I then in him be found:
Dressed in his righteousness alone,
Faultless to stand before the throne.

Edward Mote (1797-1874) wrote the chorus of this song while he was on a walk. He had the idea for it when he thought he should write a hymn based on the "Gracious Experience of a Christian." He sang it for a friend's ill wife while on a visit, and she loved it so much, she asked for a copy. Mote finished the song and sent it off to the publisher, and we sing it still today.

We find courage and strength in planting ourselves on the solid rock of Jesus Christ, our Lord. When our lives are submitted to him, we have nothing to fear. Even when trials come and everything falls away, the foundation of our faith will not be shaken. Christ's love is unshakeable.

Christ Jesus, I have planted the roots of my faith in your love. I trust you will not fail to remain steadfast and sure.

FEBRUARY 7

Higher Ground

Set your minds on the things that are above,
not on the things that are on earth.

COLOSSIANS 3:2 NASB

I'm pressing on the upward way,
New heights I'm gaining ev'ry day;
Still praying as I'm onward bound,
"Lord, plant my feet on higher ground."

My heart has no desire to stay
Where doubts arise and fears dismay;
Though some may dwell where these abound,
My prayer, my aim, is higher ground.

Lord, lift me up, and let me stand
By faith, on heaven's tableland;
A higher plane than I have found,
Lord, plant my feet on higher ground.

I want to scale the utmost height,
And catch a gleam of glory bright;
But still I'll pray till heav'n I've found,
"Lord, lead me on to higher ground."

Johnson Oatman (1856-1922) wrote over three thousand hymns. Although most of them are not remembered, a few remain well-circulated. He often focused his hymns on growth as a Christian as well as victory in Christ. These themes are both presented in "Higher Ground."

Perhaps you have known and walked with Christ for a long time. Does your relationship with him remain dynamic? Are you growing deeper in your knowledge of who he is and what he is like? As a child of God, you have access to his Spirit. There is always more to learn and more ways to grow; do so with intention today.

Lord, thank you for leading and teaching me with your presence. I am thankful to know you and continue to learn about you. I am yours, Lord; draw near to me as I draw near to you today.

He Lifted Me

I will extol You, O Lord,
for You have lifted me up,
And have not let my foes rejoice over me.
Psalm 30:1 NKJV

In loving kindness Jesus came
My soul in mercy to reclaim,
And from the depths of sin and shame
Through grace he lifted me.

From sinking sand he lifted me,
With tender hand he lifted me,
From shades of night to plains of light,
O praise his name, he lifted me!

He called me long before I heard,
Before my sinful heart was stirred,
But when I took him at his word,
Forgiven he lifted me.

His brow was pierced with many a thorn,
His hands by cruel nails were torn,
When from my guilt and grief, forlorn,
In love he lifted me.

Charles Hutchinson Gabriel (1856-1932) was musical from a young age. He taught himself to play his family's reed organ, and he began teaching singing when he was just sixteen. He not only played and taught music, but he also wrote his own. "He Lifted Me" speaks of the Savior's kindness toward us even when we feel we are sinking without hope.

Jesus is incredibly gracious with us. He pursues us before we even know to look to him. He draws us to himself with loving kindness, heals us of our pain, and removes our shame. His mercy is powerful and beautiful. How have you experienced the mercy of God meeting you in your mess?

Gracious Lord, I'm grateful you are gentle with me. You don't put me to shame; you lift me out of it. How could I begin to thank you?

The Tie That Binds

Now these three remain: faith, hope and love.
But the greatest of these is love.

1 Corinthians 13:13 NIV

Blest be the tie that binds
Our hearts in Christian love;
The fellowship of kindred minds
Is like to that above.

Before our Father's throne
We pour our ardent prayers;
Our fears, our hopes, our aims are one,
Our comforts and our cares.

When we are called to part,
It gives us inward pain;
But we shall still be joined in heart,
And hope to meet again.

From sorrow, toil, and pain,
And sin, we shall be free;
And perfect love and friendship reign
Through all eternity.

In an age of division when we draw lines instead of opening our homes, it is important to remember what truly unites us. Christ did not come so we could fight but so we would receive his love and walk the path of his truth. He summed up the Law like this: Love God with all your heart, soul, mind, and strength, and love your neighbor as yourself. We don't have to agree with each other to choose to love. We don't have to escape our pain to know the bonds of a supportive community.

John Fawcett was a Baptist minister in England during the late 1700s. When he had the opportunity to move to a larger parish with better pay, he couldn't do it. He felt called to stay and minister to his little church. May we learn to put others above our personal gain, for love is the thread holding us together.

Lord, I humble myself before you and ask for your help in loving others well. I choose to uphold unity rather than sow division.

Have Thine Own Way

"House of Israel,
can I not treat you as this potter treats his clay?"—
this is the Lord's declaration.
"Just like clay in the potter's hand,
so are you in my hand, house of Israel."

Jeremiah 18:6 CSB

Have thine own way, Lord!
Have thine own way!
Thou art the potter,
I am the clay.
Mold me and make me
After thy will,
While I am waiting,
Yielded and still.

Have thine own way, Lord!
Have thine own way!
Search me and try me,
Savior today!
Wash me just now, Lord,
Wash me just now,
As in thy presence
Humbly I bow.

Adelaide Pollard longed to do missionary work in Africa. She dreamed about serving the Lord in this way, but her financial situation wouldn't allow it. This is the backdrop to the genesis of this 1906 hymn. Allegedly, she had gone to a prayer meeting and heard someone pray, "It really doesn't matter what you do with us, Lord; just have your own way with our lives."

Have you been longing for something that doesn't seem possible? Bring it to the Lord in prayer. Ask him to soften your heart so your prayer would become, "Have thine own way, Lord." As you grow to know him more, you will discover he is completely trustworthy. He brings beauty from ashes and creates new life from the death of old dreams.

Lord, I don't want to fight for my way. I trust you. Have your way in my life.

FEBRUARY 11

Living for Jesus

Whatever you do, in word or deed,
do everything in the name of the Lord Jesus,
giving thanks to God the Father through him.

COLOSSIANS 3:17 ESV

Living for Jesus, a life that is true,
Striving to please him in all that I do;
Yielding allegiance, glad-hearted and free,
This is the pathway of blessing for me.

O Jesus, Lord and Savior, I give myself to thee,
For thou, in thy atonement, didst give thyself for me;
I own no other master, my heart shall be thy throne;
My life I give, henceforth to live, O Christ, for thee alone.

Living for Jesus who died in my place,
Bearing on Calv'ry my sin and disgrace;
Such love constrains me to answer his call,
Follow his leading and give him my all.

Living for Jesus through earth's little while,
My dearest treasure, the light of his smile;
Seeking the lost ones he died to redeem,
Bringing the weary to find rest in him.

The tune of this song was written before the text. Years later, the composer sent the music to Thomas Chisholm (1866-1960) and asked him to write words to the music with "living for Jesus" as a starting point. Chisolm did not have much in the way of formal education, but that didn't stop him from publishing many wonderful devotional poems and hymn texts.

"Living for Jesus" can be used for dedicating ourselves to the Lord. May we give ourselves to the Lord and trust our lives and trajectories with him. He is wise, kind, and good. It doesn't matter what we do for a living but how we live that truly matters.

Lord, thank you for the power of your love and the freedom of your grace. I am yours, and I choose to live for you. Be glorified in my life as much in the mundane as in the extraordinary.

Sweet Trust

"I am leaving you with a gift—peace of mind and heart.
And the peace I give is a gift the world cannot give.
So don't be troubled or afraid."

John 14:27 NLT

'Tis so sweet to trust in Jesus,
And to take him at his word;
Just to rest upon his promise,
And to know, "Thus saith the Lord."

Jesus, Jesus, how I trust him!
How I've proved him o'er and o'er!
Jesus, Jesus, precious Jesus!
O for grace to trust him more!

O how sweet to trust in Jesus,
Just to trust his cleansing blood;
And in simple faith to plunge me
Neath the healing, cleansing flood!

Yes, 'tis sweet to trust in Jesus,
Just from sin and self to cease;
Just from Jesus simply taking
Life and rest, and joy and peace.

Louisa Stead (1850-1917) penned this hymn in a time of great grief. It was published two years after her husband drowned. Though this must have been a painful time for her, she still went to her Savior with a trusting heart. No matter what we are going through, we can do the same.

Jesus promised the gift of peace to all who look to him. It doesn't matter our station in life or the status of our bank accounts. If we are healthy or ill, God is gracious toward us in the same measure. May we choose to trust him especially when grief clouds our understanding. When we lay offer our pain on the altars of our hearts, the Lord will consume it with his love.

Faithful One, thank you for the gift of your present peace. I quiet my mind before you and open my heart in surrender to your love. Fill me anew, I pray.

FEBRUARY 13

This Little Light

"Your light must shine before people in such a way
that they may see your good works,
and glorify your Father who is in heaven."

MATTHEW 5:16 NASB

This little light of mine,
I'm gonna let it shine!
This little light of mine,
I'm gonna let it shine!
This little light of mine,
I'm gonna let it shine!
Let it shine, let it shine, let it shine!

Although the author of this popular song is unknown, it has carried through many decades since its inception in the 1920s. It was used in the civil rights movement as well as in many Sunday schools. It is catchy, which makes it easy to remember, and the lyrics are simple. Its simplicity is not a detriment but a strength.

What simple truths have you clung to in your walk with the Lord? How have they shaped your life choices? When you feel overwhelmed, redirect your attention back to the Lord and his simple gospel. What one, simple thing can you do today to let your light shine? Do that. Let go of the need to do everything perfectly. His grace is enough to cover you.

Gracious Jesus, your light is like the sun, and mine is like a star reflecting your glory. May the choices I make glorify you and reveal the power of your mercy at work in my life. Let me shine for you.

Breathe on Me

"I will put my Spirit inside you
and help you live by my rules
and carefully obey my laws."
EZEKIEL 36:27 NCV

Breathe on me, breath of God,
Fill me with life anew,
That I may love the way you love,
And do what you would do.

Breathe on me, breath of God,
Until my heart is pure,
Until my will is one with yours,
To do and to endure.

Breathe on me, breath of God,
So shall I never die,
But live with you the perfect life
For all eternity.

The writer of this simple hymn from 1878 was a highly educated man. Edwin Hatch did not feel the need to fill the song with doctrine or hefty ideals. It reads more as a devotional prayer as many of the psalms of David do.

Though simple, "Breathe on Me, Breath of God" is one of the most powerful hymns we can sing. It is an invitation for God to breathe his Spirit on us so we will be strengthened to love as Christ does and to act in a way pleasing to the Lord. Before you go about your day, take some time to read or sing this hymn as a prayer of open invitation to the Holy Spirit.

Holy Spirit, thank you for the power of your life in mine. You empower me with the grace and strength of Christ, and I am refreshed and made new in your presence. Breathe on me, breath of God.

FEBRUARY 15

Nothing but the Blood

According to the law almost all things are purified with blood,
and without shedding of blood there is no remission.

HEBREWS 9:22 NKJV

What can wash away my sin?
Nothing but the blood of Jesus.
What can make me whole again?
Nothing but the blood of Jesus.

O precious is the flow
That makes me white as snow;
No other fount I know;
Nothing but the blood of Jesus.

For my pardon this I see:
Nothing but the blood of Jesus.
For my cleansing this my plea:
Nothing but the blood of Jesus.

This is all my hope and peace:
Nothing but the blood of Jesus.
This is all my righteousness:
Nothing but the blood of Jesus.

Focused on the power of Christ's redemption over sin, "Nothing but the Blood" reminds us that the sacrifice of Christ saves us from cycles of sin, shame, fear, and death. We can do nothing to add to his sacrifice, and we can't do anything to take away from it either.

First published in 1876, this hymn was accompanied by Hebrews 9:22. The authors, Robert Lowry and William Doane, sought to underscore the meaning behind the blood. Scripture—both the Old and New Testament—is filled with imagery about sacrifice and blood. Thankfully, Christ was the ultimate and perfect sacrifice, and his blood holds the final word over our sin.

Jesus Christ, your mercy is evident in the sacrifice of your life for the sins of the world. Thank you for doing what no one else could and for the hope of your resurrection life in us now.

Shelter in the Storm

You are my true tower of strength,
my safe place, my hideout,
and my true shelter.

Psalm 94:23 TPT

The Lord's our rock, in him we hide,
A shelter in the time of storm;
Secure whatever ill betide,
A shelter in the time of storm.
Mighty rock in a weary land,
Cooling shade on the burning sand,
Faithful guide for the pilgrim band
A shelter in the time of storm.

The raging storms may round us beat,
A shelter in the time of storm;
We'll never leave our safe retreat,
A shelter in the time of storm.
Mighty rock in a weary land,
Cooling shade on the burning sand,
Faithful guide for the pilgrim band
A shelter in the time of storm.

Vernon Charlesworth wrote this hymn in the late nineteenth century probably based on his study of Psalm 32:7. The psalm, as with the imagery of many psalms, focuses on God as our hiding place and safe shelter in the storm.

When you go through storms in this life, whether they be physical, financial, emotional, or any other kind, God is your shelter. Run into his presence and hide in his peace. He is faithful to defend you even and especially when you have nothing to offer of your own strength. When the storms rage, your heavenly Father is your place of peace. Hide yourself in him today and let him do what you cannot.

Rock of Ages, you are the firm foundation and rock of safety I run to. Keep me in your perfect peace. I rest in you.

FEBRUARY 17

Pass Me Not

"If I have found favor in your eyes, my lord,
do not pass your servant by."
GENESIS 18:3 NIV

Pass me not, O gentle Savior,
Hear my humble cry,
While on others thou art calling,
Do not pass me by.

Savior, Savior,
Hear my humble cry;
While on others thou art calling,
Do not pass me by.

Let me at a throne of mercy
Find a sweet relief;
Kneeling there in deep contrition,
Help my unbelief.

Trusting only in thy merit,
Would I seek thy face;
Heal my wounded, broken spirit,
Save me by thy grace.

When we are at a loss for how to move ahead with our ideas, sometimes we need the partnership and gifts of another. Instead of trying to do everything on our own, our work may go further through collaboration with the right people. Fanny Crosby wrote the lyrics to this 1868 hymn while William Doane wrote the music. In fact, they wrote many successful songs together.

God does not ignore our cries for help, and his capacity is endless. He has infinite time and attention to offer you when you ask for his help. Don't hold back from asking for what you need; he is kind and reliable, and he delights in helping you.

Savior, I'm tired of struggling on my own. That's not how you created me. You made me for community, for family, and to depend on others in my time of need even as I reach out to help others. Be near me today, Lord.

A Heart to Praise

Come, let's worship and bow down;
let's kneel before the LORD our Maker.
For he is our God,
and we are the people of his pasture,
the sheep under his care.

PSALM 95:6-7 CSB

O for a heart to praise my God,
A heart from sin set free;
A heart that's sprinkled with the blood
So freely shed for me.

A heart resigned, submissive, meek,
My great Redeemer's throne;
Where only Christ is heard to speak,
Where Jesus reigns alone.

A humble, lowly, contrite heart,
Believing, true, and clean,
Which neither life nor death can part
From him that dwells within.

Thy nature, gracious Lord, impart,
Come quickly from above;
Write thy new name upon my heart,
Thy new best name of Love.

Charles Wesley is one of the most famous hymnists in history. He wrote thousands of hymns in his lifetime. Pen and music were the friends he went to in all manner of circumstances, but he was also known as a passionate preacher and a zealous evangelist.

We can have many passions and gifts in this life, but none are our true identity. We get to express ourselves in many ways, but our worth is found in God and who he says we are. Our heavenly Father loves us, Christ pursues us, and the Spirit fills us. God declares us clean in his mercy as we surrender fully to him. Why not follow him wholeheartedly?

Great God, thank you for the power of your redemption in my life. I can't express the gratitude of my heart. Without you, I don't know where I'd be. Continue to move through my yielded life; I want to glorify you through it.

FEBRUARY 19

Follow On

Even though I walk through the valley of the shadow of death,
I will fear no evil, for you are with me;
your rod and your staff, they comfort me.

PSALM 23:4 ESV

Down in the valley with my Savior I would go,
Where the flowers are blooming and the sweet
waters flow;
Everywhere he leads me I would follow,
follow on,
Walking in his footsteps till the crown be won.

Follow, follow, I will follow Jesus,
Anywhere, everywhere, I will follow on;
Follow, follow, I will follow Jesus,
Everywhere he leads me I will follow on.

Down in the valley with my Savior I would go,
Where the storms are sweeping and the dark
waters flow;
With his hand to lead me I will never,
never fear;
Dangers cannot fright me if my Lord is near.

William Cushing wrote this hymn in 1878. It was born out of a strong desire to surrender all to Jesus in response to the one who gave his life for him. Perhaps you have felt that longing stir within your heart. Maybe you wonder what you can offer God in return for all he has done.

The answer is simple: remain openhearted to the Lord and follow him. Keep following him through the valley and the storm. Trust him when you feel his presence leading you in a direction you did not think to choose. He is full of loyal love to guide you, and he will not let you down. He doesn't need your perfection; he only needs your willingness.

Redeemer, I don't want to pave my path unless you are already leading me down it. I choose to follow you through every season of the soul and every stage of life. Be glorified in me.

FEBRUARY 20

Child of the King

The Spirit Himself testifies with our spirit that we are children of God, and if children, heirs also, heirs of God and fellow heirs with Christ, if indeed we suffer with Him so that we may also be glorified with Him.

Romans 8:16-17 NASB

My Father is rich in houses and land,
He holdeth the wealth of the world in his hands!
Of rubies and diamonds, of silver and gold,
His coffers are full, he has riches untold.

I'm a child of the King,
A child of the King,
With Jesus my Savior,
I'm a child of the King.

My Father's own Son, the Savior of men,
Once wandered on earth as the poorest of them;
But now he is reigning for ever on high,
And will give me a home in heav'n by and by.

A tent or a cottage, why should I care?
They're building a palace for me over there;
Though exiled from home, yet still may I sing:
All glory to God, I'm a child of the King.

Harriet Buell wrote this poem on her walk home from a church meeting in 1876. She was full of joy as she thought about the message she had heard. The wonderful truth is our heavenly Father is a king, and he has prepared a place for each of us in his glorious kingdom. What a reason to rejoice!

Let the words wash over you as you take time to reread them. "I'm a child of the King, a child of the King, With Jesus my Savior, I'm a child of the King." No matter what you are facing today, if you are in Christ, you are a child of the King of kings and Lord of lords. Remember who (and whose) you are and rejoice!

Heavenly Father, I delight in being your child. Thank you for seeing, knowing, and choosing me as your own. May even more joy arise as you continue to reveal this deep truth to me.

FEBRUARY 21

Wondrous Story

Come and listen, all you who fear God,
and I will tell you what he did for me.

Psalm 66:16 NLT

I will sing the wondrous story
Of the Christ who died for me.
How he left his home in glory
For the cross of Calvary.
I was lost, but Jesus found me,
Found the sheep that went astray,
Threw his loving arms around me,
Drew me back into his way.

He will keep me till the river
Rolls its waters at my feet;
Then he'll bear me safely over,
Where the loved ones I shall meet.
Yes, I'll sing the wondrous story
Of the Christ who died for me,
Sing it with the saints in glory,
Gathered by the crystal sea.

In 1886, Francis Rowley wrote this hymn during a series of revival meetings at the First Baptist Church in North Adams, Massachusetts, where he pastored. When we are spiritually refreshed and revived, when our hearts are soaring in hope and fulfilled prayers, the joy of our testimonies bubbles to the surface. This was true of Rowley too.

Where can you recognize God's hand of mercy on your life? When were you at your most faith-filled? Don't approach it as a judgment on your current reality but rather a chance to reflect and give gratitude for the faithfulness of the Lord. The one who revived you once will do it again. Share a memory that comes up, perhaps a tender moment you had forgotten, with someone dear to you today.

Faithful Father, you never stop moving in miraculous mercy, and I won't forget how you have changed my life. Thank you.

By and By

"My thoughts are not like your thoughts.
Your ways are not like my ways.
Just as the heavens are higher than the earth,
so are my ways higher than your ways
and my thoughts higher than your thoughts."

ISAIAH 55:8-9 NCV

By and by, when the morning comes,
When the saints of God are gathered home,
We'll tell the story,
How we've overcome,
For we'll understand it better by and by.

Temptations, hidden snares,
Often take us unawares,
And our hearts are made to bleed for
Any thoughtless word or deed;
And we wonder why the test
When we try to do our best,
But we'll understand it better by and by.

Charles Tindley (1851-1933) was the son of an enslaved man and a free woman. He knew what poverty was, and he worked hard to help the family from a young age. Mainly self-taught, he applied to become a Methodist minister in Philadelphia through correspondence courses. He not only served as a minister and captivating preacher but also as a songwriter. "Better By and By" is one of many hymns he wrote and used in his ministry.

We can be quick to disqualify ourselves from serving the Lord for one reason or another, but God uses all who are willing. We have unique talents and gifts we can work at and grow in, and when we offer them to the Lord, he will use them for his glory.

Father, I'm grateful you understand what I can't come close to comprehending. I want to learn from your wisdom and walk in your ways. Teach me and lead me on.

FEBRUARY 23

Man of Sorrows

He is despised and rejected by men,
A Man of sorrows and acquainted with grief.
And we hid, as it were, our faces from Him;
He was despised, and we did not esteem Him.

ISAIAH 53:3 NKJV

Man of sorrows what a name
For the Son of God, who came
Ruined sinners to reclaim:
Hallelujah, what a Savior!

Bearing shame and scoffing rude,
In my place condemned he stood,
Sealed my pardon with his blood:
Hallelujah, what a Savior!

He was lifted up to die;
"It is finished" was his cry;
Now in heaven exalted high:
Hallelujah, what a Savior!

When he comes, our glorious King,
All his ransomed home to bring,
Then anew this song we'll sing:
Hallelujah, what a Savior!

"Man of Sorrows" written by Philip Bliss in 1875, effectively moves through the gospel story and is a powerful hymn to both sing and meditate on. The term "Man of sorrows" comes from Isaiah in a prophecy of the Messiah's coming.

Take comfort in the fact that God is not put off by your grief. He knows how it feels to be full of sorrow and acquainted with grief. Though we may despise our pain, he does not. He has experienced loss and disappointment. Let's bring him our own and allow him to comfort us.

Savior, when I think about the grief, humility, and sacrifice you bore so we could know the Father in spirit and in truth, I am undone. Thank you for letting love compel you. Meet me in my sorrow as I lean into your presence today.

I Need Thee

"I am the vine; you are the branches.
If you remain in me and I in you,
you will bear much fruit;
apart from me you can do nothing."
JOHN 15:5 NIV

I need thee ev'ry hour,
Most gracious Lord;
No tender voice like thine
Can peace afford.

I need thee, oh, I need thee;
Ev'ry hour I need thee;
Oh, bless me now, my Savior,
I come to thee.

I need thee ev'ry hour,
In joy or pain;
Come quickly and abide,
Or life is vain.

I need thee ev'ry hour,
Teach me thy will;
And thy rich promises
In me fulfill.

When we realize our dependence on God, we actively humble ourselves. Though we try to control aspects of our lives, there comes a point when we realize how little power we have. Realization of this is not a bad thing; it grounds us in the faithfulness of God and throws our hopeful trust onto his power.

Annie Hawks (1835-1918), the writer of the stanzas of this hymn, was a housewife. Though a humble title, we all know mothers and wives who carry their households with devotion, tenacity, and some serious multi-tasking. Though the pressures are great, God is greater. We don't have to pretend to have everything under control. Instead, we can allow our weakness to send us running to our Savior over and over again. Oh, how we need him!

Faithful One, thank you for providing for my needs and filling in the cracks of my weakness. You are so good.

FEBRUARY 25

I Have Decided

"Why do you keep looking back to your past
and have second thoughts about following me?
If you turn back you are not fit for God's kingdom."

Luke 9:62 TPT

I have decided to follow Jesus;
I have decided to follow Jesus;
I have decided to follow Jesus;
no turning back, no turning back.

Though none go with me, I still will follow;
though none go with me, I still will follow;
though none go with me, I still will follow;
no turning back, no turning back.

The world behind me, the cross before me;
the world behind me, the cross before me,
the world behind me, the cross before me;
no turning back, no turning back.

The specific author of this declarative hymn is largely unknown. However, we do know it was written in northeastern India. It is highly likely the writer was experiencing persecution for their faith. Whatever the circumstances surrounding the inception of the hymn, it is just as powerful when we sing it today.

Have you ever reached a pivotal moment in your walk of faith where you knew you had a choice to make? Choosing to follow Christ on the path of his laid-down love is not a popular one. It requires humility, trust, and surrender. Still, when everything else fades away in this life, what are we left with? What do we want to go after with all our hearts, souls, minds, and strength? Let's not take that choice lightly but instead weigh it with wisdom, insight, and faith.

Lord Jesus, I believe you are worth following. You revealed what the Father is really like: merciful, patient, true, and kind. I choose to follow you no matter what.

Lover of My Soul

Both the Spirit and the bride say, "Come!"
Let anyone who hears, say, "Come!"
Let the one who is thirsty come.
Let the one who desires take the water of life freely.

REVELATION 22:17 CSB

Jesus, lover of my soul,
Let me to thy bosom fly,
While the nearer waters roll,
While the tempest still is high;
Hide me, O my Savior, hide,
Till the storm of life is past;
Safe into the haven guide,
O receive my soul at last!

Other refuge have I none;
Hangs my helpless soul on thee;
Leave, ah! Leave me not alone,
Still support and comfort me.
All my trust on thee is stayed,
All my help from thee I bring;
Cover my defenseless head
With the shadow of thy wing.

Charles Wesley originally published this 1740s hymn under the title "In Temptation." What can we do when we are tempted to compromise? Turn to Jesus, for with him is not only the grace and strength we are looking for but also healing, companionship, and endless love.

In Christ, we find the fullness of hope, joy, and peace. He is the embodiment of God's true nature, and he will never turn away those who come to him for help. As we draw near to Christ, we become more like him. As we adopt his ways, we reflect his likeness on the earth. How we live is just as important as what we believe, so we cannot neglect our choices in the day-to-day.

Loving Jesus, you are my refuge, source, and strength. You are the lover of my soul, and you are worthy of my attention, trust, and obedience.

Just as I Am

Have mercy on me, O God,
according to your steadfast love;
according to your abundant mercy
blot out my transgressions.

PSALM 51:1 ESV

Just as I am, without one plea,
But that thy blood was shed for me,
And that thou bidd'st me come to thee,
O Lamb of God, I come, I come.

Just as I am, and waiting not
To rid my soul of one dark blot,
To thee, whose blood can cleanse each spot,
O Lamb of God, I come, I come.

Just as I am, though tossed about
With many a conflict, many a doubt,
Fightings and fears within, without,
O Lamb of God, I come, I come.

Just as I am, thou wilt receive,
Wilt welcome, pardon, cleanse, relieve;
Because thy promise I believe,
O Lamb of God, I come, I come.

Just as we are. That is how God accepts us. We don't have to dress ourselves up or beat ourselves down. God welcomes us as we are precisely in this moment and every moment. Whatever excuses have kept us from coming to him, now is the time to abandon them. We bring him our open hearts, and he meets us there in that most holy place.

Today's hymnist, Charlotte Elliott (1789-1871), was only thirty-two when a serious illness changed her abilities. She struggled to come to Christ as she found herself limited in ways she never imagined she would be. After confessing this to evangelist Henri Cesar Malan, the encouragement she found was to come just as she was. No matter what you are struggling with today, come as you are.

Lord, just as I am, right here in this moment, I come to you. Meet me in the messiest parts of my life and speak life, truth, and peace to my troubled heart.

More Love to Thee

You will guide me with Your plan,
And afterward receive me to glory.
Whom do I have in heaven but You?
And with You, I desire nothing on earth.

PSALM 73:24-25 NASB

More love to thee, O Christ,
More love to thee!
Hear thou the prayer I make
On bended knee;
This is my earnest plea:
More love, O Christ, to thee,
More love to thee,
More love to thee!

Once earthly joy I craved,
Sought peace and rest;
Now thee alone I seek,
Give what is best;
This all my prayer shall be:
More love, O Christ, to thee,
More love to thee,
More love to thee!

Out of incredible personal grief and tragedy, Elizabeth Prentiss (1818-1878) wrote this hymn as a declaration of her devotion. While grieving the loss of two children, Prentiss was inspired to write this song of devoted surrender to the Lord. It wasn't written for the masses but in a journal she did not share with anyone for thirteen years. When it was finally printed, it struck a chord and became a popular hymn.

Even in our deepest pain, God can plant seeds that will bloom in later seasons and bring joy out of the shadows of despair. Let's trust him and echo Prentiss's words to offer "more love, O Christ, to thee," no matter what we are going through.

Merciful One, I trust you are with me in my pain. You will carry me into fields of joy once again.

March

Holy, holy, holy! Lord God Almighty!
Early in the morning our song shall rise to thee;
Holy, holy, holy! merciful and mighty,
God in three persons, blessed Trinity!

Private Faith

We do this by keeping our eyes on Jesus, the champion who initiates and perfects our faith. Because of the joy awaiting him, he endured the cross, disregarding its shame. Now he is seated in the place of honor beside God's throne.

HEBREWS 12:2 NLT

My faith looks up to thee,
Thou Lamb of Calvary,
Savior divine.
Now hear me while I pray;
Take all my guilt away;
O let me from this day
Be wholly thine!

May thy rich grace impart
Strength to my fainting heart;
My zeal inspire!
As thou hast died for me,
Oh, may my love to thee
Pure, warm, and changeless be,
A living fire!

Ray Palmer wrote this hymn in 1830. The text was written as a private expression of how Palmer felt about Christ. Even though it was not written with the intention of being published, Palmer was willing to share it with Lowell Mason when asked if he had any hymns Mason could use for a music book he was putting together.

Some of our greatest offerings begin in private expression. It takes our time, resources, and attention. It requires discipline and consistency. This is as true in our spiritual lives as it is in our physical lives. Perhaps you have personal expressions that will turn into opportunities someday. Don't neglect the power of your personal devotion; that is where integrity grows.

Savior, I offer you the truth of my heart, and I am satisfied if you alone accept and know its depths.

MARCH 2

Don't Let Go

"Then I will lead the blind along a way they never knew;
I will guide them along paths they have not known.
I will make the darkness become light for them,
and the rough ground smooth. These are the things
I will do; I will not leave my people."

Isaiah 42:16 NCV

O Love that will not let me go,
I rest my weary soul in thee.
I give thee back the life I owe,
That in thine ocean depths its flow
May richer, fuller be.

O Light that follows all my way,
I yield my flick'ring torch to thee.
My heart restores its borrowed ray,
That in thy sunshine's blaze its day
May brighter, fairer be.

O Joy that seekest me through pain,
I cannot close my heart to thee.
I trace the rainbow through the rain,
And feel the promise is not vain,
That morn shall tearless be.

George Matheson (1842-1906) was a Scottish minister, and he wrote many poems later turned into sacred songs. When he was twenty, his fiance cut off their engagement after finding out he was going blind. "O Love" was written the evening of his sister's wedding as he felt how alone he was while realizing he was not alone at all.

When we are lonely, we can turn to a love that never lets us go. God's Spirit never leaves us. The Father never forsakes his children. Christ promises to walk with us as we journey through the ups and downs of life. Even when we face disappointments and broken relationships, God will never choose to walk away from us. He is gracious, kind, patient, and persistent, and he is not a consolation prize.

Lord, your love is the most generous and powerful force in existence. I'm grateful you will never let me go; you promise to never leave me.

Thine Is the Glory

Christ is risen from the dead, and has become the firstfruits
of those who have fallen asleep.

1 Corinthians 15:20 NKJV

Thine is the glory, Resurrected One!
Endless is the victr'y now for us begun!
Angels clothed in glory rolled the stone away,
Leaving only graveclothes where his body lay.

Thine is the glory, Resurrected One!
Endless is the victr'y now for us begun!

Thine was the suff'ring, mine the endless life.
Sin holds no dominion; love wins over strife.
What then shall I shall I offer? Songs that never cease!
Thou hast won the vict'ry, glorious Prince of Peace!

A favorite hymn in Great Britain, "Thine is the Glory" is a translation of a French hymn. It was first written by Edmond Louis Budry, a Swiss writer, translator, and minister, in 1904. After its translation, it often was and still is used in funerals and Easter services in Great Britain.

The resurrection power of Christ is a hope to us no matter the day, time, or place. His resurrected life points us to the promise of our own. Christ broke the power of sin, shame, fear, and death so we can stand confident and clean in his victory. Though we grieve our losses in this life, loss is not the end of the story. There is new life and redemption for every ending. Let us take hope in he who has overcome.

Jesus Christ, you are glorious and worthy of my praise. Your resurrection life is at work in the details of my life.

MARCH 4

Stand Up

Praise be to the Lord, the God of Israel, from everlasting to everlasting.
Then all the people said "Amen" and "Praise the Lord."

1 Chronicles 16:36 NIV

Stand up, and bless the Lord,
Ye people of his choice;
Stand up, and bless the Lord your God
With heart, and soul, and voice.

Tho' high above all praise,
Above all blessing high,
Who would not fear his holy name,
And laud and magnify?

O for the living flame,
From his own altar brought,
To touch our lips, our minds inspire,
And wing to heav'n our thought!

Stand up and bless the Lord,
The Lord your God adore;
Stand up, and bless his glorious name
Henceforth for evermore.

Originally written in 1824 by James Montgomery for the Sheffield Red Hill Wesleyan Sunday School Anniversary, the first two lines read, "Stand up, and bless the Lord, ye children of His choice." It was only changed to "people" when it was published the following year. Whether young or old, we can stand up in the company of believers and bless the name of the Lord our God.

No matter where we are, God sees the stance of our hearts. Even if we cannot get on our feet, we can raise our hearts to him. He sees through the exterior to the inner places of our hearts and straight to our intentions. Offer him praise, for he is worthy.

Great God, I worship you simply because you are worthy of it. You have been good, faithful, and true to me. I choose to turn my heart to you today. Be honored in my life.

Take Time to Be Holy

"Seek first the kingdom of God and his righteousness,
and all these things will be provided for you."

MATTHEW 6:33 CSB

Take time to be holy, speak oft with thy Lord;
Abide in him always, and feed on his Word.
Make friends of God's children, help those
who are weak,
Forgetting in nothing his blessing to seek.

Take time to be holy, the world rushes on;
Spend much time in secret, with Jesus alone.
By looking to Jesus, like him thou shalt be;
Thy friends in thy conduct his likeness shall see.

Take time to be holy, let him be thy guide;
And run not before him, whatever betide.
In joy or in sorrow, still follow the Lord,
And, looking to Jesus, still trust in his Word.

Take time to be holy, be calm in thy soul,
Each thought and each motive beneath his
control.
Thus led by his Spirit to fountains of love,
Thou soon shalt be fitted for service above.

William Longstaff was born the son of a wealthy ship merchant in 1822. He became involved in his church and gave generously to Christian causes. He attended a church service where the sermon was based on 1 Peter 1:16: "Be ye holy: for I am holy." In response, he wrote what holiness meant to him in a simple poem. This is the text of "Take Time to Be Holy."

In a world that never stops moving, we can always find something to keep us busy. However, we must not neglect to give time to the Lord and his fellowship. As we grow in Christ, abiding in him and following his instructions, we find purpose, fulfillment, and inspiration. Be sure to take time today with your God. He always has time for you.

Generous One, thank you for always receiving me when I come to you. I want to grow strong in faith and grow deep in the knowledge of who you are.

MARCH 6

The Very Thought

To know the love of Christ that surpasses knowledge,
that you may be filled with all the fullness of God.

EPHESIANS 3:19 ESV

Jesus, the very thought of thee
With sweetness fills the breast;
But sweeter far thy face to see,
And in thy presence rest.

O hope of every contrite heart,
O joy of all the meek,
To those who fall, how kind thou art!
How good to those who seek!

But what to those who find? Ah, this
Nor tongue nor pen can show;
The love of Jesus, what it is,
None but his loved ones know.

Jesus, our only joy be thou,
As thou our prize wilt be;
Jesus, be thou our glory now,
And through eternity.

The love of Christ is not some knowledge to attain. It is a force. If we only spoke of love or its experience intellectually, we would be missing out. How much more is this true of the love of God? Love is experienced in relationship. It is in the patience of a parent, the humble apology of a loved one, and the joy of sharing ourselves with those dear to us.

This hymn was originally written by Bernard of Clairvaux in 1100. He had abandoned his wealth and status to live as a monk. It can only be assumed that Christ's love led him to such sacrifice. Jesus' love is pure. It has no hidden motivation, and it is better than any love we have known. We have tasted and seen its beauty, but there is more in its depths. The same love that led to Bernard's devotion is available to us and streams from the Father in waves of unending glory.

Glorious One, there are no limits to your love. I ask for more of it today.

Mighty Power

In the beginning God created
the heavens and the earth.
GENESIS 1:1 NASB

We sing the mighty power of God
That made the mountains rise,
That spread the flowing seas abroad
And built the lofty skies.
We sing the wisdom that ordained
The sun to rule the day;
The moon shines full at his command,
And all the stars obey.

There's not a plant or flower below
But makes your glories known,
And clouds arise and tempests blow
By order from your throne;
While all that borrows life from you
Is ever in your care,
And everywhere that we can be,
You, God, are present there.

God is the Creator, artist, originator, and mastermind behind all creation. He is the source of all life. Within creation, we find hints of his wisdom and majesty. Think about all the new discoveries unfolding even now. We are just beginning to explore the depths of the ocean and the limits of our universe. All of it points to his power.

Isaac Watts (1674-1748) wrote this poem for children, but it is just as powerful for adults. If we want to reengage with the wonder of our youth, a great way to do that is to consider creation and its order. When we look at the diversity and intricacies of nature, awe leads us to worship the source behind it.

Creator, you are wise, innovative, and powerful. You are more than I can imagine and greater than I know. I am in awe of you as I consider the works of your hands. Be glorified in your creation!

MARCH 8

Till We Meet Again

Now I entrust you to God and the message of his grace that is able to build you up and give you an inheritance with all those he has set apart for himself.

ACTS 20:32 NLT

God be with you till we meet again;
Loving counsels guide, uphold you,
May the Shepherd's care enfold you;
God be with you till we meet again.

Till we meet, till we meet,
Till we meet at Jesus' feet.
Till we meet, till we meet,
God be with you till we meet again.

God be with you till we meet again;
When life's perils thick confound you,
Put unfailing arms around you;
God be with you till we meet again.

God be with you till we meet again;
Keep love's banner floating o'er you,
Smite death's threat'ning wave before you;
God be with you till we meet again.

Jeremiah Rankin wrote this hymn in 1880 specifically as a Christian goodbye. Often used when commissioning missionaries or when people move on to other places, it is a blessing and a benediction for parting.

We would do well to bless others when we part ways in life. We can wish others the best even if their absence will be greatly felt. Though technology has done much in the way of connecting us no matter where in the world we are, it is still beneficial to mark goodbyes with a blessing. Make this a part of your practice and consider its effects in your relationships.

Spirit, you bind your people together in love even across distances. Help me to bless others both in significant and small partings. I'm grateful for your presence through it all.

Crown Him

They sang the song of Moses, the servant of God, and the song of the Lamb:
"You do great and wonderful things, Lord God Almighty.
Everything the Lord does is right and true, King of the nations."
REVELATION 15:3 NCV

Crown him with many crowns,
The Lamb upon his throne.
Hark! How the heavenly anthem drowns
All music but its own.
Awake, my soul, and sing
Of him who died for thee,
And hail him as thy matchless king
Through all eternity.

Crown him the Lord of life,
Who triumphed o'er the grave,
And rose victorious in the strife
For those he came to save;
His glories now we sing
Who died and rose on high,
Who died eternal life to bring,
And lives that death may die.

Though many variations of this hymn exist, the original text was written by Matthew Bridges in 1851. It is easy to see why it is so popular, for it is a joyous declaration and invitation to worship our Lord Jesus Christ. He is the one "who triumphed o'er the grave, and rose victorious." He is the God who died and rose so we could rise with him into eternal life.

Sometimes we must do as the writer did and direct our souls to put our trust in God. "Awake, my soul, and sing" is a perfect place to start if we find we are disconnected from the power and purpose of Christ's sacrifice. He is still victorious, still near, and still working in us. He is worthy of our praise, so let's offer it.

Jesus, I crown you with my offering of praise. Be honored in my life and in all creation.

MARCH 10

Can It Be

There is therefore now no condemnation to those who are in Christ Jesus, who do not walk according to the flesh, but according to the Spirit.

Romans 8:1 NKJV

And can it be that I should gain
An int'rest in the Savior's blood?
Died he for me, who caused his pain?
For me, who him to death pursued?
Amazing love! How can it be
That thou, my God, should die for me?

Amazing love! How can it be
That thou, my God, should die for me!

No condemnation now I dread;
Jesus, and all in him is mine!
Alive in him, my living head,
And clothed in righteousness divine,
Bold I approach th'eternal throne,
And claim the crown, through Christ my own.

Written in 1738 by Charles Wesley, "And Can It Be" remains a classic hymn sung worldwide today. He wrote it to celebrate his conversion that very same year. With that in mind, the theme of personal salvation rings clearly.

Think about your salvation story. Do you remember what it was like at first? As you meditate on your journey with the Lord, allow your heart to remember the wonder, humility, and joy you felt as you discovered God died died for the sins of the world and for you.

Savior, thank you for your love that led you to the cross and for the power of your mercy that broke the power of the grave. Your resurrection life is alive and well in me, and I am thankful.

Come Almighty King

"When the Counselor comes,
the one I will send to you from the Father—
the Spirit of truth who proceeds from the Father—
he will testify about me."

John 15:26 CSB

Come, thou almighty King,
Help us thy name to sing;
Help us to praise.
Father all-glorious,
O'er all victorious,
Come and reign over us,
Ancient of Days.

To thee, great one in three,
Eternal praises be
Hence evermore!
Thy sov'reign majesty
May we in glory see,
And to eternity
Love and adore.

The text of this hymn is anonymous and dates back before 1757. It is a British hymn and seems to be patterned after their national anthem, "God Save the King." God is our great King, and his reign knows no end. The hymn amplifies the triune nature of God—Father, Son, and Spirit—and his rule over all.

No matter what earthly powers have authority, our hope does not rest in them. Our true hope is in our God and King, the one who created it all and who redeemed it by the blood of the Lamb, Christ our true King. May we honor him with our trust and not fear when the governments of earth fail.

King Jesus, you are the wisest ruler, and I trust you more than the leaders of this earth. May your will be done on earth as it is in heaven.

By and By

Those the LORD has rescued will return.
They will enter Zion with singing;
everlasting joy will crown their heads.
Gladness and joy will overtake them,
and sorrow and sighing will flee away.

ISAIAH 35:10 NIV

There's a land that is fairer than day,
And by faith we can see it afar,
For the Father waits over the way
To prepare us a dwelling place there.

In the sweet by and by,
We shall meet on that beautiful shore;
In the sweet by and by,
We shall meet on that beautiful shore.

We shall sing on that beautiful shore
The melodious songs of the blest;
And our spirits shall sorrow no more—
Not a sigh for the blessing of rest.

To our bountiful Father above
We will offer our tribute of praise
For the glorious gift of his love
And the blessings that hallow our days.

Friends Sanford Fillmore Bennet and Joseph Webster wrote this hymn in only thirty minutes in 1868. Bennet had noticed his friend seemed sad, and he asked him what was the matter. Webster's response was, "It's no matter; it will be all right by and by." Bennet was immediately inspired and wrote the whole of the hymn before offering it to Webster who, in turn, wrote the music just as swiftly.

In the time between now and then, between promise and fulfillment, we find "the sweet by and by." Time will pass whether we pay attention to it or not, but we can find peace and rest in the knowledge that the Father prepares us along the way. He is actively working in our lives, and we can rest in his ability to continue moving in mercy.

Father, thank you for your faithfulness and incomparable wisdom. I trust you with what I can't control for you are trustworthy and true.

Arms of Jesus

He will tend his flock like a shepherd;
he will gather the lambs in his arms;
he will carry them in his bosom,
and gently lead those that are with young.

ISAIAH 40:11 ESV

Safe in the arms of Jesus,
Safe on his gentle breast,
There by his love o'ershaded,
Sweetly my soul shall rest.
Hark! 'Tis the voice of angels,
Borne in a song to me,
Over the fields of glory,
Over the jasper sea.

Safe in the arms of Jesus,
Safe from corroding care,
Safe from the world's temptations,
Sin cannot harm me there.
Free from the blight of sorrow,
Free from my doubts and fears;
Only a few more trials,
Only a few more tears.

On his way to a Sunday School Convention, William Doane brought some music to Fanny Crosby to see if she could finish a hymn. Thankfully for Doane, Fanny was able to write "Safe in the Arms of Jesus" quickly enough for him to bring it with him. A simple message tailored for children, this hymn from 1868 speaks to the hearts of those who have that child within them.

Christ is the Good Shepherd who gathers helpless lambs into his arms. He holds them close to his chest, and he gently leads all who follow. Let's follow our gentle Shepherd today and trust him to carry us through the harsh terrain of this life when our legs give way.

Good Shepherd, when I have no strength, carry me close to your heart. I trust you.

MARCH 14

We Would See Jesus

"Look!" Stephen said. "I can see the heavens opening and the Son of Man standing at the right hand of God to welcome me home!"

ACTS 7:56 TPT

We would see Jesus, for the shadows lengthen
Across this little landscape of our life;
We would see Jesus, our weak faith to strengthen
For the last weariness, the final strife.

We would see Jesus, the great rock foundation
Whereon our feet were set with sov'reign grace;
Nor life nor death, with all their agitation,
Can thence remove us, if we see his face.

We would see Jesus; other lights are paling,
Which for long years we have rejoiced to see;
The blessings of our pilgrimage are failing;
We would not mourn them, for we go to thee.

We would see Jesus: this is all we're needing;
Strength, joy, and willingness come with the sight;
We would see Jesus, dying, risen, pleading;
Then welcome day, and farewell mortal night.

There is a hymn for any occasion. In our living and dying, there is always reason to reach toward the Lord who is nearer than we know. Anna Warner wrote this song about the approach of death in 1852. This may be uncomfortable to think about, but it is best to come to peace with it and be mindful about how we can approach death well and with surrender.

We don't have to fear death; Christ has overcome it. He has already gone through all we have or will one day experience, and that includes dying. Do we trust him to guide us lovingly into death as he does everything else? Our earthly end is only the beginning of a new chapter: everlasting life in his presence. We have his love, his face, and his glory to look forward to.

Jesus, it is difficult for me to think about death. Help me to trust you with my days, for you know their number. I look forward to seeing your face in the end.

Day Is Over

In peace I will both lie down and sleep,
For You alone, LORD, have me dwell in safety.
PSALM 4:8 NASB

Now the day is over,
Night is drawing nigh;
Shadows of the evening
Steal across the sky.

Jesus, give the weary
Calm and sweet repose;
With your tend'rest blessing
May my eyelids close.

Thro' the long night-watches
May your angels spread
Their bright wings above me,
Watching round my bed.

When the morning wakens,
Then may I arise
Pure and fresh and sinless
In your holy eyes.

Sabine Baring-Gould, the writer of the text of this 1865 hymn, was an author, archaeologist, artist, and teacher. His creativity shines through the poem and directs our attention to the experience of night falling and the wait until morning dawns again.

Perhaps you find yourself in a dark night of the soul. If so, take heart and courage in the hope of a new day dawning. It is coming; morning is on its way, and when it awakens, you will rise with the joy that daylight brings. In the meantime, rest in the tender arms of Jesus who keeps watch over you by night.

Keeper of my soul, watch over me in the night seasons of my life. Hold me close and remind me of the hope still mine in you. I trust you will lead me through and watch over my soul as I lean on you.

MARCH 16

Secret Presence

You hide them in the shelter of your presence,
safe from those who conspire against them.
You shelter them in your presence,
far from accusing tongues.

PSALM 31:20 NLT

In the secret of his presence how my soul delights to hide!
Oh, how precious are the lessons which I learn at Jesus' side!
Earthly cares can never vex me, neither trials lay me low;
For when Satan comes to tempt me, to the secret place I go,
To the secret place I go.

Would you like to know the sweetness of the secret of the Lord?
Go and hide beneath his shadow: this shall then be your reward;
And whene'er you leave the silence of that happy meeting place,
You must mind and bear the image of the master in your face,
Of the master in your face.

Ellen Lakshmi Goreh was the daughter of an Indian reverend and was adopted after her mother died in 1853. She spent much of her life in England until she returned in 1880 to do mission work among her fellow Indian women. She published a few hymns, and "In the Secret of His Presence" is the best known.

This song paints a vivid picture of devotion and an affectionate relationship with the Lord. Take Goreh's lead and do as she did when saying, "Only this I know: I tell him all my doubts, my griefs, and fears." He can take your honesty, and he will listen patiently and encourage your heart in hope.

Lord, I come to you with an open heart that wants to know you more. I lay it all out before you: the truth of my fears, hopes, and everything in between. Meet me in this place.

Love Divine

Because he was full of grace and truth,
from him we all received one gift after another.

John 1:16 NCV

Love divine, all loves excelling,
Joy of heav'n, to earth come down,
Fix in us thy humble dwelling,
All thy faithful mercies crown.
Jesus, thou art all compassion,
Pure, unbounded love thou art.
Visit us with thy salvation;
Enter ev'ry trembling heart.

Finish, then, thy new creation;
True and spotless let us be.
Let us see thy great salvation
Perfectly restored in thee.
Changed from glory into glory,
Till in heav'n we take our place,
Till we cast our crowns before thee,
Lost in wonder, love and praise.

Charles Wesley's "Love Divine" is a sung prayer. It is addressed to divine love: Jesus Christ who is the personification of God's nature. He is full of compassion for all who come to him, and this remains true in every age. No matter where you are today, "love divine" meets you with the compassion of his heart and the salvation of his sacrifice.

Whether you are familiar with this hymn or not, use it as a prayer to personally connect with the Lord today. The Spirit breathes peace into your heart as you let go of the need to control the narrative and allow the Lord to be God. He can handle the details; he can handle it all.

Savior, thank you for the power of your presence at work in the world and in my heart and life. I praise you, for I am fearfully and wonderfully made, and you take good care of me.

MARCH 18

Peace Like a River

The peace of God, which surpasses all understanding,
will guard your hearts and minds through Christ Jesus.

PHILIPPIANS 4:7 NKJV

When peace like a river attendeth my way,
When sorrows like sea billows roll;
Whatever my lot, thou hast taught me to say,
"It is well, it is well with my soul."

Though Satan should buffet, though trials
should come,
Let this blest assurance control:
That Christ has regarded my helpless estate,
And has shed his own blood for my soul.

My sin oh, the bliss of this glorious thought!
My sin, not in part, but the whole,
Is nailed to the cross, and I bear it no more;
Praise the Lord, praise the Lord, O my soul!

O Lord, haste the day when my faith
shall be sight,
The clouds be rolled back as a scroll;
The trump shall resound and the Lord shall
descend;
Even so, it is well with my soul.

This hymn was born out of tragedy. In 1873, Horatio Spafford was to travel from the United States to Europe with his family. Business held him back, but his family went on without him. Tragically, the ship they were on collided with another, and it sank within twelve minutes. His wife was saved, but his four daughters did not make it. As he passed the spot where the ship sank on the way to meet his wife, he began to write the hymn.

Even in times of incredible grief, sorrow, and pain, we can know the all-surpassing peace of Christ. Peace is not dependent on our circumstances. It is found in the surrender of our hearts. May we be able to say, like Spafford did, "It is well with my soul" no matter the troubles we face.

Father, I know you are near in my heartbreak. I trust your peace is plentiful enough to fill and sustain me. Meet me with the power of your presence.

Redeemer Guide Me

"This God, our God forever and ever—
he will always lead us."

Psalm 48:14 CSB

Guide me, O my great Redeemer,
Pilgrim through this barren land;
I am weak, but you are mighty;
Hold me with your powerful hand.
Bread of heaven, bread of heaven,
Feed me now and evermore,
Feed me now and evermore.

Open now the crystal fountain,
Where the healing waters flow.
Let the fire and cloudy pillar
Lead me all my journey through.
Strong deliverer, strong deliverer,
Ever be my strength and shield,
Ever be my strength and shield.

William Williams wrote this hymn in Welsh with the title "Lord, Lead Me Through the Wildnerness; A prayer for strength to go through the wilderness of the world" in the eighteenth century. Williams was originally training to be a medical professional, but he changed course after an encounter with an evangelist.

In every transition, we can ask the Lord to lead us. The unknown future is already known to our great Redeemer. He is full of wisdom, clarity, and grace. We can trust him to guide us as we listen for his voice. We can trust him to redirect us in the wilderness where we cannot see more than a step ahead. The one who faithfully guided the Israelites through the desert guides us today as we look to him and lean on his leadership.

Great Jehovah, you are Alpha and Omega, my Savior and wise counsel. There is nothing you can't do. I trust you with every part of my life. Lead me on.

MARCH 20

Moment by Moment

God did not appoint us to suffer wrath but to receive salvation through our Lord Jesus Christ.
He died for us so that, whether we are awake or asleep, we may live together with him.

1 THESSALONIANS 5:9-10 NIV

Dying with Jesus, by death reckoned mine;
Living with Jesus, a new life divine;
Looking to Jesus till glory doth shine,
Moment by moment, O Lord, I am thine.

Moment by moment I'm kept in his love;
Moment by moment I've life from above;
Looking to Jesus till glory doth shine;
Moment by moment, O Lord, I am thine.

Never a trial that he is not there,
Never a burden that he doth not bear,
Never a sorrow that he doth not share,
Moment by moment, I'm under his care.

Never a weakness that he doth not feel,
Never a sickness that he cannot heal;
Moment by moment, in woe or in weal,
Jesus, my Savior, abides with me still.

D.W. Whittle (1840-1901) heard a preacher say he did not like the hymn "I Need Thee Every Hour" because he really needed the Lord every moment. Inspired by the preacher's statement, Whittle penned the hymn "Moment by Moment" that very evening. Whether or not we connect with the theme of turning to the Lord every hour or minute, our need remains the same.

As we tune in to the present moment, we can bring our attention to what is true here and now. The air around us offers oxygen. The ground beneath us holds us. The presence of God keeps us in the love of Christ. Practice bringing your attention to the presence of God. Focus on the gratitude of those moments and not on the regret of moments when you are drawn to other things.

Present One, I want to be more aware of your goodness with me. Awaken my senses as I train them to turn to you throughout the day.

Beauty of the Earth

Keep it up, sun and moon!
Don't stop now, all you twinkling stars of light!
Psalm 148:3 TPT

For the beauty of the earth,
For the glory of the skies,
For the love which from our birth
Over and around us lies.

Christ, our Lord, to you we raise
This, our hymn of grateful praise.

For the wonder of each hour
Of the day and of the night,
Hill and vale and tree and flower,
Sun and moon and stars of light,

For yourself, best gift divine,
To the world so freely given,
Agent of God's grand design:
Peace on earth and joy in heaven.

Folliott Pierpoint wrote this text in 1863 as he wandered the English countryside outside his native city of Bath. As he admired the beauty in the hills and the Avon river, he was inspired by God's gifts in both creation and the church. Awe of God's creation can lead us to see the connections of God's hand in our lives and communites.

As we enter a new spring season, we come out of the dark days of winter into newness of life sprouting and light growing longer each day. As we notice growth in the world around us, may we also see growth within. Dormancy does not last forever; new life is sprouting all around.

Creator, as I spend time tuning in to your handiwork in the world around me, I can't help but be grateful that your wisdom and creativity is also at work in your people. Thank you.

MARCH 22

Standing on Promises

Since we have these promises, beloved,
let us cleanse ourselves from every defilement of body and spirit,
bringing holiness to completion in the fear of God.

2 CORINTHIANS 7:1 ESV

Standing on the promises of Christ, my King,
Through eternal ages let his praises ring;
Glory in the highest, I will shout and sing,
Standing on the promises of God.

Standing, standing,
Standing on the promises of God, my Savior;
Standing, standing,
I'm standing on the promises of God.

Standing on the promises of Christ, the Lord,
Bound to him eternally by love's strong cord,
Overcoming daily with the Spirit's sword,
Standing on the promises of God.

Standing on the promises I cannot fall,
List'ning ev'ry moment to the Spirit's call,
Resting in my Savior as my all in all,
Standing on the promises of God.

Russell Kelso Carter (1849-1928) was a star athlete in his youth and an instructor and athletics coach at the Pennsylvania Military Academy. At age thirty, he was diagnosed with a critical heart condition that had no cure. He was facing his mortality, and in that process, he surrendered his heart to the Lord and decided to stand on God's promises in faith. He chose to believe God's promises were true, and he miraculously lived a long, healthy life.

Have you been drowning under your circumstances? What does God's Word have to say about his unfailing nature? Spend time in the presence of God and in his Word today and stand on his promises.

Christ Jesus, your promises are true, and I believe your nature is more constant than my understanding of it. Transform my heart in faith and speak your words of promise over me. I will stand on them.

Take My Life

I heard the voice of the Lord, saying,
"Whom shall I send, and who will go for Us?"
Then I said, "Here am I. Send me!"

Isaiah 6:8 NASB

Take my life and let it be
Consecrated, Lord, to thee.
Take my moments and my days;
Let them flow in endless praise,
Let them flow in endless praise.

Take my voice and let me sing
Always, only, for my King.
Take my lips and let them be
Filled with messages from thee,
Filled with messages from thee.

Take my will and make it thine;
It shall be no longer mine.
Take my heart it is thine own;
It shall be thy royal throne,
It shall be thy royal throne.

Written as a personal consecration to Christ, the couplets Frances Havergal (1836-1879) wrote became the beloved hymn we know and sing worldwide today. "Take My Life" is a beautiful hymn of surrender and sanctification. When we offer the Lord our lives, not just as a grand gesture but day by day and moment by moment, he receives us and offers everything he is to us. In fact, our surrender is receiving what he is always ready to give us.

Perhaps you have fought against letting go of an area of your life. The one who created you does not demand your surrender. He invites it. His ways are better than yours, and his plans are always for your good. Trust him. You will find the pleasantness of his presence refreshes your weary soul.

Lord, I choose to give you access to every area of my life. Take it and mold it with your mercy, and may I become a reflection of your kindness.

MARCH 24

All Glory

The crowds that went ahead of him and those that followed shouted,
"Hosanna to the Son of David!"
"Blessed is he who comes in the name of the Lord!"
"Hosanna in the highest heaven!"

MATTHEW 21:9 NIV

All glory, laud, and honor
To you, Redeemer, King,
To whom the lips of children
Made sweet hosannas ring.
You are the King of Israel
And David's royal Son,
Now in the Lord's name coming,
The King and Blessed One.

To you before your passion
They sang their hymns of praise;
To you, now high exalted,
Our melody we raise.
As you received their praises,
Accept the prayers we bring,
For you delight in goodness,
O good and gracious King!

Written by Theodulph, the Biship of Orleans, around 820, this hymn is most often used on Palm Sunday for which it was written. It is based on the triumphal entry of Jesus when he enters Jerusalem as described in Matthew 21.

We can easily skip over this important prophetic fulfillment in the lead-up to Easter. Looking back, we can see how fickle we humans are. Instead of brushing past Jesus' celebrated entrance to Jerusalem, let's take time to meditate on it. We can offer Christ all glory, laud, and honor as we join the song of sweet hosannas.

Christ Jesus, you are worthy of all praise and honor today and every day. Be glorified in my life and in the earth. I join with all creation in crying out hosanna to God in the highest!

Eye on the Sparrow

"Look at the birds. They don't plant or harvest or store food in barns,
for your heavenly Father feeds them.
And aren't you far more valuable to him than they are?"

MATTHEW 6:26 NLT

Why should I feel discouraged,
Why should the shadows come,
Why should my heart be lonely,
And long for heav'n and home;
When Jesus is my portion?
My constant Friend is he;
His eye is on the sparrow,
And I know he watches me;
His eye is on the sparrow,
And I know he watches me.

I sing because I'm happy,
I sing because I'm free;
For his eye is on the sparrow,
And I know he watches me.

Civilla Martin wrote this poem in 1905 after visiting an ill friend. Both the ill woman and her husband were limited health-wise, but they were also full of joy, comfort and inspiration that they shared with others. Martin wanted to know the secret of their hopefulness in the midst of challenges, and her friend's response was the last two lines of the refrain: "His eye is on the sparrow, and I know he watches me."

The sparrow is a small bird, but it does not go unnoticed by God. Neither do any of us. He knows what we need and what we are struggling with. He is our constant provider, overwhelming comfort, and faithful companion. When worry creeps in, remind your heart of his steadfast love and presence.

Comforter, I want to live with generosity and joy no matter my limitations or circumstances. You are the source of all I need, and I depend on you. Thank you for your overwhelming generosity.

MARCH 26

All the Way

"When he brings all his sheep out, he goes ahead of them, and they follow him because they know his voice."

JOHN 10:4

All the way my Savior leads me—
What have I to ask beside?
Can I doubt his tender mercy,
Who through life has been my guide?
Heav'nly peace, divinest comfort,
Here by faith in him to dwell!
For I know, whate'er befall me,
Jesus doeth all things well;
For I know, whate'er befall me,
Jesus doeth all things well.

Fanny Crosby wrote this hymn directly after a remarkable experience in 1875. Needing five dollars for something and not knowing how she would get it, she prayed God would provide. Not long after, she had a man call on her at her home, and when he shook hands with her as he was leaving, he left a five dollar bill in her hand. There was no explanation for Fanny in this instance but that God had heard her prayer and impressed on that man to give to her.

God knows big needs as well as little ones. He does not overlook a single one. Take time today to pray for seemingly insignificant things you don't know how to fulfill and trust the Lord to provide in one way or another. Don't forget to write down the answers; they will serve as encouragement in the future.

Faithful Lord, I'm grateful for testimonies of your faithfulness. I trust you care about the seemingly insignificant things taking up room in my heart and mind.

Old Rugged Cross

"For God so loved the world
that He gave His only begotten Son,
that whoever believes in Him
should not perish but have everlasting life."

JOHN 3:16 NKJV

On a hill far away stood an old rugged cross,
The emblem of suffering and shame;
And I love that old cross where the dearest
and best
For a world of lost sinners was slain.

So I'll cherish the old rugged cross,
Till my trophies at last I lay down;
I will cling to the old rugged cross,
And exchange it some day for a crown.

In that old rugged cross, stained with blood
so divine,
A wondrous beauty I see,
For 'twas on that old cross Jesus suffered
and died,
To pardon and sanctify me.

To that old rugged cross I will ever be true,
Its shame and reproach gladly bear;
Then he'll call me some day to my home
far away,
Where his glory forever I'll share.

George Bennard wrote "The Old Rugged Cross" over a series of evangelistic meetings he held in 1912 and 1913. The text was born out of his contemplation of the cross and meditation on John 3:16. It became incredibly popular perhaps because of the beautiful meaning of the cross and the power of its symbolism in our lives.

The power of the cross is not in its shame as "the emblem of suffering." Its power is that the God of creation would allow himself to be subject to it, take our place, and break the power of sin over us. Romans 8:31 says, "If God is for us, who can be against us?" If God gave himself for us, no one can overpower his sacrifice. We are completely purified and sanctified by him.

Savior, thank you for undergoing the awful humiliation of the cross for our freedom. You are powerfully kind and merciful.

Bread of Life

"I am the Bread of Life.
Come every day to me and you will never be hungry.
Believe in me and you will never be thirsty."

JOHN 6:35 TPT

Break now the bread of life, dear Lord, to me,
As once you broke the loaves beside the sea.
Beyond the sacred page I seek you, Lord;
My spirit waits for you, O living Word.

Bless your own Word of truth, dear Lord,
to me,
As when you blessed the bread by Galilee.
Then shall all bondage cease, all fetters fall;
And I shall find my peace, my all in all!

You are the bread of life, dear Lord, to me,
Your holy Word the truth that rescues me.
Give me to eat and live with you above;
Teach me to love your truth, for you are love.

O send your Spirit now, dear Lord, to me,
That he may touch my eyes and make me see.
Show me the truth made plain within your Word,
For in your book revealed I see you, Lord.

Mary Lathbury wrote this hymn in 1877 as a reflection on Scripture and a prayer to illuminate our understanding of Jesus: both what he did and who he was and is. How has the Bread of Life fed your heart? Has the power of Christ's ministry met you in your need?

Jesus is the way, the truth, and the life. He is the living reflection of the Father. He offered us wisdom, mercy, and endless grace. May we press in to know him more in spirit and truth. His Word of truth still speaks to us today, and his presence carries the same power he moved in when he ministered on the earth and rose from the grave.

Jesus, you are the Bread of Life. You are the provider for all I need. Not only do I trust you, but I need you more and more. Fill me with the nourishment of your Word and the refreshing waters of your Spirit.

O Sacred Head

They twisted together a crown of thorns,
put it on his head, and placed a staff in his right hand.
And they knelt down before him and mocked him:
"Hail, king of the Jews!"
MATTHEW 27:29 CSB

O sacred head, now wounded,
With grief and shame weighed down,
Now scornfully surrounded
With thorns, thine only crown!
O sacred head, what glory,
What bliss till now was thine!
Yet, though despised and gory,
I joy to call thee mine.

What language shall I borrow
To thank thee, dearest friend,
For this, thy dying sorrow,
Thy pity without end?
Oh, make me thine forever,
And should I fainting be,
Lord, let me never, never
Outlive my love to thee.

We must look at the suffering of Christ—meditate on it—if we want to know the power of his sacrifice in our lives. He gave up everything, including his dignity, so we could know the Father's love without hindrance. Look for the beauty within the suffering, for there is always redemption, light, and love in the details.

As you read through today's hymn, which comes out of a medieval monk's meditation on Christ's crucifix, allow yourself to see the pain without trying to shield yourself from it. Jesus is acquainted with suffering, and you can find comfort in his fellowship when you are faced with your own.

Jesus Christ, thank you for the power of your sacrifice. I don't like to linger long on the pain you went through, the humiliation you endured, or the discouragement those around you must have felt. Reveal your goodness through the suffering and give me eyes to see the gift of your presence within it.

MARCH 30

Power in the Blood

God was pleased to have all his fullness dwell in him,
and through him to reconcile to himself all things,
whether things on earth or things in heaven,
by making peace through his blood, shed on the cross.

Colossians 1:19-20 NIV

Would you be free from the burden of sin?
There's pow'r in the blood, pow'r in the blood;
Would you o'er evil a victory win?
There's wonderful pow'r in the blood.

There is pow'r, pow'r, wonder-working pow'r
In the blood of the Lamb;
There is pow'r, pow'r, wonder-working pow'r
In the precious blood of the Lamb.

Would you be whiter, yes brighter than snow?
There's pow'r in the blood, pow'r in the blood;
Sin-stains are lost in its life-giving flow
There's wonderful pow'r in the blood.

Would you do service for Jesus, your King?
There's pow'r in the blood, pow'r in the blood;
Would you live daily his praises to sing?
There's wonderful pow'r in the blood.

Lewis Edgar Jones wrote this hymn in 1899 at a camp meeting in Maryland. Inspired by the message, he focused the song on the "wonder-working" power of Christ's blood. When we feel burdened by sin and overwhelmed by what's going wrong in the world, we can turn our attention to Christ's overcoming power and sacrifice.

Reflect on how you've experienced the power of Christ's loving sacrifice in your life. How has it affected your attitude, focus, or lifestyle? Allow yourself to challenge areas where you have felt defeated and submit them to Christ and his offer of liberty in his love. He offers freedom from cycles of fear, sin, shame, and defeat.

Savior, your sacrifice is sufficient for every area of my life and for the sins of the whole world. Why would I fear when you have overcome even death?

Christ Is Risen Today

"He is not here, for he has risen, as he said.
Come, see the place where he lay."
Matthew 28:6 esv

Christ the Lord is risen today, alleluia!
Earth and heaven in chorus say, alleluia!
Raise your joys and triumphs high, alleluia!
Sing, ye heavens, and earth reply, alleluia!

Love's redeeming work is done, alleluia!
Fought the fight, the battle won, alleluia!
Death in vain forbids him rise, alleluia!
Christ has opened paradise, alleluia!

Hail the Lord of earth and heaven, alleluia!
Praise to thee by both be given, alleluia!
Thee we greet triumphant now, alleluia!
Hail the Resurrection, thou, alleluia!

King of glory, soul of bliss, alleluia!
Everlasting life is this, alleluia!
Thee to know, thy power to prove, alleluia!
Thus to sing, and thus to love, alleluia!

What triumph is in the resurrection of Christ! What overwhelming relief mingled with incredible joy at his victory over the grave! As we celebrate Christ's resurrection on Easter, may we allow ourselves to feel the delight of this incredible hope, for his resurrection life is the pathway to our own in his kingdom.

Although Charles Wesley wrote this hymn in 1739, the alleluias were added later by editors. The introduction of each one allows us to praise God for each line of the text. It is a song of rejoicing, and every line reflects a reason to rejoice. The next time you find yourself struck by a phrase or sentence, perhaps add an alleluia to punctuate it.

Redeemer, you are worthy of all praise and honor. You did everything you aimed to do, revealed the Father's love, and provided a way to experience unhindered fellowship through the Spirit. Alleluia!

April

When peace like a river, attendeth my way,
When sorrows like sea billows roll
Whatever my lot, thou hast taught me to say
It is well, it is well, with my soul.

The Fountain Opened

"On that day a fountain will be opened for the house of David and for the inhabitants of Jerusalem, for sin and for defilement."

Zechariah 13:1 NASB

There is a fountain filled with blood
Drawn from Immanuel's veins;
And sinners, plunged beneath that flood,
Lose all their guilty stains:
Lose all their guilty stains,
Lose all their guilty stains;
And sinners, plunged beneath that flood,
Lose all their guilty stains.

The dying thief rejoiced to see
That fountain in his day;
And there may I, though vile as he,
Wash all my sins away:
Wash all my sins away,
Wash all my sins away;
And there may I, though vile as he,
Wash all my sins away.

William Cowper (1731-1800), a well-known English poet, struggled with depression for much of his life. His mother died when he was six, and it affected his whole life. Coming to Christ did not cure Cowper's depression, but that does not mean he did not find meaning, comfort, and hope in the person of Christ. This very hymn came out of a severe depressive episode. Even when we are in the grips of our struggles, our voices matter. God loves us, and our worth is undiminished in his love.

Pain and sorrow do not have to be things we seek to escape. We can come to Christ as we are and receive his comfort, strength, hope, and life even as we struggle. He will always meet us in the messy middle.

Lord, may I know the power of your love with me in my darkest moments. I trust you receive me as I am, and you purify me with the power of your blood. Thank you.

APRIL 2

Perfect Peace

You will keep in perfect peace all who trust in you,
all whose thoughts are fixed on you!

Isaiah 26:3 NLT

Peace, perfect peace, in this dark world of sin?
The blood of Jesus whispers peace within.

Peace, perfect peace,
by thronging duties pressed?
To do the will of Jesus, this is rest.

Peace, perfect peace,
death shadowing us and ours?
Jesus has vanquished death and all its powers.

Peace, perfect peace, our future all unknown?
Jesus we know, and he is on the throne.

It is enough: earth's struggles soon shall cease,
and Jesus call to heaven's perfect peace.

This simple hymn was written by Bishop Edward Bickersteth (1825-1906) at the bedside of a dying relative. He wanted to offer hope in those last days of life, so he penned a poem and read it directly to the dying man. Whether we are facing our mortality, the death of a dream, or the transition to a new way of life, God meets all who trust him with his perfect peace.

When you find yourself overwhelmed by life, direct your thoughts to Christ. He is your ever-present help in times of trouble. His peace is not the fleeting calm we find in this world. It is deep like the waters that feed our rivers. It does not cease to flow. Fix your thoughts on God, and as you do, perfect peace will settle on your heart.

Prince of Peace, there is no peace like the kind you give. You don't take it away when I fail or falter. You don't change your nature depending on your mood. You are always kind, loving, wise, and powerful. I look to you for all I need today.

Revive Us Again

God is strong and can help you not to fall. He can bring you before his glory without any wrong in you and can give you great joy. He is the only God, the One who saves us. To him be glory, greatness, power, and authority through Jesus Christ our Lord for all time past, now, and forever. Amen.

JUDE 1:24-25 NCV

We praise thee, O God, for the Son of thy love,
For Jesus who died, and is now gone above.

Hallelujah! Thine the glory, hallelujah! Amen!
Hallelujah! Thine the glory, revive us again.

We praise thee, O God, for thy Spirit of light
Who has shown us our Savior and scattered
our night.

We praise thee, O God, for the joy thou
hast giv'n
To thy saints in communion, these foretastes
of heav'n.

Revive us again, fill each heart with thy love.
May each soul be rekindled with fire from
above.

William Mackay (1839-1885) was a Scottish doctor. His mother prayed he would offer his life to the Lord, but he was not interested as a young man. He even pawned the Bible his mother had given him. One day, a gravely injured laborer was brought into the hospital, and there was no hope for his recovery. Even so, the young man asked for his Bible. After the young man passed away, there was no one to give his one belonging to. When William Mackay opened the Bible, he realized it was his own! He saw his mother's inscription, and it changed him forever. Shortly after committing his life to Christ, he wrote this song.

God is creative in the ways he reaches out to us, and he does not forget the prayers of his saints. He hears you, and he moves in marvelous mercy. Let's trust him to do it in his time and his way.

Merciful Father, thank you for the relentless kindness of your heart.

APRIL 4

Did My Savior Bleed

For three hours, beginning at noon, darkness came over the earth. About three o'clock, Jesus shouted with a mighty voice in Aramaic, "Eli, Eli, lama sabachthani?"— that is, "My God, My God, why have you turned your back on me?"

Mark 15:33-34 TPT

Alas! And did my Savior bleed,
And did my Sovereign die!
Would he devote that sacred head
For sinners such as I?

Was it for crimes that I have done,
He groaned upon the tree?
Amazing pity! Grace unknown!
And love beyond degree!

Thus might I hide my blushing face
While his dear cross appears;
Dissolve my heart in thankfulness,
And melt mine eyes to tears.

But drops of tears can ne'er repay
The debt of love I owe.
Here, Lord, I give myself away;
'Tis all that I can do.

Our salvation does not depend on our goodness but on Christ's. His sacrifice is the atonement for every one of our sins. As we come under his mercy and yield our lives to him in love, he removes our sins as far as the east is from the west. We don't have to strive to earn his love; he offers it freely.

Meditate on the love of Christ through his sacrifice. He knew what he was doing when he submitted to the Father's plan. He suffered so we might have full and unhindered fellowship with the Father through his atonement. Praise God that you are washed in Christ's blood and can stand before your Creator. As Isaac Watts wrote, "Here, Lord, I give myself away [to you]; 'tis all that I can do."

Savior, thank you for choosing love in everything you did including dying on the cross for the sins of the world. I am indebted to your love as you invite me to fellowship with you. I am yours.

When We Get There

"God will wipe away every tear from their eyes;
there shall be no more death, nor sorrow, nor crying.
There shall be no more pain, for the former things have passed away."

Revelation 21:4 NKJV

Sing the wondrous love of Jesus,
Sing his mercy and his grace;
In the mansions bright and blessed
He'll prepare for us a place.

When we all get to heaven,
What a day of rejoicing that will be!
When we all see Jesus,
We'll sing and shout the victory!

Let us then be true and faithful,
Trusting, serving ev'ry day;
Just one glimpse of him in glory
Will the toils of life repay.

Onward to the prize before us!
Soon his beauty we'll behold;
Soon the pearly gates will open—
We shall tread the streets of gold.

Eliza Edmund Hewitt (1851-1920) knew disappointment. Her teaching career was cut short by a spinal condition that made her bedridden for years. Though she was in pain, she wanted to be useful to her church. She studied English literature and started writing poems for the children's department. This is one hymn from that time.

Even in our disappointment, God can redirect our paths. He can use us no matter where we are or what state we are in. His love empowers us in our weakness and gives us fresh vision, hope, and meaning. If you find yourself starting over in some way, this is not your end. It is a new beginning.

Father, even as I long for the day I stand face to face with you in your kingdom, I have hope that you are not done with me yet on this earth. Renew my passion for you and this life.

APRIL 6

Power of Jesus' Name

For this reason God highly exalted him
and gave him the name that is above every name.

PHILIPPIANS 2:9 CSB

All hail the power of Jesus' name!
Let angels prostrate fall.
Bring forth the royal diadem,
And crown him Lord of all.
Bring forth the royal diadem,
And crown him Lord of all!

Oh, that with all the sacred throng
We at his feet may fall!
We'll join the everlasting song
And crown him Lord of all.
We'll join the everlasting song
And crown him Lord of all.

Edward Perronet's (1721-1792) hymn has become an international anthem of Christendom. It is a poetic praise offering all glory and honor to Christ who is Lord over all creation. Declaring God's praises can bring us back to the heart of our faith and remind us of God's greatness. As we glorify his name, our hearts declare the truth of his lordship.

Let every worry and care melt away as you focus on the greatness and goodness of God for these few moments. Meditate on the vastness of the universe and the hand of the Creator putting it all into motion. Allow yourself to see from God's perspective, and your own will shift.

Majestic One, you are the Lord of all, and I worship you today. I put all my attention on you, the author and finisher of my faith.

Before the Throne

Who then is the one who condemns? No one.
Christ Jesus who died—more than that, who was raised to life—
is at the right hand of God and is also interceding for us.

ROMANS 8:34 NIV

Before the throne of God above
I have a strong and perfect plea;
A great High Priest whose name is Love,
Who ever lives and pleads for me.
My name is graven on his hands,
My name is written on his heart.
I know that while in heav'n he stands
No tongue can bid me thence depart.

Behold him there, the risen Lamb,
My perfect, spotless righteousness,
The great unchangeable I AM,
The King of glory and of grace.
At one with him, I cannot die;
My soul is purchased by his blood.
My life is hid with Christ on high,
With Christ my Savior and my God.

Charitie Bancroft (1841-1923) was the daughter of a reverend in Ireland. She wrote many poems, and some were turned into hymns. "Before the Throne of God Above" is beloved for its rich imagery of Christ as our intercessor. He stands between us and the Father to plead our case. We can find strength in his love for us, for he has already cleansed our sin with his sacrifice.

Pick one of the verses of this hymn to meditate on today. As you go throughout your day, bring your mind back to it and ask the Lord to illuminate his truth in deeper ways within your heart.

Loving God, thank you for interceding for me before the throne of the Father. As I turn my attention to you through the day, open my understanding of who you are in greater ways.

Search Me O God

Create in me a clean heart, O God,
and renew a right spirit within me.
Cast me not away from your presence,
and take not your Holy Spirit from me.

Psalm 51:10-11 ESV

Search me, O God, and know my heart today;
Try me, O Savior, know my thoughts, I pray.
See if there be some wicked way in me;
Cleanse me from ev'ry sin and set me free.

I praise thee, Lord, for cleansing me from sin;
Fulfill thy Word, and make me pure within.
Fill me with fire where once I burned with shame;
Grant my desire to magnify thy name.

Lord, take my life and make it wholly thine;
Fill my poor heart with thy great love divine.
Take all my will, my passion, self, and pride;
I now surrender; Lord, in me abide.

James Edwin Orr (1912-1987) was a missionary and evangelist who also served as a chaplain in the U.S. Air Force during World War II. Along with his wife, they evangelized in 150 countries over the course of their ministry. Orr wasn't known for his hymn writing but rather his published works on revival work. "Search Me, O God" is one of the few hymns he wrote.

Written like a psalm, "Search Me, O God" is an invitation for the Lord to transform our hearts in his wise presence. His love reaches every space and fills every crack. There isn't a cell left untouched by the presence of his grace. Consider beginning your day with this prayer and allow the Lord to pour out his presence in you to renew and transform your heart and mind.

Lord, thank you for your cleansing love that removes the guilt of my failures. You are stronger than my weakness, and you don't hold my weakness against me.

Strong to Save

The voice of the LORD is on the waters;
The God of glory thunders,
The LORD is over many waters.
The voice of the LORD is powerful,
The voice of the LORD is majestic.

PSALM 29:3-4 NASB

Eternal Father, strong to save,
Whose arm does bind the restless wave,
Who bids the mighty ocean deep
Its own appointed limits keep;
O hear us when we cry to thee
For those in peril on the sea.

O Savior, whose almighty Word
The winds and waves submissive heard,
Who walked upon the foaming deep,
And calm amid the rage did sleep;
O hear us when we cry to thee
For those in peril on the sea.

O Holy Spirit, who did brood
Upon the waters dark and rude,
And bid their angry tumult cease,
And give for wild confusion peace;
O hear us when we cry to thee
For those in peril on the sea.

Due to its sea-faring themes, this hymn has been adopted by naval forces across the globe. It was written in 1860 in England by William Whiting, and it became a favorite of both civilian and military sailors in English-speaking countries. You don't have to be a sailor to connect with the themes though; the Trinity is the main focus of this hymn.

Humans like to reduce God to what is "knowable." A father is easy to relate to. Jesus was a man, and his sacrifice was visceral. The Holy Spirit is perhaps the most difficult for believers in the West to relate to, but the Spirit is the one with us now in power. May we not forget the Holy Spirit's divinity and foster a closer relationship with our comforter, teacher, and friend.

Holy Spirit, I'm grateful to know you are God as much as the Father is God and Jesus is God. I honor you and your work in this world.

APRIL 10

Face to Face

You have endowed him with eternal blessings
and given him the joy of your presence.

PSALM 21:6 NLT

Face to face with Christ, my Savior,
Face to face—what will it be
When with rapture I behold him,
Jesus Christ who died for me?

Only faintly now I see him
With the darkened veil between,
But a blessed day is coming
When his glory shall be seen.

What rejoicing in his presence,
When are banished grief and pain;
When the crooked ways are straightened
And the dark things shall be plain.

Face to face—oh, blissful moment!
Face to face—to see and know;
Face to face with my Redeemer,
Jesus Christ who loves me so.

Carrie Breck had the heart of a worshiper though she could not hold a tune. She put her praise in prose, and she wrote over two thousand poems. After she completed "Face to Face" in 1898, she sent it to friend and musician Grant Tullar. Remarkably, he had just composed a tune that fit her poem just right.

We carry within us the longing for all things to be made right. One day, when we stand before the Lord face to face, we shall see him fully. We will know what we only catch glimpses of now. We will behold him and be transformed by him. No matter what we go through, the longing for that day pulls in our chest. God is faithful, and his promises are true. We do not hope in vain.

Glorious God, the longing for your physical presence is stronger some days than others. When the world weighs me down, renew my hope by reminding me of the truth of your coming. My hope is in you.

God Will Take Care

"Five sparrows are sold for only two pennies,
and God does not forget any of them.
But God even knows how many hairs you have on your head.
Don't be afraid. You are worth much more than many sparrows."

LUKE 12:6-7 NCV

Be not dismayed whate'er betide,
God will take care of you;
Beneath his wings of love abide,
God will take care of you.

God will take care of you,
Through ev'ry day, o'er all the way;
He will take care of you,
God will take care of you.

Through days of toil when heart doth fail,
God will take care of you;
When dangers fierce your path assail,
God will take care of you.

No matter what may be the test,
God will take care of you;
Lean, weary one, upon his breast,
God will take care of you.

Civilla Martin wrote the text of this 1904 hymn inspired by a statement her son made. She was sick, and her husband was meant to preach that day. Walter, her husband, struggled with whether he should leave her or not. Their son encouraged his father, pointing out that if God wanted him to preach that day, he would take care of Civilla while he was gone. Walter went to preach, Civilla got better, and she wrote this hymn that very day.

No matter what you are going through or how alone you may feel, God will take care of you. His presence does not leave you, and he will not turn a blind eye to your need. He is a good father and plentiful provider. Trust him to take care of you and yours.

Faithful Father, thank you for your presence with me no matter where I am or what I am facing. I trust you to take care of me and those around me.

Old Time Religion

"Stand in the ways and see,
And ask for the old paths, where the good way is,
And walk in it;
Then you will find rest for your souls."

JEREMIAH 6:16 NKJV

Give me that old time religion,
Give me that old time religion,
Give me that old time religion,
It's good enough for me.

It was good for Paul and Silas,
It was good for Paul and Silas,
It was good for Paul and Silas,
It's good enough for me.

It was good for the Hebrew children,
It was good for the Hebrew children,
It was good for the Hebrew children,
It's good enough for me.

Makes me love ev'rybody,
Makes me love ev'rybody,
Makes me love ev'rybody,
It's good enough for me.

When we hear the term "Old Time Religion," perhaps we think of our grandparents. Maybe we think of ancient prophets. Maybe we picture of cold cathedrals and empty pews. Whatever image this phrase conjurs, "Old Time Religion" simply means the roots of our faith. It's the faith that captured Paul's attention on the road and the faith that carried the Hebrew people out of their captivity and through the desert. It's the faith of those who choose to walk the path of Christ's love still.

Christ is the center of our faith. He was present at the beginning of creation and always will be. He is the one who was, is, and never ceases. When we awaken to the love of God, we cannot help but be drawn in by his kindness.

Jesus Christ, you are the foundation of my faith, and you always will be. I won't turn from you.

Praise to the Lord

Let everyone everywhere join in the crescendo
of ecstatic praise to Yahweh!
Hallelujah! Praise the Lord!

Psalm 150:6 TPT

Praise to the Lord, the Almighty, the King of
creation!
O my soul, praise him, for he is your health
and salvation!
Come, all who hear; now to his temple
draw near,
Join me in glad adoration.

Praise to the Lord, above all things so
wondrously reigning;
Sheltering you under his wings, and so gently
sustaining!
Have you not seen all that is needful has been
Sent by his gracious ordaining?

Praise to the Lord, who will prosper your work
and defend you;
Surely his goodness and mercy shall daily
attend you.
Ponder anew what the Almighty can do,
If with his love he befriends you.

Praise to the Lord! O let all that is in me
adore him!
All that has life and breath, come now with
praises before him.
Let the Amen sound from his people again;
Gladly forever adore him.

This German chorale was written by Joachim Neander and published in 1680. Loosely based on Psalms 103 and 150, it is a strong hymn of praise to our God. All creation is encouraged to praise God, for he is the King of creation who shelters those who look to him and defends those who rely on him.

We don't have to be victims of our moods or circumstances. We can direct our souls in praise as King David did and as we are encouraged to do in this hymn. As we join in praise of the one who is worthy of our adoration, we offer him the sacrifice of our praise. In any moment, we can choose to throw off our cynicism and foul mood and direct our hearts in praise to the one worthy every moment. As we do, we may find our hearts and minds transformed in his presence.

King of Creation, I spend too much time caught up in my thoughts and feelings. I will set them aside today and bow my heart in your presence.

My Savior's Love

God, who is rich in mercy, because of his great love that he had for us, made us alive with Christ even though we were dead in trespasses. You are saved by grace!

Ephesians 2:4-5 CSB

I stand amazed in the presence
Of Jesus the Nazarene,
And wonder how he could love me,
A sinner, condemned, unclean.

How marvelous! How wonderful!
And my song shall ever be;
How marvelous! How wonderful!
Is my Savior's love for me!

For me it was in the garden
He prayed, "Not my will, but thine;"
He had no tears for his own griefs,
But sweat drops of blood for mine.

When with the ransomed in glory
His face I at last shall see,
'Twill be my joy through the ages
To sing of his love for me.

Charles Gabriel (1856-1932) was extremely musical growing up. He taught himself to sing and play numerous instruments. He didn't stop there. He became a teacher and composer. He wrote an estimated seven thousand songs in his lifetime.

The marvelous love of Christ is something we can never meditate on too often. If it feels rote, we need a fresh revelation of its power. God is love, and his love is ever-expanding. We cannot reach the depths or heights of it. If we spend our whole lives focused on the love of God, we will be continuously nourished and challenged by it.

Christ Jesus, I want to know your love in deeper ways today not only with my mind and understanding but also with my experience and heart. Expand my knowledge of your love as you wash over me with your presence.

Friend for Sinners

"The Son of Man came eating and drinking, and you say,
'Here is a glutton and a drunkard, a friend of tax collectors and sinners.'
But wisdom is proved right by all her children."

Luke 7:34-35 NIV

Jesus! What a friend for sinners!
Jesus! Lover of my soul;
Friends may fail me, foes assail me,
He, my Savior, makes me whole.

Hallelujah! What a Savior!
Hallelujah! What a friend!
Saving, helping, keeping, loving,
He is with me to the end.

Jesus! What a strength for weakness!
Let me hide myself in him;
Tempted, tried, and sometimes failing,
He, my strength, my vict'ry wins.

Jesus! What a help in sorrow!
While the billows o'er me roll,
Even when my heart is breaking,
He, my comfort, helps my soul.

Wilbur Chapman, an evangelist and minister for most of his life, preached with Dwight L. Moody at the World's Fair and conducted his own revivals. With Luke 7:34 as his inspiration, Chapman wrote this hymn in 1910. It was based on one of his lifelong messages: Jesus is a friend of sinners.

Each stanza focuses on an attribute of Jesus: his love, strength, help, and forgiveness. We can take what we need when we need it, for Jesus Christ offers us the fullness of himself whenever we come to him. He is gracious. What do you need most from him today?

Lord Jesus, thank you for being a friend to all: the unlovely, the hard to get along with, and the vulnerable. Thank you for being my friend.

My Redeemer Lives

If we have been united with him in a death like his,
we shall certainly be united with him in a resurrection like his.

ROMANS 6:5 ESV

I know that my Redeemer lives!
What comfort this sweet sentence gives!
He lives, he lives, who once was dead;
He lives, my everliving head!

He lives to grant me rich supply;
He lives to guide me with his eye;
He lives to comfort me when faint;
He lives to hear my soul's complaint.

He lives and grants me daily breath;
He lives, and I shall conquer death;
He lives my mansion to prepare;
He lives to bring me safely there.

He lives, all glory to his name!
He lives, my Savior, still the same.
Oh, the sweet joy this sentence gives:
I know that my Redeemer lives!

Samuel Medley started his career as a sailor in the Royal Navy in England, but he was forced to redirect when he was severely wounded and almost lost his leg. He converted to Christianity and joined active ministry. He wrote this hymn in 1775, and it became a favorite both in Great Britain and America.

The entire hymn is focused on the fact that Christ, our Redeemer, lives. He is not dead. He is living and active in this world and in our lives. What comfort, joy, and hope this truth brings to our hearts as we set our lives before him. He lives, and because he does, we can walk with courage.

Lord Jesus, you are the head of my life, for I have surrendered to your love. I don't want to live to satisfy my selfishness but to know your love and live it in full. I am yours.

Morning Gilds the Sky

Through Him then, let's continually offer up a sacrifice of praise to God, that is, the fruit of lips praising His name.

HEBREWS 13:15 NASB

When morning gilds the sky,
Our hearts awaking cry:
May Jesus Christ be praised!
In all our work and prayer
We ask his loving care:
May Jesus Christ be praised!

Let earth's wide circle round
In joyful notes resound:
May Jesus Christ be praised!
Let air and sea and sky
From depth to height reply:
May Jesus Christ be praised!

Then let us join to sing
To Christ, our loving King:
May Jesus Christ be praised!
Be this the eternal song
Through all the ages long:
May Jesus Christ be praised!

Originating as an anonymous text in German, Edward Caswall translated it into English, and it was first published in 1854. The poem focuses on different times of the day to draw our attention to the fact that Jesus Christ should be praised through them all. In the morning, evening, and every moment between, "May Jesus Christ be praised!"

Wherever this finds you today, whatever time of day, can you set your heart on the presence of Christ? Can you offer him praise through whatever you are experiencing or what lies ahead? Lay down your burdens and do whatever is before you—work, cleaning, caring for others, resting—as unto the Lord. Let it all be worship.

Lord, I offer you my actions and my heart. May it all serve to praise you.

Christ Arose

Very early on Sunday morning the women went to the tomb, taking the spices they had prepared. They found that the stone had been rolled away from the entrance. So they went in, but they didn't find the body of the Lord Jesus.

Luke 24:1-3 NLT

Low in the grave he lay, Jesus my Savior,
Waiting the coming day, Jesus my Lord!

Up from the grave he arose;
With a mighty triumph o'er his foes;
He arose a victor from the dark domain,
And he lives forever, with his saints to reign.
He arose! He arose! Hallelujah! Christ arose!

Vainly they watch his bed, Jesus my Savior,
Vainly they seal the dead, Jesus my Lord!

Death cannot keep its prey, Jesus my Savior;
He tore the bars away, Jesus my Lord!

Robert Lowry (1826-1899) was a reverend and hymnist. Though he would have rather preached the gospel to a receptive congregation than write a hymn, his hymns have outlasted him. They have preached and comforted more souls than he could have in his lifetime. What we give our time, energy, and dedication to ripples outward from our lives.

"Christ Arose" allows us to reflect on the time directly after Jesus' burial. In that space, when his friends were grieving his death and had yet to experience the power of his resurrection, we find tensions that are with us still. Christ has already overcome every obstacle to bring us into the liberty of his lasting love. He arose! Hallelujah! Joy is coming.

Redeemer, thank you for the power of your life over death. Even in areas that seem destroyed, you sow seeds of redemption. I look to you.

Grace Greater than Sin

If he chose them by grace, it is not for the things they have done.
If they could be made God's people by what they did,
God's gift of grace would not really be a gift.

ROMANS 11:6 NCV

Marvelous grace of our loving Lord,
Grace that exceeds our sin and our guilt!
Yonder on Calvary's mount out-poured—
There where the blood of the Lamb was spilt.

Grace, grace, God's grace,
Grace that will pardon and cleanse within;
Grace, grace, God's grace,
Grace that is greater than all our sin!

Sin and despair, like the sea-waves cold,
Threaten the soul with infinite loss;
Grace that is greater—yes, grace untold—
Points to the Refuge, the mighty Cross.

Marvelous, infinite, matchless grace,
Freely bestowed on all who believe!
All who are longing to see his face,
Will you this moment his grace receive?

Full of theological heft, Julia Johnston's 1910 hymn describes the doctrine of grace and our justification by faith through Christ. In the book of Romans, Paul speaks often of both of the power of God's grace and the sufficiency of his sacrifice.

There is relief in embracing God's grace. We cannot earn it, and we cannot lose it. It is an offering and gift we can receive as we come to Christ again and again. Are you tired today? Receive God's grace. Have you messed up? There is more grace for you. Stop trying to earn God's favor and simply accept the grace he offers as a good father offers his love to his children at all times.

Lord, I don't want to strive for your attention or affection. I believe you when you say I don't have to. I believe you are the source of all goodness, all life, and of everything I need. I receive your grace moment by moment.

All Blessings Flow

God is the triumphant King; all the powers of the earth are his.
So sing your celebration songs of highest praise
to the glorious Enlightened One!

Psalm 47:7 TPT

Praise God, from whom all blessings flow;
Praise him, all creatures here below;
Praise him above, ye heav'nly host;
Praise Father, Son, and Holy Ghost.
Amen.

This short hymn was written within a trio of hymns for morning, evening, and midnight masses. Bishop Thomas Ken penned them in 1674, and "Praise God" was the doxology, the final stanza, for each of the hymns. Many of us know it as a stand-alone doxology, but it is also included as a final stanza for some hymns.

This hymn calls on every part of creation, on earth and in heaven, to offer praise to the triune God. All good things come from God. James 1:17 puts it this way: "Every good gift and every perfect gift is from above, and comes down from the Father of lights, with whom there is no variation or shadow of turning" (NKJV). Practice turning your heart in gratitude to the giver of good gifts who showers his love on you in practical ways and unending measure.

God, I praise you for little gifts and overwhelmingly large ones. I thank you for the goodness you have planted in my life and in the world around me.

Down at the Cross

God forbid that I should boast except in the cross of our Lord Jesus Christ,
by whom the world has been crucified to me, and I to the world.

Galatians 6:14 NKJV

Down at the cross where my Savior died,
Down where for cleansing from sin I cried,
There to my heart was the blood applied;
Glory to his name!

Glory to his name,
Glory to his name;
There to my heart was the blood applied;
Glory to his name!

I am so wondrously saved from sin,
Jesus so sweetly abides within;
There at the cross where he took me in;
Glory to his name!

Come to this fountain so rich and sweet,
Cast thy poor soul at the Savior's feet;
Plunge in today, and be made complete;
Glory to his name!

There is no shortage of hymns meditating on the crucifixion of Christ and the power of that sacrifice. "Down at the Cross," also known as "Glory to His Name," is Elisha Hoffman's addition to this canon. He wrote the poem in 1878, and John Stockton set it to music.

Reading through the text of this hymn, we move from meditation on Christ's sacrifice, to the power of his redemption, to the grace of God that covers us, and to the endless love we find in Christ's fellowship. Do as the hymnist encourages; "Plunge in today, and be made complete."

Savior, your sacrifice covers every debt of my soul, and I do not need to do a thing more but come to you with a yielded heart. I am yours; I lay myself at your feet. Fill me with the power of your presence as I sing glory to your name.

APRIL 22

Love Lifted Me

He brought me up from a desolate pit,
out of the muddy clay,
and set my feet on a rock,
making my steps secure.

Psalm 40:2 CSB

I was sinking deep in sin,
Far from the peaceful shore,
Very deeply stained within,
Sinking to rise no more;
But the master of the sea
Heard my despairing cry,
From the waters lifted me—
Now safe am I.

Love lifted me,
Love lifted me,
When nothing else could help,
Love lifted me;
Love lifted me,
Love lifted me,
When nothing else could help,
Love lifted me.

James Rowe was born in 1865 to an English copper miner and emigrated to the US in his mid-twenties. He was a prolific writer and published more than nine thousand hymns, poems, recitations, and other works in his lifetime. "Love Lifted Me" is based mostly on Matthew 14 where the disciples encountered Jesus walking on stormy waters.

Who cannot relate to the feeling of sinking Peter had when he took his eyes off Jesus? Instead of looking to him, we become overwhelmed by fear and the loss of control we feel. Let's lift our eyes to the Lord who reaches out his arms to lift us up. When nothing else can help, the Lord's love still lifts us.

Redeemer, your love is better than anything I've ever known. I don't want to resist your help, leadership, or love today. Lift me up and save me, Lord. I need you.

Tell the Story

"You also must testify,
for you have been with me from the beginning."

John 15:27 NIV

I love to tell the story
Of unseen things above,
Of Jesus and his glory,
Of Jesus and his love.
I love to tell the story
Because I know it's true;
It satisfies my longings
As nothing else can do.

I love to tell the story;
'Twill be my theme in glory
To tell the old, old story
Of Jesus and his love.

Oftentimes, there is a seasonal stanza included as verse two in this hymn by Kate Hankey and William Fischer. There are four options for Christ's birth, death, resurrection, and the great commission. No matter the time of year, the gospel story meets us where we are.

Hankey wrote the text in the 1860s while dealing with a prolonged illness. It is part of a longer poem she penned on the life of Christ. When we are not feeling our best, we still participate in the greater story God has written and continues to write. We are his people, and he uses us as much in times of weakness as in times of strength. Let's draw hope from his promised presence and keep telling the stories of his goodness.

Great God, there is no one else like you who uses weak things to shame the strong. I am yours. Use me, just as I am today, for your glory as I share your story.

Love of God

See what kind of love the Father has given to us,
that we should be called children of God; and so we are.
The reason why the world does not know us
is that it did not know him.

1 John 3:1 ESV

The love of God is greater far
Than tongue or pen can ever tell;
It goes beyond the highest star,
And reaches to the lowest hell.
The wand'ring child is reconciled
By God's beloved Son.
The aching soul again made whole,
And priceless pardon won.

O love of God, how rich and pure!
How measureless and strong!
It shall forevermore endure—
The saints' and angels' song.

Frederick Lehman (1868-1953) dedicated the majority of his life to writing sacred songs. He was inspired to write "The Love of God" after hearing a preacher quote an adapted portion of an eleventh-century Jewish poem. This would become the third stanza, evocative in its illustration of the endlessness of God's love.

Whether this hymn is one of your favorites or a new discovery, read through it today. Perhaps listen to a version of it while you go about your day. Allow your thoughts to meditate on the power and breadth of God's love so "measureless and strong."

Loving Father, I want to know the power, breadth, and strength of your love in deeper ways every day. If there is no limit, then I must know you more. Open my understanding and allow me to encounter your love in fresh ways.

How I Love Jesus

"She will give birth to a Son; and you shall name Him Jesus, for He will save His people from their sins."

MATTHEW 1:21 NASB

There is a name I love to hear,
I love to sing its worth;
It sounds like music in my ear,
The sweetest name on earth.

O how I love Jesus,
O how I love Jesus,
O how I love Jesus,
Because he first loved me!

It tells me of a Savior's love,
Who died to set me free;
It tells me of his precious blood,
The sinner's perfect plea.

It tells of one whose loving heart
Can feel my deepest woe;
Who in each sorrow bears a part
That none can bear below.

The stanzas of this hymn were written by Frederick Whitfield in 1855. The refrain, however, is anonymous and was also paired with other hymns in the late nineteenth century. Emphasis on the name of Jesus is a fixture in our Christian tradition. We whisper his name, and his Spirit comes in close. We call on his name, and he breaks strongholds of fear.

Jesus Christ is the same yesterday, today, and forever. With that in mind, we can call on him and count on him as the Savior of the world. His resurrection power is still at work in each of our stories. Let's sing with those who have gone before and raise our voices, proclaiming, "O how I love Jesus!"

Lord Jesus, you have drawn me to your heart with kindness, and you never stop. I'm grateful for the power of your love that breaks down barriers and relieves me of the need to strive. You are enough, and you say I am enough in you.

APRIL 26

At Calvary

In my insolence, I persecuted his people.
But God had mercy on me
because I did it in ignorance and unbelief.
Oh, how generous and gracious our Lord was!
He filled me with the faith and love that come from Christ Jesus.

1 Timothy 1:13-14 NLT

Years I spent in vanity and pride,
Caring not my Lord was crucified,
Knowing not it was for me he died on Calvary.

Mercy there was great and grace was free,
Pardon there was multiplied to me,
There my burdened soul found liberty—
At Calvary.

By God's Word at last my sin I learned—
Then I trembled at the Law I'd spurned,
Till my guilty soul imploring turned to Calvary.

Now I've giv'n to Jesus ev'rything,
Now I gladly own him as my King,
Now my raptured soul can only sing of Calvary.

O the love that drew salvation's plan!
O the grace that brought it down to man!
O the mighty gulf that God did span at
Calvary.

William Newell (1868-1956) was a well-educated man and follower of Christ. He served as the Assistant Superintendent of the Moody Bible Institue in Chicago. On his way to class one day, the words for "At Calvary" came to him. He wrote them down quickly on the back of an envelope. When we are struck with inspiration, we would do well to take a quick minute to scribble down the idea. We never know what it will become.

The apostle Paul is one of the best examples we have of a life redeemed and transformed. He persecuted those who followed Christ. It wasn't until he had a dramatic encounter with Christ that he turned his life around, but after that, he was forever changed. Consider your transformation in the mercy and grace of God.

Redeemer, you do what no one else can do. I trust you with my life, direction, and heart. You are my Redeemer, and you change me for the better.

Battle Hymn of the Republic

The God of Israel spoke; the Rock of Israel said to me:
"Whoever rules fairly over people, who rules with respect for God,
is like the morning light at dawn, like a morning without clouds.
He is like sunshine after a rain that makes the grass sprout from the ground."

2 Samuel 23:3-4 NCV

Mine eyes have seen the glory of the coming of the Lord;
He is trampling out the vintage where the grapes of wrath are stored;
He hath loosed the fateful lightning of his terrible swift sword:
His truth is marching on.

Glory! Glory! Hallelujah!
Glory! Glory! Hallelujah!
Glory! Glory! Hallelujah!
His truth is marching on.

He has sounded forth the trumpet that shall never call retreat;
He is sifting out the hearts of all before his judgment seat;
O be swift, my soul, to answer him; be jubilant, my feet!
Our God is marching on.

In the beauty of the lilies Christ was born across the sea,
With a glory in his bosom that transfigures you and me;
As he died to make us holy, let us die that all be free!
While God is marching on.

Written at the beginning of the Civil War, Julia Howe's battle hymn was meant as a patriotic song and not a hymn for public worship. The tune "Glory, Hallelujah!" was already being used by troops, but the lyrics were decidedly morbid. Howe's pastor asked if she could write more uplifting lyrics after they overheard the troops' rendition in Washington. She was inspired and, after writing it within a day, sent it off for publishing as a poem.

The song became an anthem for the Union Army and the north at large. One does not have to be in a physical battle to feel the power of this song. God's truth marches on no matter who opposes it, and his truth resists our feeble attempts at control. No matter what happens, his truth will carry on undeterred. Glory, Hallelujah!

Word of Truth, I trust your truth will remain even when we misinterpret it. Be glorified and align my heart in your love. Thank you.

Near the Cross

In Christ Jesus you who once were far off
have been brought near by the blood of Christ.

EPHESIANS 2:13 NKJV

Jesus, keep me near the cross,
There a precious fountain;
Free to all, a healing stream,
Flows from Calv'ry's mountain.

In the cross, in the cross
Be my glory ever,
Till my ransomed soul shall find
Rest beyond the river.

Near the cross, a trembling soul,
Love and mercy found me;
There the Bright and Morning Star
Shed his beams around me.

Near the cross! I'll watch and wait,
Hoping, trusting ever;
Till I reach the golden strand,
Just beyond the river.

Fanny Crosby (1820-1915) wrote under many pseudonymns as well as her name, and she wrote over eight thousand hymns. She was blind from the age of six weeks, but that did not keep her parents from educating her or encouraging her endeavors. She became a teacher and an accomplished writer. Covering a wide breadth of subjects in her works, she continues to impact how we approach the Lord through her hymns today.

As Crosby shows us, our greatest treasure is found in Christ. He is worth every surrender, sacrifice, and movement of love in his name. May we offer him our hearts as he reveals to us his own in deeper ways.

Savior, your cross and resurrection are the power of your testimony. I yield to your love, for I know it is better than life. You are better to us than we could dream.

Praise Him

Come on, everyone!
Let's sing for joy to the Lord!
Let's shout our loudest praises
to our God who saved us!

Psalm 95:1 TPT

Praise him, praise him! Jesus, our blessed redeemer!
Sing, O earth, his wonderful love proclaim!
Hail him, hail him! Highest archangels in glory!
Strength and honor give to his holy name!
Like a shepherd, Jesus will guard his children.
In his arms he carries them all day long.

Praise him! Praise him! Tell of his excellent greatness.
Praise him! Praise him! Ever in joyful song.

Praise him, praise him! Jesus, our blessed redeemer!
Heav'nly portals loud with hosannas ring!
Jesus, Savior, reigneth forever and ever!
Crown him, crown him! Prophet, and priest, and king!
Christ is coming, over the world victorious.
Pow'r and glory unto the Lord belong.

Another hymn by Fanny Crosby, "Praise Him!" directs us to offer Jesus our unhindered adoration. Echoing many psalms that do the same, this hymn encourages creation to join in the universal song of praise to our great Creator.

What can you offer praise to Jesus for in this moment? Think of every little thing you are grateful for whether it be as simple as the breath in your lungs, the acceptance you've found in God's love, or the touch of a loved one. Pour out your praise in specific ways, and allow your heart to lead you.

Jesus, you are worthy of my praise both when I'm grateful and when I'm struggling to find anything to give thanks for. There is always goodness present, for you are present with me. Here's my praise, Lord. Here's my thanks, for you are good and your love endures forever.

Since Jesus Came

You were washed, you were sanctified, you were justified in the name of the Lord Jesus Christ and by the Spirit of our God.

1 Corinthians 6:11 csb

What a wonderful change in my life has been wrought
Since Jesus came into my heart!
I have light in my soul for which long I have sought,
Since Jesus came into my heart!

Since Jesus came into my heart,
Since Jesus came into my heart,
Floods of joy o'er my soul like the sea billows roll,
Since Jesus came into my heart.

I'm possessed of a hope that is steadfast and sure,
Since Jesus came into my heart!
And no dark clouds of doubt now my pathway obscure,
Since Jesus came into my heart!

I shall go there to dwell in that city, I know,
Since Jesus came into my heart!
And I'm happy, so happy, as onward I go,
Since Jesus came into my heart!

Rufus McDaniel was ordained in 1873. As many of us connect strongly to music, so did he. He found joy in church music. In the 1880s, he started to write hymns of his own. He wanted to be a blessing to others and glorify God through each one. This particular hymn was written in 1913 after the tragic loss of his youngest son.

Reading the uplifting lyrics of this hymn, one would never know they were born out of grief. It is not necessary for us to resist the sorrow that comes over us in times of great trouble, but it is also not wrong to express the joy we have in Christ. He is the same in every season. As we invite him to rule and reign over our hearts, may we know the joy that McDaniel so freely wrote about.

Jesus, you are my comforter, friend, and great reward. You are my Savior, King, and teacher. You are everything I need. Where there is sorrow, there are also planted seeds of your joy.

May

Great is thy faithfulness, O God my Father;
There is no shadow of turning with thee;
Thou changest not, thy compassions, they fail not;
As thou hast been thou forever will be.

The Church's One Foundation

Don't you know that you yourselves are God's temple
and that God's Spirit dwells in your midst?

1 Corinthians 3:16 NIV

The Church's one foundation
Is Jesus Christ, her Lord;
She is his new creation
By water and the Word.
From heav'n he came and sought her
To be his holy bride;
With his own blood he bought her,
And for her life he died.

The Church shall never perish.
Her dear Lord to defend,
To guide, sustain, and cherish,
Is with her to the end.
Tho' there be those that hate her
And strive to see her fail,
Against both foe and traitor
She ever shall prevail.

This hymn is a defense of the historic accuracy and authority of many Old Testament books. Samuel Stone was inspired by the written defense Bishop Gray made against these challenges in 1866. He based the hymn on the ninth article of the Catholic faith, which follows the Apostles' Creed: "The Holy Catholic [Universal] Church; the Communion of Saints; He is the Head of this Body."

With Christ as the firm foundation of our faith, we join with others around the world in declaring we are all part of the same body of Christ. He is our head, and beyond any differences, he is where all paths lead. He is the leader of the global church. Consider how you can look past differences with others today and extend grace and kindness.

King Jesus, you are the truth. You are a firm foundation steadier than any thoughts or opinions I have. I stand on your truth and choose to walk out your love.

Sweet Name of Jesus

The name of the LORD is a strong tower;
the righteous man runs into it and is safe.
PROVERBS 18:10 ESV

How sweet the name of Jesus sounds
In a believer's ear!
It soothes our sorrows, heals our wounds,
And drives away our fear.

It makes the wounded spirit whole
And calms the troubled breast;
'Tis manna to the hungry soul,
And to the weary, rest.

O Jesus, shepherd, guardian, friend,
My prophet, priest, and King,
My Lord, my life, my way, my end,
Accept the praise I bring.

How weak the effort of my heart,
How cold my warmest thought;
But when I see you as you are,
I'll praise you as I ought.

John Newton based his hymn on Song of Solomon 1:3: "Your anointing oils are fragrant; your name is oil poured out." The name of Jesus is a fragrant perfume sweet to our senses and satisfying to our souls. His love is a balm that heals our wounds, relieves our sorrows, and fills us with peace.

Jesus is not only our Savior but our "shepherd, guardian, friend, Prophet, Priest, and King." He is the perfect parent, the wisest advisor, and the most reliable help. Whatever we need, he is the perfect solution. Instead of looking for fulfillment in things that don't truly satisfy, let's focus on Christ. He knows what we need and how to guide us into his goodness at every turn.

Jesus, I have found comfort for my weary soul in your presence before, and I long for a sweet taste of your love today. Fill me up with your goodness. I rely on you, and I will follow your guidance.

Be Still My Soul

I have certainly soothed and quieted my soul;
Like a weaned child resting against his mother,
My soul within me is like a weaned child.

PSALM 131:2 NASB

Be still, my soul; the Lord is on your side;
Bear patiently the cross of grief or pain;
Leave to your God to order and provide;
In ev'ry change he faithful will remain.
Be still, my soul; your best, your heav'nly friend
Through thorny ways leads to a joyful end.

Be still, my soul; your God will undertake
To guide the future as he has the past;
Your hope, your confidence, let nothing shake;
All now mysterious shall be bright at last.
Be still, my soul; the waves and winds still know
His voice who ruled them while he lived below.

It is not anyone's responsibility to soothe and quiet our souls. Yes, we need the support of loved ones; we were built for it. Still, no one can choose how we align our hearts but us. May we not overlook the agency we have to choose how we approach others and the Lord. We can remind our souls of the faithfulness of God and find our rest in him.

Not much is known of the author of this poem except that Katharina von Schlegel was born in 1697 in Germany. Her poem was translated into English by Jane Borthwick in 1855. We don't have to know much about the writer to connect to this hymn however. It elicits a quiet comfort as we focus our attention on the constancy of Christ even in the midst of pain.

Faithful One, I quiet my soul before you and look to the truth of who you are.

God's Wondrous Grace

That is why I am suffering here in prison.
But I am not ashamed of it, for I know the one in whom I trust,
and I am sure that he is able to guard what I have entrusted to him
until the day of his return.

2 Timothy 1:12 NLT

I know not why God's wondrous grace
To me is daily shown,
Nor why, with mercy, Christ in love
Redeemed me for his own.

But "I know whom I have believed,
And am persuaded that he is able
To keep that which I've committed
Unto him against that day."

I know not how the Spirit moves,
Convincing us of sin,
Revealing Jesus through the Word,
Creating faith in him.

I know not when my Lord may come,
At night or noon-day fair,
Nor if I'll walk the vale with him,
Or meet him in the air.

Though there is much we do not know, we can cling to one thing with unabashed faith. "I know whom I have believed," Daniel Webster Whittle wrote, "and am persuaded that he is able." Christ is able to do far more than we could ask or imagine, let alone keep us close to him through the mercy of his heart.

There is a tender mystery in fellowship with the Lord. He offers peace we can't explain, revelation of his Word through the Spirit, and unending grace. We do not know when he will return, but we wait with hope knowing we have access to him through his Spirit. We don't need all the logical answers to follow him, for he draws us in with loving kindness and transforms our lives with generous grace. Throw anchor of your hope into the sea of his faithfulness and trust him with your life.

Constant One, I trust you with all I have and all I am. I believe you are real, true, and faithful.

Were You There

The women who had come from Galilee with Jesus followed Joseph and saw the tomb and how Jesus' body was laid.

Luke 23:55 NCV

Were you there when they crucified my Lord?
Were you there when they crucified my Lord?
Oh, sometimes it causes me to tremble,
tremble, tremble.
Were you there when they crucified my Lord?

Were you there when they nailed him to the tree?
Were you there when they nailed him to the tree?
Oh, sometimes it causes me to tremble,
tremble, tremble.
Were you there when they nailed him to the tree?

Were you there when God raised him from the tomb?
Were you there when God raised him from the tomb?
Oh, sometimes it causes me to tremble,
tremble, tremble.
Were you there when God raised him from the tomb?

A meditative hymn on the sacrifice of Christ, "Were You There" is an African American spiritual that most likely dates back before the Civil War. It was first published in 1899, but it began as an oral tradition learned and passed on by those who heard it.

In the cross of Christ and his subsequent burial and resurrection, there is cause for awe. As you meditate on what Jesus did, you can keep it simple. Listen to, sing, or read through this hymn and give it space to breathe. As you focus your attention on the words of the song, direct your heart to God. Whether or not you tremble, may you feel the awe his presence brings.

Gracious Jesus, you are worthy of my attention. I give you these moments, my open heart, and my focus as I meditate on this hymn. Move in me as I do.

Wonderful Words of Life

Simon Peter answered Him,
"Lord, to whom shall we go?
You have the words of eternal life."

John 6:68 NKJV

Sing them over again to me,
Wonderful words of life;
Let me more of their beauty see,
Wonderful words of life;
Words of life and beauty
Teach me faith and duty.

Beautiful words, wonderful words,
Wonderful words of life;
Beautiful words, wonderful words,
Wonderful words of life.

Christ, the blessed one, gives to all
Wonderful words of life;
Sinner, list to the loving call,
Wonderful words of life;
All so freely given,
Wooing us to heaven.

Peter's statement in John 6:68 echoes through this 1874 hymn by Philip Bliss: "Lord, to whom shall we go? You have the words of eternal life." We can go to Jesus and drink from the wells of his wisdom just as his followers did. Jesus promised in John 15:26, "But when the Helper comes, whom I shall send to you from the Father, the Spirit of truth who proceeds from the Father, He will testify of Me." We have the Spirit, and he testifies and teaches us with the truth of Christ.

A wonderful way to listen for the Lord and learn his voice is to get to know Jesus through the Scriptures. We can read the gospels a thousand times and still find truth that challenges us. Let's not give up reading the Word and asking the Lord to speak directly to our hearts with his "beautiful words, wonderful words, wonderful words of life."

Word of Life, you are the source of life. Speak directly to my heart today.

He Hideth My Soul

He will conceal me in his shelter in the day of adversity;
he will hide me under the cover of his tent;
he will set me high on a rock.

Psalm 27:5 csb

A wonderful Savior is Jesus my Lord,
A wonderful Savior to me.
He hideth my soul in the cleft of the rock,
Where rivers of pleasure I see.

He hideth my soul in the cleft of the rock
That shadows a dry, thirsty land.
He hideth my life in the depths of his love,
And covers me there with his hand,
And covers me there with his hand.

When clothed in his brightness, transported
I rise
To meet him in clouds of the sky,
His perfect salvation, his wonderful love,
I'll shout with the millions on high.

Fanny Crosby fostered a deep relationship with the Lord. Having lost her sight as an infant, she did not know what anyone's face looked like, but that didn't stop her from putting her hope in the beautiful truth that Jesus' would be the first face she saw when standing before him in glory.

We don't have to wait until we stand face to face with the Lord to know him. We get to press in to the fellowship of his presence and worship him in spirit and truth now. We have a wonderful hope we have in him now and forevermore.

Glorious Jesus, whatever my limitations, I don't find my identity in them. I am rooted in you, and my hope is in your everlasting love. Reveal yourself to me in truth as I look to you throughout my days.

Jesus Saves

O Lord, how blessed are the people
who know the triumphant shout,
for they walk in the radiance of your presence.

PSALM 89:15 TPT

We have heard the joyful sound:
Jesus saves! Jesus saves!
Spread the tidings all around:
Jesus saves! Jesus saves!
Bear the news to ev'ry land,
Climb the steeps and cross the waves;
Onward! 'Tis our Lord's command;
Jesus saves! Jesus saves!

Waft it on the rolling tide:
Jesus saves! Jesus saves!
Tell to sinners far and wide:
Jesus saves! Jesus saves!
Sing, ye islands of the sea;
Echo back, ye ocean caves;
Earth shall keep her jubilee:
Jesus saves! Jesus saves!

Priscilla Owens (1829-1907) worked in public schools for the majority of her career. She also wrote many hymns, most of them written for children. She devoted her life to teaching children, and this did not stop with her day job. This particular hymn was written for a Sunday school mission anniversary.

"Jesus saves" is a refrain we can sing no matter our age. He is Savior to the child as well as the elder. There is no age requirement for his kingdom. May we not disqualify ourselves from his family or service, for he uses all who are willing. As we look to him throughout our lives, he will guide us with a steady hand. He is our song of victory. Praise the Lord, Jesus saves!

Lord Jesus, help my heart remain humble in your love, knowing no one is excluded from your salvation. All who look to you are radiant.

Wonderful Grace of Jesus

We believe it is through the grace of our Lord Jesus
that we are saved, just as they are.
ACTS 15:11 NIV

Wonderful grace of Jesus,
Greater than all my sin;
How shall my tongue describe it,
Where shall its praise begin?
Taking away my burden,
Setting my spirit free,
For the wonderful grace of Jesus reaches me.

Wonderful the matchless grace of Jesus,
Deeper than the mighty rolling sea,
Higher than the mountain, sparkling like a
fountain,
All sufficient grace for even me;
Broader than the scope of my transgressions,
sing it!
Greater far than all my sin and shame.
O magnify the precious name of Jesus, praise
his name!

The grace of God is hard to wrap our heads around. It is more generous than we are. It is unending; there are no limits to God's grace. It is outrageous in its effects. Every time we come to the Lord, we are met by grace. We could never outrun it, and we can't mess up so badly that his grace is not enough to cover us.

Grace takes away the burden of sin, and it liberates the soul once held captive. Haldor Lillenas' 1918 hymn makes this clear in its verses. It also reminds us that the grace of God reaches even those that society reviles. Grace is the gift we receive when we come to Christ and enter his family. What wonderful grace!

Gracious Lord, thank you for the gift of knowing you, being transformed in your love, and for being called your very own. May I fight to not sell your grace short, for it is astounding and always available.

He Keeps Me Singing

Addressing one another in psalms and hymns and spiritual songs, singing and making melody to the Lord with your heart.

Ephesians 5:19 ESV

There's within my heart a melody;
Jesus whispers sweet and low,
"Fear not, I am with you, peace, be still,"
In all of life's ebb and flow.

Jesus, Jesus, Jesus,
Sweetest name I know,
Fills my every longing,
keeps me singing as I go.

All my life was wrecked by sin and strife,
Discord filled my heart with pain,
Jesus swept across the broken strings,
Stirred the slumbering chords again.

Feasting on the riches of his grace,
Resting 'neath his sheltering wing,
Always looking on his smiling face,
That is why I shout and sing.

Luther Bridgers was a minister who sometimes wrote hymns. He published "He Keeps Me Singing" in 1910. Though it is unclear whether the following incident happened before or after the hymn was written, Bridgers faced devastating news when he received notice that his wife and children died in a housefire while he was at a conference away from home. Regardless of the timeline, the sentiment of this hymn rings true in times of mourning and joy.

May you find peace as you connect with the Lord through this hymn today. Jesus promises to be with you through every trial and storm as well as in times of celebration. Call on his name, no matter your season, for his name is sweet and his presence even sweeter.

Jesus, thank you for your presence in my life. You are the best thing I know. I rely on your help and wisdom in every high and low. You are my God. I call on you.

Showers of Blessing

Will You not revive us again,
So that Your people may rejoice in You?
Psalm 85:6 NASB

There shall be showers of blessing:
This is the promise of love;
There shall be seasons refreshing,
Sent from the Savior above.

Showers of blessing,
Showers of blessing we need:
Mercy-drops round us are falling,
But for the showers we plead.

There shall be showers of blessing,
Precious reviving again;
Over the hills and the valleys,
Sound of abundance of rain.

There shall be showers of blessing:
Oh, that today they might fall,
Now as to God we're confessing,
Now as on Jesus we call!

Daniel Webster Whittle was a major in the Union Army. He went to war with a New Testament from his mother tucked in his knapsack. When he was injured and had his arm amputated, he needed a way to pass the time. Finding the Bible, he read through it several times. When a dying man begged for someone to pray for him, Whittle was moved to pray for the first time. He confessed his own sins and then prayed for the young man who peacefully passed as he did.

This hymn is fruit of a life surrendered to the Lord. After Major Whittle left the service, he went to work with D.L. Moody's ministry. He wrote many songs in that time of which this is one. May you receive the showers of blessing Christ rains down on everyone who looks to him. His presence is near, and he offers you himself. There is no greater blessing.

Great God, rain on me the blessing of your presence and refresh my heart in you.

Deep Love of Jesus

This is real love—not that we loved God,
but that he loved us and sent his Son
as a sacrifice to take away our sins.

1 John 4:10 NLT

O the deep, deep love of Jesus!
Vast, unmeasured, boundless, free,
Rolling as a mighty ocean
In its fullness over me.
Underneath me, all around me,
Is the current of thy love;
Leading onward, leading homeward,
To thy glorious rest above.

O the deep, deep love of Jesus!
Spread his praise from shore to shore;
How he loveth, ever loveth,
Changeth never, nevermore;
How he watches o'er his loved ones,
Died to call them all his own;
How for them he intercedeth,
Watcheth o'er them from the throne.

Samuel Francis was a merchant, preacher, and hymn writer in the late nineteenth and early twentieth centuries. This is his best-known hymn but that is all we know for sure of its origin. We find a familiar refrain and hopeful message in its text: "O the deep, deep love of Jesus."

The love of God is endless. "Vast, unmeasured, boundless, free." If you were to put words to the love of Christ today, trying to describe it in a creative way, what words would you use? Perhaps words fall short and an image is a stronger connector for you. Imagine the lengths of this love and then dream bigger. We cannot exaggerate the love of God.

Christ Jesus, I am in awe of the love you give and the love you are. Open my understanding in new ways today as I meditate on the greatness of your mercy.

Gather at the River

The angel showed me the river of the water of life.
It was shining like crystal and was flowing from the throne of God
and of the Lamb down the middle of the street of the city.
The tree of life was on each side of the river.

REVELATION 22:1-2 NCV

Shall we gather at the river,
Where bright angel feet have trod;
With its crystal tide forever
Flowing by the throne of God?

Yes, we'll gather at the river,
The beautiful, the beautiful river;
Gather with the saints at the river
That flows by the throne of God.

On the margin of the river,
Washing up its silver spray,
We will walk and worship ever,
All the happy golden day.

Soon we'll reach the shining river,
Soon our pilgrimage will cease;
Soon our happy hearts will quiver
With the melody of peace.

Robert Lowry wrote this hymn in 1864. He was meditating on Revelation 22:1-2 and the metaphor of the river. He wondered why hymn writers said so much about the "river of death" and less about the pure water of life coming from the throne of God. We don't go to the river of death but the river of life.

When we are in the fullness of God's kingdom in the age to come, we will gather at that river. We will see its crystal waters and the tree of life growing on its shores. We will know powerful, perfect peace, and we will gather with those who have gone before and will come after us. No more sadness, pain, or suffering. We will be made perfect, just as God is perfect, and we will dwell with him forever in that place.

Glorious One, thank you for the hope I have in you. My heart longs to know you more.

Wonderful Peace

May the Lord of peace Himself give you peace always in every way.
The Lord be with you all.

2 Thessalonians 3:16 NKJV

Far away in the depths of my spirit tonight
Rolls a melody sweeter than psalm;
In celestial-like strains it unceasingly falls
O'er my soul like an infinite calm.

Peace! Peace! Wonderful peace,
Coming down from the Father above;
Sweep over my spirit forever, I pray,
In fathomless billows of love.

I am resting tonight in this wonderful peace,
Resting sweetly in Jesus' control;
For I'm kept from all danger by night and
  by day,
And his glory is flooding my soul.

And methinks when I rise to that city of peace,
Where the author of peace I shall see,
That one strain of the song which the
ransomed will sing,
In that heavenly kingdom shall be.

After several days of camp meetings with other believers, Reverend Warren Cornell (1858-1936) wrote the beginnings of this hymn with joy overflowing his heart. At some point, he dropped the note he'd penned the poem on. Reverend Cooper, who was hosting the camp meetings, found it. He took it to the organ, set it to music, and finished the verses. From this divine cooperation, we have "Wonderful Peace."

Out of the overflow of our hearts, we can offer God new praises. As we give him our words, he inspires and fills us with his wonderful peace. He is always moving in fresh waves of mercy. We can offer him our fresh response as he does.

Wonderful Lord, I am in awe of your wisdom, power, and loving kindness. Thank you for your peace that passes all understanding.

MAY 15

In His Hands

The Lord, the Most High, is awe-inspiring,
a great King over the whole earth.
He subdues peoples under us
and nations under our feet.

Psalm 47:2-3 csb

He's got the whole world in his hands.
He's got the whole world in his hands.
He's got the whole world in his hands.
He's got the whole world in his hands.

He's got the wind and the rain in his hands...
He's got the little tiny baby in his hands...
He's got you and me, brother, in his hands...
He's got you and me, sister, in his hands...

This anonymous spiritual rose out of the African American oral tradition. It became popular among other cultures in the 1940s and 1950s when it was recorded and performed by artists such as Frank Warner and Laurie London. It has been covered many times over and become a beloved song for many.

When the world feels like a harsh place and the news is preoccupied with what's wrong in the world, a simple perspective shift can help our hearts rest in the sovereignty of God. "He's got the whole world in his hands." He's got it all. He's got all the things we cannot control, and more importantly, he's got us.

Sovereign Lord, I trust you hold me in your hands. You've got my family. You've got my community. You've got the world. I trust you, and I choose to rest in your peace as I follow your lead in living out your love in my life.

Lily of the Valley

A friend loves at all times,
and a brother is born for a time of adversity.
PROVERBS 17:17 NIV

I have found a friend in Jesus, he's ev'rything
to me,
He's the fairest of ten thousand to my soul;
The Lily of the Valley—in him alone I see
All I need to cleanse and make me fully whole.
In sorrow he's my comfort, in trouble he's
my stay,
He tells me ev'ry care on him to roll;
He's the Lily of the Valley,
The Bright and Morning Star,
He's the greatest of ten thousand to my soul.

He will never, never leave me nor yet forsake
me here,
While I live by faith and do his blessed will;
A wall of fire about me, I've nothing now
to fear—
With his manna he my hungry soul shall fill.
Then sweeping up to glory I'll see his
blessed face,
Where rivers of delight shall ever roll;
He's the Lily of the Valley, the Bright and
Morning Star,
He's the greatest of ten thousand to my soul.

The term "lily of the valley" comes from a poetic verse in Song of Solomon. Lilies were used in Solomon's time as emblems of purity. Christ is the purest offering. He is without blemish before God and before men. He is the pure, spotless lamb.

The blessed truth ringing in verse three is an encouragement to every heart needing courage: "He will never, never leave me nor yet forsake me here." No matter the troubles we face or the trials we walk through, we are never alone in our battles. Jesus fights for us, leads us, and always remains victorious. Before him, the Lily of the Valley, the Bright and Morning Star, we will one day stand. May we live for him now and know his goodness even on mundane days.

Lily of the Valley, you are beautiful and kind. You are strong and undeterred. I want to know you more than I want to be right. Lead me.

Closer Walk with Thee

I'm not defeated by my weakness, but delighted! For when I feel my weakness and endure mistreatment—when I'm surrounded with troubles on every side and face persecution because of my love for Christ—I am made yet stronger. For my weakness becomes a portal to God's power.

2 Corinthians 12:10 TPT

I am weak but thou art strong;
Jesus, keep me from all wrong;
I'll be satisfied as long
As I walk, let me walk close to thee.

Just a closer walk with thee,
Grant it, Jesus, is my plea,
Daily walking close to thee,
Let it be, dear Lord, let it be.

Thro' this world of toil and snares,
If I falter, Lord, who cares?
Who with me my burden shares?
None but thee, dear Lord, none but thee.

When my feeble life is o'er,
Time for me will be no more;
Guide me gently, safely o'er
To thy kingdom shore, to thy shore.

This anonymous hymn recognizes our humanity and the strength we find in fellowship with Christ, and it can be sung as a prayer. When we are weak, burdened down by life, or grieving, the comfort of Christ is not a consolation prize. It is the power of God at work in us and the love of God reaching us where we are. We can lay our burdens at his feet and rest in his presence.

Even when our willpower runs out, God's grace is abundant. It is always more than we need. Let's quit trying to earn our way into God's kingdom and instead receive the gift of his grace to empower us in our weakness. He is enough, more than enough, and that is exceedingly good news to grab hold of.

Lord Jesus, I want to know you more and walk closer with you every day. I don't want to lose sight of what truly matters. Teach, guide, and be near me, Lord.

Feel the Spirit

"God is spirit, and those who worship him must worship in spirit and truth."

John 4:24 ESV

Ev'ry time I feel the Spirit
Moving in my heart, I will pray.
Yes, ev'ry time I feel the Spirit
Moving in my heart, I will pray.

Upon the mountain when my God spoke,
Out of God's mouth came fire and smoke.
All around me, it looked so fine,
I asked my Lord if all was mine.

Jordan River, chilly and cold,
It chills the body, but not the soul.
There ain't but one train that's on this track,
It runs to heaven and runs right back.

Originating in the south before the Civil War, this African American spiritual is a beautiful picture of faith. Our spiritual lives are not based just on what we think about God but what we know about God and experience of him. The Spirit moved in ancient days, and the Spirit moves today. Every time we sense his presence, we can pray.

Following Christ is all about knowing him. In the fellowship of his Spirit, we grow in understanding, are transformed in his love, and garner grace to persevere. The Spirit is mysterious, and yet the Spirit is God. Let's not neglect the beauty of experiencing deep friendship with the Spirit who fills our lives with light, life, joy, and peace.

Holy Spirit, whenever I sense you today, I will turn my heart to you in prayer. Please move in me.

Fight the Good Fight

In all these things we overwhelmingly conquer
through Him who loved us.

ROMANS 8:37 NASB

Fight the good fight with all your might,
Christ is your strength and Christ your right.
Lay hold on life, and it shall be
Your joy and crown eternally.

Run the straight race through God's good grace;
Lift up your eyes, and seek his face.
Life with its way before us lies;
Christ is the path and Christ the prize.

Cast care aside, lean on your guide;
His boundless mercy will provide.
Lean, and the trusting soul shall prove
Christ is its life and Christ its love.

Faint not, nor fear, his arms are near;
He changes not, and you are dear.
Only believe, and you will see
That Christ is Lord eternally.

John Monsell (1811-1875) was a prolific Irish poet who wrote three hundred hymns. This hymn is based on 1 Timothy 6:12, Paul's encouragement to Timothy: "Fight the good fight of faith; take hold of the eternal life to which you were called." Fighting the fight of faith is not with fists or sword; it is a race we run. We fight to persevere in the strength of Christ.

When we cast our trust on the Lord Jesus Christ, we believe what he says is true, what he did still ripples into our lives, and he is God eternal. Let's keep our eyes fixed on him and let go of the distractions that lure us away from our great Prince of peace.

Shepherd, I depend on you to help me through the twists and turns of this life. I will continue to run the race set before me knowing you are with me as my guide, coach, and strength. My fight of faith is to keep my focus on you.

Resting Place

Everyone who calls on the
name of the Lord will be saved.

Acts 2:21 NLT

My faith has found a resting place,
From guilt my soul is freed;
I trust the ever-living One,
His wounds for me shall plead.

I need no other argument,
I need no other plea,
It is enough that Jesus died,
And that he died for me.

Enough for me that Jesus saves,
This ends my fear and doubt;
A sinful soul, I come to him,
He'll never cast me out.

My heart is leaning on the Word,
The written Word of God,
Salvation by my Savior's name,
Salvation thro' his blood.

Eliza Hewitt wrote many hymns in her rehabilitation, and this is one of her best known. It was first published in 1891. Knowing she dealt with a debilitating spinal issue that kept her from teaching, it is remarkable she did not give in to despair. Instead, she found new ways to bring meaning and joy to her life and to serving the Lord.

At its heart, the faith of Christianity is simple: it is in Jesus Christ our Lord. He took our place, removed our guilt and shame, and liberated us in the power of his death and resurrection. He lives to make intercession for us. He is our ever-present help, constant companion, and God. He is a resting place for every soul who comes to him.

Lord Jesus, I yield my heart to you knowing you are kind, true, and faithful. I put my trust in you and let my heart rest in your love.

The Voice of Jesus

"Come to me,
all of you who are tired and have heavy loads,
and I will give you rest."
MATTHEW 11:28 NCV

I heard the voice of Jesus say,
"Come unto me and rest;
Lay down, O weary one,
Lay down your head upon my breast."
I came to Jesus as I was,
So weary, worn, and sad;
I found in him a resting place,
And he has made me glad.

I heard the voice of Jesus say,
"Behold, I freely give
The living water, thirsty one;
Stoop down and drink and live."
I came to Jesus, and I drank
Of that life-giving stream;
My thirst was quenched, my soul revived,
And now I live in him.

Each verse of this hymn from 1846 is based on statements Jesus made in his ministry. They are straight from the gospel as the living words of our God and Savior. He beckons us to rest and lay our burdens at his feet. He offers us the living waters of his salvation. He is the light of the world, and he shines brightly in every season and change.

Reading through Horatius Bonar's hymn, allow yourself to hear the invitation Christ offers and take him up on it. Find a resting place in his love. Fill up on the living waters of his presence. Follow his loving light. Christ is the answer for everything you need today and every day.

All-Sufficient One, you are my daily bread and the living water that satisfies my soul. You are my resting place where I am made whole. I heed your call, and I take you up on all you offer. Thank you.

Faith Is the Victory

He brought me to the banqueting house,
And his banner over me was love.

SONG OF SOLOMON 2:4 NKJV

Encamped along the hills of light,
Ye Christian soldiers, rise
And press the battle ere the night
Shall veil the glowing skies.
Against the foe in vales below
Let all our strength be hurled;
Faith is the victory, we know,
That overcomes the world.

Faith is the victory!
Faith is the victory!
Oh, glorious victory
That overcomes the world.

When John Yates (1837-1900) left his work as a salesman to become the editor of a local newspaper and a commissioned writer for a famous singer, he penned the words to this song. Yates had a talent for poetry, and his mother encouraged him to keep writing. Because of her encouragement, we have this hymn today.

Faith is the victory because it is rooted and grounded in Christ's love and sacrifice. We don't hope in vain. No, our hope is in Christ, and we can take him at his word, for he is faithful and fulfills his promises. His banner over us is love, and we cannot escape it.

Lord, thank you for the banner of your love over my life. I am surrounded by you, and I am kept in your perfect peace. I don't need to know all the answers to every question. You are my firm foundation, and I trust you with it all.

MAY 23

Sing of the Mercies

This forever-song I sing of the gentle love of God!
Young and old alike will hear about
your faithful, steadfast love—never failing!

PSALM 89:1 TPT

I will sing of the mercies of the Lord forever,
I will sing, I will sing,
I will sing of the mercies of the Lord forever,
I will sing of the mercies of the Lord.
With my mouth will I make known
Thy faithfulness, thy faithfulness,
With my mouth will I make known
Thy faithfulness to all generations,
I will sing of the mercies of the Lord forever,
I will sing of the mercies of the Lord.

Though this song was composed by James Fillmore around the turn of the twentieth century, it only became popular during the 1960s when people often sang simple Sciptural choruses in worship. Its simplicity does not take away from the depth of it; if that were true, many of the psalms would be seen in the same way.

Let us sing of the mercies of the Lord, for he is worthy. Let's glorify his name and tell of his faithfulness, for he never fails. This hymn is straight out of Psalm 89. Take some time to read through the psalm and sing its simple message throughout your day. His mercies are new every morning; that means his mercies are fresh for you now.

Lord, your mercy refreshes my soul and revives my heart. I trust your faithful love finds me wherever I am and whatever I am doing. I turn to you and give you praise. Thank you for your nearness to me.

Come Every Soul

"The Spirit of the Lord is on me, because he has anointed me to preach good news to the poor. He has sent me to proclaim release to the captives and recovery of sight to the blind, to set free the oppressed."

Luke 4:18 CSB

Come, every soul by sin oppressed,
There's mercy with the Lord;
And he will surely give you rest,
By trusting in his Word.
Only trust him, only trust him,
Only trust him now.

He will save you, he will save you,
He will save you now.

Come then and join this holy band,
And on to glory go,
To dwell in that celestial land,
Where joys immortal flow.
I will trust him, I will trust him,
I will trust him now.

After withdrawing from pastoral work due to his ill health, John Stockton began compiling and publishing gospel hymnals. In 1875, he began writing both text and music for many of the songs. One of these was "Come, Every Soul." It is an invitation to each and every one of us no matter who we are.

The gospel is also an open invitation. Jesus came to set the sinner free and to liberate the opressed. His love is not reserved for the elite. In fact, Jesus spent much time with the outcasts of society and garnered harsh criticism from the religious elite his day. His grace is for all, so let's humble ourselves before him and partner with his heart. There are no class systems in his kingdom. We are all saved by grace, and that grace is available in abundant measure for all who receive it.

Gracious Jesus, I'm grateful you welcome all who come to you. May my heart remain humble in your love. Help me not judge others but love them as you do.

Tell Me the Story

Beginning with Moses and all the Prophets,
he explained to them what was said
in all the Scriptures concerning himself.

LUKE 24:27 NIV

Tell me the story of Jesus,
Write on my heart every word;
Tell me the story most precious,
Sweetest that ever was heard.
Tell how the angels, in chorus,
Sang as they welcomed his birth,
"Glory to God in the highest!
Peace and good tidings to earth."

Tell me the story of Jesus,
Write on my heart every word;
Tell me the story most precious,
Sweetest that ever was heard.

This hymn, written by Fanny Crosby and composed by John Sweney, was first published in 1880. Homer Rodeheaver was a singer-evangelist known to sing this song in dugouts on battlefields and in barracks during World War I while stationed in France. It had a lasting effect on many who heard it, and it brought peace to many souls.

In our battles, we can find solace, relief, and courage in the story of Jesus. His life was not a fairy tale or fable but a lived reality. The power of his love remains as strong today as it was when it resurrected him from the grave. He is with us wherever we go.

Jesus, I will not forget the power of your life, ministry, death, or resurrection. You are life, breath, hope, and peace to my heart and to the world. Thank you.

Where He Leads Me

A scribe came up and said to him,
"Teacher, I will follow you wherever you go."
MATTHEW 8:19 ESV

I can hear my Savior calling,
I can hear my Savior calling,
I can hear my Savior calling,
"Take thy cross and follow, follow me."

Where he leads me I will follow,
Where he leads me I will follow,
Where he leads me I will follow,
I'll go with him, with him all the way.

I'll go with him through the garden,
I'll go with him through the garden,
I'll go with him through the garden,
I'll go with him, with him all the way.

He will give me grace and glory,
He will give me grace and glory,
He will give me grace and glory,
And go with me, with me all the way.

Reverend Ernest Blandly was a Salvation Army officer. In 1889, he had a choice: a comfortable post at an established church or an assignment on the New York City waterfront in an area known as Hell's Kitchen. While he could have chosen what was comfortable, he chose to follow God to the more challenging post.

We can trust that where the Lord leads, he goes with us. We cannot avoid challenges in this life, and trying to remain safe in our comfortable lives may block us from the world the Lord wants us to partake in. His love is enough to supply all we need. Rise above fear and follow the Lord with courage, for he is with you all the way.

Faithful One, I take up my cross and follow you. I don't have to be comfortable to know your peace. I want to know your love more than I want to remain the same. Thank you for your constant presence.

He Who Reigns Above

"Naked I came from my mother's womb,
And naked I shall return there.
The Lord gave and the Lord has taken away.
Blessed be the name of the Lord."

Job 1:21 NASB

All praise to him who reigns above
In majesty supreme,
Who gave his Son for man to die,
That he might man redeem!

Blessed be the name, blessed be the name,
Blessed be the name of the Lord;
Blessed be the name, blessed be the name,
Blessed be the name of the Lord!

His name above all names shall stand,
Exalted more and more,
At God the Father's own right hand,
Where angel hosts adore.

His name shall be The Counselor,
The mighty Prince of Peace,
Of all earth's kingdoms conqueror,
Whose reign shall never cease.

This hymn echoes the statement Job made to God: "Blessed be the name of the Lord." In good and harsh times, in plenty and want, through every gift and sacrifice, the name of the Lord is worthy to be praised.

William Clark (1854-1925) adapted this hymn from an earlier version which took some of the text of Charles Wesley's "O for a Thousand Tongues to Sing." Ralph Hudson wrote the refrain. It is unkown why Clark rewrote the verses, but his is the version we sing most often these days. The Lord is worthy of our praise no matter what is going on in the world or in our lives. May we join with those who have suffered before us and still proclaimed, "Blessed be the name of the Lord!"

Lord, I am thankful for life. I am thankful for your faithfulness. I am thankful for you. Be glorified!

Ye That Love the Lord

Sing a new song of praise to him;
play skillfully on the harp,
and sing with joy.
Psalm 33:3 NLT

Come, we that love the Lord,
And let our joys be known.
Join in a song with sweet accord,
Join in a song with sweet accord,
And thus surround the throne,
And thus surround the throne.

We're marching to Zion,
Beautiful, beautiful Zion.
We're marching upward to Zion,
The beautiful city of God.

Then let our songs abound,
And ev'ry tear be dry.
We're marching thro' Immanuel's ground,
We're marching thro' Immanuel's ground,
To fairer worlds on high,
To fairer worlds on high.

Isaac Watts is often described by scholars as the "father of English hymnody." Born in the late seventeenth century, he pioneered the practice of adapting Scripture for use as devotional poetry. Many of these poems were turned into hymns we still sing today. The refrain to "Come, Ye That Love the Lord" was added in the nineteenth century by gospel song writer Robert Lowry.

As we heed the invitation to come to the Lord today, let's focus our full attention on him and offer the praise of our hearts. Every day is a step closer to his heavenly kingdom. As we journey through this life, we have Christ as our vision and his promises as our hope. March on with him.

Lord Jesus, you are the vision of my life, and your faithfulness is my foundation. I choose to keep following you.

MAY 29

Joy Unspeakable

You have not seen Christ, but still you love him.
You cannot see him now, but you believe in him.
So you are filled with a joy that cannot be explained,
a joy full of glory.

1 Peter 1:8 NCV

I have found his grace is all complete;
He supplieth every need.
While I sit and learn at Jesus' feet,
I am free, yes, free indeed.

It is joy unspeakable and full of glory,
Full of glory, full of glory.
It is joy unspeakable and full of glory;
O the half has never yet been told!

I have found the pleasure I once craved;
It is joy and peace within.
What a wondrous blessing! I am saved
From the awful gulf of sin.

I have found that hope so bright and clear,
Living in the realm of grace.
O the Savior's presence is so near;
I can see his smiling face.

Barney Warren was a minister and hymn writer who wrote over two thousand hymns and children's songs. "Joy Unspeakable" has stood the test of time. As you read through the words of the hymn, allow your heart to follow the directives.

The grace of God is so great, it is a joy that transcends description. It is full of glory, and we know glory cannot be hemmed in by words. The grace of God cannot be captured by words; it must be experienced. Give yourself the time and space to experience and receive God's grace today, for it meets you where you are.

Gracious One, you are my living hope, guiding light, and exceeding joy. Fill me with the power and pleasure of your presence. I live for you.

Make Me a Blessing

"Heal the sick, cleanse the lepers,
raise the dead,cast out demons.
Freely you have received, freely give."

MATTHEW 10:8 NKJV

Out in the highways and byways of life,
Many are weary and sad;
Carry the sunshine where darkness is rife,
Making the sorrowing glad.

Make me a blessing, make me a blessing.
Out of my life may Jesus shine;
Make me a blessing, O Savior, I pray.
Make me a blessing to someone today.

Tell the sweet story of Christ and his love,
Tell of his pow'r to forgive;
Others will trust him if only you prove
True, ev'ry moment you live.

Give as 'twas given to you in your need,
Love as the master loved you;
Be to the helpless a helper indeed,
Unto your mission be true.

When Jesus comissioned his disciples to go and minister, he did not just send them with his message but also with his power. He told them to heal the sick, raise the dead, and cast out demons. When the Lord sends us out, it is always with both message and power to prove his love.

Ira Wilson studied at the Moody Bible Institute in the early twentieth century. After attending the bible college, he worked for a publishing company and also composed many hymns. With a background in theology and evangelism, Wilson's "Make Me a Blessing" reflects these values. The Christian life isn't simply to make personal connection with the Lord but also to reach out in generosity, serve others in love, and share the truth of Christ's hopeful message.

Jesus, make me a blessing for your name. Move in and through me with your power so you may be glorified.

Left Thy Throne

He entered into the world he created,
yet the world was unaware.
John 1:10 TPT

Thou didst leave thy throne and thy kingly
crown,
When thou camest to earth for me;
But in Bethlehem's home was there found
no room
For thy holy nativity.
O come to my heart, Lord Jesus,
There is room in my heart for thee.

The foxes found rest, and the birds their nest
In the shade of the forest tree;
But thy couch was the sod, O thou Son of God,
In the deserts of Galilee.
O come to my heart, Lord Jesus,
There is room in my heart for thee.

Emily Elliott, the daugter of a reverend and editor of the Church Missionary Juvenile Instructor, wrote and contributed to many hymns over the years. "Thou Didst Leave Thy Throne" contrasts the glory Jesus came from and the dishonor he endured while on earth. What a beautiful mystery that God would humble himself and allow himself to be ridiculed for us. What love, grace, and incomparable kindness he shows us!

Consider your life now and what it would be like if you left it all behind to face the unknown. The Lord loved you enough to set aside his glory and take the shame of the cross so you could be free in his mercy and covered by his grace. Will you come to him and take the invitation he offers you?

Savior, while there was no room in Bethlehem for your birth, I make room in my heart for you now. I believe you are worth every sacrifice and surrender.

June

Be Thou my vision, O Lord of my heart;
Naught be all else to me, save that thou art
Thou my best thought, by day or by night;
Waking or sleeping, thy presence my light.

The Sweetest Name

Far above every ruler and authority, power and dominion,
and every title given, not only in this age
but also in the one to come.

Ephesians 1:21 CSB

There have been names that I have loved
to hear,
But never has there been a name so dear
To this heart of mine, as the name divine,
The precious, precious name of Jesus.

Jesus is the sweetest name I know,
And he's just the same as his lovely name,
And that's the reason why I love him so;
Oh, Jesus is the sweetest name I know.

There is no name in earth or heav'n above,
That we should give such honor and such love
As the blessed name, let us all acclaim,
That wondrous, glorious name of Jesus.

And some day I shall see him face to face
To thank and praise him for his wondrous
grace,
Which he gave to me, when he made me free,
The blessed Son of God called Jesus.

Lela Long (1896-1951) wrote this hymn after hearing a missionary doctor tell a story from his service in China. An elderly woman traveled a great distance to see him, and he recognized her from having treated her several weeks prior. She came back to ask the name of the one whom he had introduced to her. That person had come to live in her heart and bring her happiness. He told her "Jesus," and she repeated it over and over again. This inspired Lela Long to pen this song about the sweetness of Jesus' name.

Jesus is a person and not just a name. He is living, active, and makes himself at home in the hearts of those who receive him. He brings joy, peace, and healing. Call on that sweetest name today and enter into deeper fellowship with him.

Jesus, you have transformed my life in your living love. I can't express my gratitude. Draw nearer to me as I turn to you today.

Happy Day

Jesus Christ, who is the faithful witness,
the firstborn from the dead,
and the ruler of the kings of the earth.
To him who loves us and has freed us from our sins by his blood.

Revelation 1:5 NIV

O happy day that fixed my choice
On thee, my Savior and my God!
Well may this glowing heart rejoice,
And tell its raptures all abroad.

Happy day, happy day,
When Jesus washed my sins away!
He taught me how to watch and pray,
And live rejoicing every day;
Happy day, happy day,
When Jesus washed my sins away!

High heaven that hears the solemn vow,
That vow renewed shall daily hear;
Till in life's latest hour I bow,
And bless, in death, a bond so dear.

Many of the hymns Philip Doddridge wrote in his lifetime in the eighteenth century were written to accompany his sermons. Isaac Watts, one of the early revivalists, was a mentor to Doddridge. Under his influence, Doddridge became an author and hymn writer. The hymn "Happy Day" is about the covenant he made with the Lord and the wonder of its effects in his life.

Have you made a covenant with God? Have you surrendered your life to his leading? If you have known the fellowship of his presence, the goodness of his grace, and the power of his love in your life, give him thanks today. He is not finished working his mercy in the details of your life.

Merciful Jesus, I'm grateful to know you. You pursue me with such love, I can't turn away from your kindness. I love you.

Stand Up for Jesus

Share in suffering as a good soldier of Christ Jesus.

2 Timothy 2:3 ESV

Stand up, stand up for Jesus
Ye soldiers of the cross;
Lift high his royal banner,
It must not suffer loss.
From vict'ry unto vict'ry
His army he shall lead
Till ev'ry foe is vanquished
And Christ is Lord indeed.

Stand up, stand up for Jesus,
The trumpet call obey;
Forth to the mighty conflict
In this his glorious day.
Ye that are men now serve him
Against unnumbered foes;
Let courage rise with danger
And strength to strength oppose.

At the deathbed of his friend and colleague, Dudley Tyng, George Duffield was inspired to write this hymn in his honor in 1858. Tyng's last message was that those who hear it should stand up for Jesus. This, in context with his anti-slavery stance in a time when it was unpopular, should remind us that standing up for Jesus can mean standing up for him within religious arenas as much as in the world.

Jesus is the bedrock of our faith. We follow his life, ministry, and Word rather than interpretations from those who lose sight of his true message. Let's stand up for Jesus when it is unpopular. We are called to align our lives with his love even when it costs us. Jesus is the one we follow and not powerful people.

Jesus, I choose to follow you, know you and your ways, and stand up for you. I will not settle for fitting in with those who use your name in ways that compromise your values. I choose you.

I Will Sing of My Redeemer

He gave himself for us to redeem us from all lawlessness
and to cleanse for himself a people for his own possession,
eager to do good works.

Titus 2:14 CSB

I will sing of my Redeemer
And his wondrous love to me;
On the cruel cross he suffered,
From the curse to set me free.
Sing, O sing of my Redeemer!
With his blood he purchased me;
On the cross he sealed my pardon,
Paid the debt, and made me free.

I will tell the wondrous story,
How my lost estate to save,
In his boundless love and mercy,
He the ransom freely gave.
I will praise my dear Redeemer,
His triumphant power I'll tell:
How the victory he gives me
Over sin and death and hell.

Philip Bliss was traveling with his wife to Chicago to sing at services at Moody's Tabernacle in 1876. On the way, a train wreck and subsequent fire caused them both to perish. This hymn was found in their trunk which survived the wreckage. The power of the Redeemer's love is as true in our devastation as it is in our thriving.

When we pass from this life, we get to stand before our Redeemer. We offer him the sacrifice of our praises in pain and suffering now, but when we are in the fullness of his presence, praise will flow as a response to his glory. Let's not wait to sing of the Redeemer's love, for he is present with us. One day, every tear will be wiped from our faces, and pain will be but a memory.

Redeemer, thank you for the power of your love that reaches me in unending measure every moment. I offer you my praise whether as a natural overflow of gratitude or a sacrifice in the midst of trouble. I trust you.

Washed in the Blood

"Come now, let's settle this," says the LORD.
"Though your sins are like scarlet,
I will make them as white as snow.
Though they are red like crimson,
I will make them as white as wool."

ISAIAH 1:18 NLT

Have you been to Jesus for the cleansing power?
Are you washed in the blood of the Lamb?
Are you fully trusting in his grace this hour?
Are you washed in the blood of the Lamb?

Are you washed in the blood,
In the soul cleansing blood of the Lamb?
Are your garments spotless?
Are they white as snow?
Are you washed in the blood of the Lamb?

When the Bridegroom cometh will your robes
be white?
Are you washed in the blood of the Lamb?
Will your soul be ready for the mansions bright,
And be washed in the blood of the Lamb?

Throughout the Old Testament, the blood of sacrificial animals covered the sins of the people. Jesus' sacrifice was the ultimate payment. No blood need be shed to cover our faults, sin, or shame, for he was the spotless lamb for the whole world. His blood was sufficient for all people over all time. Elisha Hoffman's question rings out through his 1878 hymn: "Are you washed in the blood, in the soul cleansing blood of the Lamb?"

When we walk in the power of Jesus' sacrifice, we walk as those who have no hidden shame to hold us back. We have been liberated in his love, and we get to dwell in Christ's perfect sacrifice all the days of our lives. Peace, joy, and hope is ours in him.

Lamb of God, thank you for the power of your blood that covers my sin. I have found true freedom in you, and I can't thank you enough.

He Is Lord

"As surely as I live," says the LORD,
"Everyone will bow before me;
everyone will say that I am God."
ROMANS 14:11 NCV

He is Lord, he is Lord!
He is risen from the dead and he is Lord!
Ev'ry knee shall bow, ev'ry tongue confess
That Jesus Christ is Lord.

This familiar chorus has been used around the world to proclaim the lordship of Christ. Written by Steve Vest in 1969, it is a younger hymn than most in the public domain. Instead of copyrighting the song, Steve Vest decided to make its use free of charge for everyone. It is based on 1 Timothy 6:15: "He is the blessed and only Ruler, the King of all kings and the Lord of all lords." Christ is alive, and in his resurrection life, we find our lives restored.

There will come a day when every knee will bow before Christ and every tongue confess he is Lord. We don't have to wait for that day to honor him as our Lord and Savior. Take hold of the gift of his grace and receive him as Redeemer, teacher, and guide. He is faithful to all who look to him.

Lord of lords, you are King above all, and I choose to bow my knee to you in honor and reverence. I choose to live for you.

Bright and Beautiful

"Why do you worry about clothing?
Consider the lilies of the field, how they grow:
they neither toil nor spin;
and yet I say to you that even Solomon in all his glory
was not arrayed like one of these."

Matthew 6:28-29 NKJV

All things bright and beautiful,
All creatures great and small,
All things wise and wonderful,
The Lord God made them all.

Each little flow'r that opens,
Each little bird that sings,
God made their glowing colors,
God made their tiny wings.

The cold wind in the winter,
The pleasant summer sun,
The ripe fruits in the garden,
God made them, ev'ry one.

God gave us eyes to see them,
And lips that we might tell
How great is God Almighty,
Who has made all things well.

Cecil Alexander wrote many hymns based around faith practices like the Apostles' Creed, baptism, communion, the Ten Commandments, and more. She also wrote poetry, visited the poor, and helped found a school for the deaf. This hymn from 1848 is different from her theologically heavy ones. This one feels as if she lost herself in the beauty of nature.

God is the Creator of all things great and small. This hymn is Alexander's explanation of the phrase "maker of heaven and earth" within the Apostles' Creed. No matter the season, God is the Creator of each one. We can find his fingerprints in the world around us, so let's look for his handiwork and praise him for it.

Creator God, you made all things bright and beautiful. Not even the smallest insect is without your help or creative intention. Open my eyes to see your glory in the world.

King and Shepherd

"Returning home, he called all his friends and neighbors together and said, 'Let's have a party! Come and celebrate with me the return of my lost lamb. It wandered away, but I found it and brought it home.'"

Luke 15:6 TPT

The King of love my shepherd is,
Whose goodness faileth never.
I nothing lack if I am his,
And he is mine forever.

Where streams of living water flow,
My ransomed soul he leadeth;
And where the verdant pastures grow,
With food celestial feedeth.

Perverse and foolish, oft I strayed,
But yet in love he sought me;
And on his shoulder gently laid,
And home, rejoicing, brought me.

Thou spreadst a table in my sight;
Thy unction grace bestoweth;
And oh, what transport of delight
From thy pure chalice floweth!

Jesus is the Good Shepherd. He watches over and cares for our souls. His Word says if one of his lambs wanders away from the flock, he goes after the one. Nothing escapes his notice. He is better at guiding, healing, and restoring us than we know. He leads us to places where we can find deep soul rest. He restores us and gives us all we need to flourish.

When Henry Baker was in his dying days in 1877, the last words he spoke were the third stanza of this hymn he composed: "Perverse and foolish, oft I strayed, but yet in love he sought me… And home, rejoicing, brought me." What a powerful statement to end a life, and what an invaluable truth to cling to today.

Good Shepherd, lead me to your waters of life that restore and rejuvenate my soul. I look to you for everything I need, and I trust you.

Loud Hosanna

They took palm branches and went out to meet him.
They kept shouting:
"Hosanna! Blessed is he who comes in the name of the Lord—
the King of Israel!"

John 12:13 csb

Hosanna, loud hosanna
The little children sang;
Through pillared court and temple
The lovely anthem rang.
To Jesus, who had blessed them,
Close folded to his breast,
The children sang their praises,
The simplest and the best.

"Hosanna in the highest!"
That ancient song we sing,
For Christ is our Redeemer,
The Lord of heaven, our King.
O may we ever praise him
With heart and life and voice,
And in his blissful presence
Eternally rejoice.

While this hymn is about the triumphal entry of Jesus into Jerusalem, it also does something other hymns on that topic typically do not: it focuses on the role of children. Jesus welcomes little children to come to him as readily as he does adults. There were probably many children running through the throng as Jesus entered Jerusalem, and they welcomed him with loud hosannas.

Jesus is kind and gentle with us just as a loving caregiver is with their children. He does not turn us away even when we are wild. When we come to him, we can come just as we are, and he will receive us.

Gentle Jesus, you are the King of creation, and you still tenderly care for everyone who comes to you. Thank you for your incomparable love and for receiving me as I am and not how anyone thinks I should be.

Let God Guide

Cast your cares on the LORD
and he will sustain you;
he will never let the righteous be shaken.

PSALM 55:22 NIV

If you but trust in God to guide you
And place your confidence in him,
You'll find him always there beside you
To give you hope and strength within;
For those who trust God's changeless love
Build on the rock that will not move.

Only be still and wait his pleasure
In cheerful hope with heart content.
He fills your needs to fullest measure
With what discerning love has sent;
Doubt not our inmost wants are known
To him who chose us for his own.

Sing, pray, and keep his ways unswerving,
Offer your service faithfully,
And trust his Word; though undeserving,
You'll find his promise true to be.
God never will forsake in need
The soul that trusts in him indeed.

George Neumark faced many trials in his seventeenth-century life even though he was educated as a tutor, poet, and archivist. When he was twenty, after struggling to find employment, he became a tutor for a judge. Relieved and grateful, he wrote this hymn as a poem of thanks to the Lord.

When we face uncertainty, whether it be financial, physical, or emotional, we can trust the Lord to guide us. He will not forsake or overlook us. He is our faithful Father, constant comfort, and reason to hope.Throw all your cares at his feet and trust him to care for you; he will do so perfectly.

Faithful One, I trust you to guide me through the unknowns of this life. I will not let worry keep me from finding peace in your loyal love. I trust you will come through for me again.

JUNE 11

My Shepherd Will Supply

Surely goodness and mercy shall follow me
all the days of my life,
and I shall dwell in the house of the LORD
forever.

PSALM 23:6 ESV

My Shepherd, you supply my need,
Most holy is your name;
In pastures fresh you make me feed,
Beside the living stream.
You bring my wand'ring spirit back.
When I forsake your ways;
You lead me, for your mercy's sake,
In paths of truth and grace.

Your sure provisions gracious God
Attend me all my days;
Oh, may your house be my abode,
And all my work be praise.
Here would I find a settled rest,
While others go and come;
No more a stranger, nor a guest,
But like a child at home.

Psalm 23 is a popular psalm. Many hymns are based on its message of God as a good shepherd guiding us to streams of living water. He leads us to rest, and we can trust him to lift our burdens as we allow his peace to settle over us. The presence of God is our shelter no matter where we are or what we go through.

Isaac Watts' 1719 hymn provokes a sense of peace as we are encouraged to trust God to guide us in his love. We can walk confidently and expect God to lead us at every turn. With the pressure to perform off our shoulders, we can simply live. As we live yielded to his love, we experience restoration and the peace of his presence.

Shepherd of my soul, I trust you to lead me back to you when I wander, and I trust you to correct me when needed. Continue to guide me in your goodness.

The Strife Is O'er

Sing a new song to the LORD,
For He has done wonderful things,
His right hand and His holy arm
have gained the victory for Him.

PSALM 98:1 NASB

The strife is o'er, the battle done;
The victory of life is won;
The song of triumph has begun.
Alleluia!

The powers of death have done their worst,
But Christ their legions has dispersed.
Let shouts of holy joy outburst.
Alleluia!

He closed the yawning gates of hell;
The bars from heaven's high portals fell.
Let hymns of praise his triumph tell.
Alleluia!

Lord, by the stripes which wounded thee,
From death's dread sting thy servants free,
That we may live and sing to thee.
Alleluia!

An anonymous writer penned these words in Latin, and it was published in a Jesuit collection in 1695. They were translated into English in 1859 by Francis Pott. The entire hymn is about the victory of Christ over death. Alleluia! His victory is also ours.

Christ did not stay in the grave after his burial. He conquered death and rose to life on the third day. His resurrection life is the new life we find in him. There is hope, power, and joy in his redemption work in our lives. As we experience trials in this life, let us never forget the triumph of Christ over death is our great hope and freedom as well.

Redeemer, thank you for conquering sin and death. You rose above shame, abuse, and corruption. In you, all things are made new including me.

JUNE 13

No East or West

"I tell you this, that many Gentiles will come from all over the world—from east and west—and sit down with Abraham, Isaac, and Jacob at the feast in the Kingdom of Heaven."

MATTHEW 8:11 NLT

In Christ there is no east or west,
In him no south or north,
But one great fellowship of love
Throughout the whole wide earth.

In Christ shall true hearts ev'rywhere
Their high communion find.
His service is the golden cord
Close binding humankind.

Join hands, then, people of the faith,
Whate'er your race may be.
All children of the living God
Are surely kin to me.

In Christ now meet both east and west,
In him meet south and north.
All Christly souls are joined as one
Tthroughout the whole wide earth.

William Dunkerly (1852-1941) was a businessman who also wrote many poems and verses. He wrote under pseudonymns, including John Oxenham, to whom this hymn is attributed. Although publishers rejected the volume of poems this work was included in, he self-published it and sold hundreds of thousands of copies. When we are passionate about what we do, we can find creative alternatives when others don't support us.

In Christ, there is no distinction of class, race, or gender. He loves us all. It is that simple. May we learn to love as Christ does: unashamedly and without parameters. The kingdom of Christ is diverse, and that is beautiful.

Great God, where I have put dividing lines in my heart and excuses for my lack of love, break through my biases. I want to love the way you do. I want it more than I want to be comfortable.

What Wondrous Love

I heard all creatures in heaven and on earth
and under the earth and in the sea saying:
"To the One who sits on the throne and to the Lamb
be praise and honor and glory and power forever and ever."
REVELATION 5:13 NCV

What wondrous love is this, O my soul,
O my soul!
What wondrous love is this, O my soul!
What wondrous love is this that caused the
Lord of bliss
To bear the dreadful curse for my soul, for
my soul,
To bear the dreadful curse for my soul!

When I was sinking down, sinking down,
sinking down,
When I was sinking down, sinking down,
When I was sinking down beneath God's
righteous frown,
Christ laid aside his crown for my soul, for
my soul,
Christ laid aside his crown for my soul.

We do not know the writer of this hymn first published in 1811. We do know it is a traditional American folk song. Simple in structure and text, it encourages us to look at the fact that God left his throne to save our souls. Why would he do such a thing? Because of his wondrous love.

Many wordsmiths have tried to describe the wonderful love of God through the centuries. Words fall short, however, when trying to describe the Lord and his nature. We catch glimpses of his glory, but he exists outside of our encapsulations of his goodness. He cannot be tied down by our descriptions. Allow yourself to imagine how great he could be and realize he is better than your mind can comprehend. Join with creation and sing praises to his glorious name.

Lord, I glorify your name, and I thank you for loving me more than I can imagine.

Draw Me Nearer

"No longer do I call you servants, for a servant does not know
what his master is doing; but I have called you friends,
for all things that I heard from My Father I have made known to you."

John 15:15 NKJV

I am thine, O Lord, I have heard thy voice,
And it told thy love to me;
But I long to rise in the arms of faith,
And be closer drawn to thee.

Draw me nearer, nearer, nearer, blessed Lord,
To the cross where thou hast died;
Draw me nearer, nearer, nearer, blessed Lord,
To thy precious, bleeding side.

Consecrate me now to thy service, Lord,
By the pow'r of grace divine;
Let my soul look up with a steadfast hope,
And my will be lost in thine.

Oh, the pure delight of a single hour
That before thy throne I spend,
When I kneel in prayer, and with thee, my God,
I commune as friend with friend!

Fanny Crosby's hymns are ubiquitous. She wrote over eight thousand before her death in 1915. She often partnered with different composers, and one was William Doane. Once, while visiting Doane in Cincinatti, they talked at length about the nearness of God in their lives. That night, the words of this hymn came to her. Doane wrote them down the next morning as she recited them, and he set them to music.

The nearness of God is a gracious gift. Every moment, we can draw nearer to God in fellowship. Just as we get to know people better the more time we spend with them, the same is true of our relationship with the Lord. Take time to draw nearer to him today, for his love reaches out at all times.

Loving Lord, draw nearer to me as I draw near to you today.

Unshakeable

My fellow believers, when it seems as though you are facing nothing but difficulties, see it as an invaluable opportunity to experience the greatest joy that you can!

James 1:2 TPT

My life flows on in endless song,
Above earth's lamentation.
I catch the sweet, though far-off hymn
That hails a new creation.

Through all the tumult and the strife,
I hear that music ringing.
It finds an echo in my soul.
How can I keep from singing?

No storm can shake my inmost calm
While to that rock I'm clinging.
Since Love is lord of heav'n and earth,
How can I keep from singing?

The peace of Christ makes fresh my heart,
A fountain ever springing!
All things are mine since I am his!
How can I keep from singing?

This hymn offers a powerful perspective. Scripture encourages us to experience deep joy even in the midst of great difficulty. In storm, sickness, or conflict, God is present with us. Even as they rage, the peace of God, which transcends our understanding, fills our souls with unshakeable trust.

When troubles are shaking your world, tune in to the presence of God with you. His love is a firm foundation that cannot be removed from your life. Stand on him and trust him to guide you through the fiercest storm. Jesus slept like a baby in the bottom of a boat while it was tossed by waves that threatened to capsize it. If he could rest in peace then, so can his Spirit within you give you peace.

Prince of Peace, I cling to you. You are my solid rock in a spinning world. Ground me in your loving truth and keep me in your perfect peace.

JUNE 17

Heart of God

Let us approach the throne of grace with boldness,
so that we may receive mercy and find grace
to help us in time of need.

HEBREWS 4:16 CSB

There is a place of quiet rest,
Near to the heart of God,
A place where sin cannot molest,
Near to the heart of God.

O Jesus, blest Redeemer,
Sent from the heart of God,
Hold us, who wait before thee,
Near to the heart of God.

There is a place of comfort sweet,
Near to the heart of God,
A place where we our Savior meet,
Near to the heart of God.

There is a place of full release,
Near to the heart of God,
A place where all is joy and peace,
Near to the heart of God.

Cleland McAfee (1866-1944) was preparing his message for Sunday while wondering how he could also prepare a song (he was the choir director too) to support it. This was no ordinary Sunday however. That week, two of his young neices had died within a day of each other from diphtheria. As he thought about what to say to a grieving community, "Near to the Heart of God" was his only answer.

When we are going through times of great grief or shock, it does not help to to ignore the pain we experience. Instead, we can press in to the heart of God. Simply being near him brings comfort. He holds us in our grief, and he will not let us go.

Comforter, I'm grateful for your close presence. Wrap around me in times of great sorrow and hold me close in your loyal love. Your nearness is what my heart needs.

Jesus Paid It All

"Watch and pray so that you will not fall into temptation. The spirit is willing, but the flesh is weak."

MARK 14:38 NIV

I hear the Savior say,
"Thy strength indeed is small,
Child of weakness, watch and pray,
Find in me thine all in all."

Jesus paid it all,
All to him I owe;
Sin had left a crimson stain,
He washed it white as snow.

Lord, now indeed I find
Thy pow'r and thine alone,
Can change the leper's spots
And melt the heart of stone.

And when, before the throne,
I stand in him complete,
"Jesus died my soul to save,"
My lips shall still repeat.

Jesus knows our weaknesses well. He isn't surprised by our penchant to wander or become distracted. He does, however, call us to watch and pray. He knows we need him, and he is our help in every trouble. Instead of growing complacent, we can draw near to him with our attention and tune our hearts to his.

Elvina Hall wrote this beloved hymn in 1865 on the flyleaf of a hymnal while at a Sunday morning service. It wasn't published until 1868, and it has been altered many times over. Still, the theme of Jesus' finished work on the cross, that all we need is found in him, rings true through the ages. May we look to Jesus as often as we think of him knowing his power can heal the sick, raise the dead, and liberate the captive.

Jesus, you are my Savior. I trust you more than any other. Fill my life with the miracle of your mercy at work and strengthen me in my weakness. I rely on you.

JUNE 19

I'd Rather Have Jesus

"No one can serve two masters,
for either he will hate the one and love the other,
or he will be devoted to the one and despise the other.
You cannot serve God and money."

MATTHEW 6:24 ESV

I'd rather have Jesus than silver or gold;
I'd rather be his than have riches untold;
I'd rather have Jesus than houses or lands.
I'd rather be led by his nail pierced hand

Than to be the king of a vast domain
Or be held in sin's dread sway.
I'd rather have Jesus than anything
This world affords today.

I'd rather have Jesus than men's applause;
I'd rather be faithful to his dear cause;
I'd rather have Jesus than worldwide fame.
I'd rather be true to his holy name.

He's fairer than lilies of rarest bloom;
He's sweeter than honey from out the comb;
He's all that my hungering spirit needs.
I'd rather have Jesus and let him lead.

Rhea Miller (1894-1966) devoted herself to teaching piano. She offered her services to pastors' children free of charge so they might have something to contribute to church services as they grew older. "I'd Rather Have Jesus" was inspired by her own father's testimony. He was an alcoholic, and it was incredibly destructive to his relationships. When he finally surrendered his life to the Lord, he experienced a great transformation. He was said to have testified that he would rather have Jesus than all the silver or gold in the world.

Knowing Jesus—the power of his salvation, comfort of his presence, and kindness of his love—is worth more than all the treasures this world holds.

Savior, thank you for the power of your love in my life. You are my liberator from fear, sin, and shame, and I can't thank you enough. Empower me with your Spirit and fill my heart with your kindness today.

Whiter than Snow

Wash me thoroughly from my guilt
And cleanse me from my sin.
Psalm 51:2 NASB

Lord Jesus, I long to be perfectly whole;
I want thee forever to live in my soul,
Break down every idol, cast out every foe;
Now wash me and I shall be whiter than snow.

Whiter than snow, yes, whiter than snow,
Now wash me, and I shall be whiter than snow.

Lord Jesus, look down from thy throne in the skies,
And help me to make a complete sacrifice;
I give up myself, and whatever I know,
Now wash me and I shall be whiter than snow.

Psalm 51 is David's prayer to the Lord after he sinned with Bathsheba. It is a guilty man's prayer for pardon from a magnanimous God. We must take responsibility for our failures to truly repent. As we humble ourselves before the Lord and others, he lifts us up and removes the stain of our sins. His mercy cleanses us, and we are clean.

"Whiter than Snow" was written by James Nicholson in 1872. He based it on David's psalm of confession. James Nicholson was deeply involved in his church though he worked as a postal clerk. We don't have to work in full-time ministry to have an effect for the kingdom of Christ. We can serve the Lord where we are and not where we imagine we should be.

Merciful Christ, in you I find forgiveness, hope, and peace. Wash me, and I will be clean. Renew me, and I will rise in hope. I am yours.

JUNE 21

The Trouble I See

This High Priest of ours understands our weaknesses,
for he faced all of the same testings we do, yet he did not sin.

Hebrews 4:15 NLT

Nobody knows the trouble I've seen,
Nobody knows but Jesus.
Nobody knows the trouble I've seen,
Glory hallelujah.

Sometimes I'm up, sometimes I'm down,
Oh, yes, Lord!
Sometimes I'm almost to the ground,
Oh, yes, Lord!

Although you see me going 'long so,
Oh, yes, Lord!
I have my troubles here below,
Oh, yes, Lord!

This African American spiritual is well-known though it was not printed in many hymnals. It is important to know the Lord sees our troubles. He understands our struggles. He knows every single one, and he walks through them with us. We can lean on the loving support of our Father and people in our lives. Though we have troubles, we also have tremendous hope.

Although no one can relate to our distinct troubles the way Jesus does, we are not alone in them. We can take comfort in the presence of God meeting us in every sorrow and trial. He does not make us walk alone either. He puts us in families and communities where we can rely on each others' support.

Faithful Father, you walk with me through the ups and downs of this life, and I don't take your companionship for granted. Be near in my griefs and victories. Make me a support for those in my life as well.

Hidden in My Heart

Your word is like a lamp for my feet
and a light for my path.
PSALM 119:105 NCV

Thy Word is a lamp to my feet,
A light to my path alway,
To guide and to save me from sin,
And show me the heav'nly way.

Thy Word have I hid in my heart,
That I might not sin against thee;
That I might not sin, that I might not sin,
Thy Word have I hid in my heart.

At morning, at noon, and at night
I ever will give thee praise;
For thou art my portion, O Lord,
And shall be thro' all my days!

Thro' him whom thy Word hath foretold,
The Savior and Morning Star,
Salvation and peace have been bro't
To those who have strayed afar.

This hymn was written by Ernest Sellers and published in 1908. It was inspired by various verses of Psalm 119 which focuses on the power of God's Word for the believer. We must not only be hearers of the Word but also doers as James points out in the first chapter of his epistle. The starting point for being a doer is to not only listen to the Word but hide it in our hearts. Once we do, we can take action.

What do we hold dear in the thoughts, values, and priorities of our lives? Out of our hearts, our lives reflect the stories we hold dear. If our lives do not match our ideals, it's time to evaluate our values and how we can prioritize them in our daily schedules.

Word of God, you are the living and active Spirit in our midst. I don't want to live my life half-heartedly. I get to choose what is important to me, and I want to reflect the power of your character in my life. Let love lead me.

JUNE 23

The Christian Race

I have fought the good fight,
I have finished the race,
I have kept the faith.
2 TIMOTHY 4:7 NKJV

Awake, my soul, stretch every nerve,
And press with vigor on;
A heavenly race demands thy zeal,
And an immortal crown.

A cloud of witnesses around
Hold thee in full survey;
Forget the steps already trod,
And onward urge thy way.

'Tis God's all-animating voice
That calls thee from on high;
'Tis his own hand presents the prize
To thine aspiring eye.

That prize, with peerless glories bright,
Which shall new lustre boast
When victors' wreaths and monarchs' gems
Shall blend in common dust.

First published in 1755, this hymn echoes Paul's encouragement throughout his letters to continue to run the race. With Christ as our vision, we can keep pressing toward the goal. When we spend too much time ruminating on the past, we can lose sight of the power of the present moment. When we get too caught up in future possibilities, we lose our ability to remain grounded in what is true now.

Yes, we are running the race of life, and we do it with our eyes fixed on Christ. Every step of the journey is valuable. Let's not rush past the gifts we have here even as we press on. We can keep our hearts rooted in faith and become proactive in current reality.

Lord, thank you for the power of your presence that removes the shame of my past, meets me in my present reality, and gives me hope for what is to come. You are in it all. Strengthen me in your Word today.

God of Grace and Glory

At last we have freedom, for Christ has set us free!
We must always cherish this truth and firmly refuse
to go back into the bondage of our past.

GALATIANS 5:1 TPT

God of grace and God of glory,
On your people pour your pow'r;
Crown your ancient Church's story,
Bring its bud to glorious flow'r.
Grant us wisdom, grant us courage
For the facing of this hour.

Lo, the hosts of evil round us
Scorn the Christ, assail his ways.
From the fears that long have bound us
Free our hearts to faith and praise.
Grant us wisdom, grant us courage
For the living of these days.

Cure your children's warring madness;
Bend our pride to your control;
Shame our wanton, selfish gladness,
Rich in things and poor in soul.
Grant us wisdom, grant us courage
Lest we miss your kingdom's goal.

This hymn was written by Pastor Harry Fosdick in 1930. It was written as an opening hymn for the church he led on the banks of the Hudson in New York. It is a prayer for God's help. It includes petitions that God help his church to live out his power and love in practical ways. This includes generosity and courage to prioritize helping the poor.

It takes some maneuvering to look at Jesus' life and miss the power of his ministry to those society deemed unloveable and unworthy. We cannot claim to love Christ and live like him but ignore those in dire need of social support and physical help. Even as we pray for wisdom and courage to live the way Jesus would, we can take steps to help those around us.

Jesus, your love is not just an idea but a powerfully practical force. May I move in your love as I help the vulnerable and look for ways to be inclusive.

JUNE 25

Jesus Is the World

I enter your house by the abundance of your faithful love;
I bow down toward your holy temple
in reverential awe of you.

Psalm 5:7 CSB

Jesus is all the world to me,
My life, my joy, my all;
He is my strength from day to day,
Without him I would fall:
When I am sad, to him I go,
No other one can cheer me so;
When I am sad, he makes me glad,
He's my friend.

Jesus is all the world to me,
And true to him I'll be;
Oh, how could I this friend deny,
When he's so true to me?
Following him I know I'm right,
He watches o'er me day and night;
Following him by day and night,
He's my friend.

Will Thompson (1847-1909) started his own publishing company after having his songs rebuffed by an existing publisher. He was both a lyricist and composer, and ideas and themes often came to him at random times. He would jot down the idea no matter where he was. In this hymn, "Jesus Is All the World to Me," we catch a glimpse of Thompson's relationship with Christ. God is an overflowing fountain of mercy, creativity, and wisdom. We should never stop going to him for our needs and the needs of those around us.

There is no better friend than Jesus the faithful Savior. He does not turn us away when we are weak. He welcomes us to him and draws us close with his kindness whenever we turn to him. Even his correction is laced with a tender father's kindness.

Jesus, you are all the world to me. I have no better friend than you, and you never fail to follow through on your promises. I trust you through ease and strife.

The Lord Bless You

"The Lord bless you and keep you;
the Lord make his face shine on you
and be gracious to you;
the Lord turn his face toward you
and give you peace."

Numbers 6:24-26 NIV

The Lord bless you and keep you;
The Lord lift his countenance upon you,
And give you peace;
The Lord make his face to shine upon you,
And be gracious unto you.
Amen, amen.

This song is a blessing straight from Scripture. It is popularly known as the priestly blessing from Numbers 6, and it was God's message to Moses to give to Aaron and his sons. One musical version of this biblical benediction was composed by John Rutter in 1981. It was written for four vocal parts as well as the organ, and it is most often performed by choirs.

Whether we sing hymns alone, with groups of people, or hear them performed by others, the meaning behind them remains the same. May you receive this blessing over you today as you read, listen, or sing. Pray it over your loved ones. Benedictions can be powerful tools of blessing in our lives and relationships.

Lord God, thank you for the peace you offer and the grace you give. As I receive from you, I have more to offer others. I am grateful for this partnership. Be honored in my life.

JUNE 27

Father's Love Begotten

To which of the angels did God ever say,
"You are my Son, today I have begotten you"? Or again,
"I will be to him a father, and he shall be to me a son"?

HEBREWS 1:5 ESV

Of the Father's love begotten
Ere the worlds began to be,
He is Alpha and Omega,
He the source, the ending he,
Of the things that are, that have been,
And that future years shall see
Evermore and evermore.

Oh, that birth forever blessed
When the virgin, full of grace,
By the Holy Ghost conceiving,
Bore the Savior of our race,
And the babe, the world's Redeemer,
First revealed his sacred face
Evermore and evermore.

The roots of this hymn go all the way back to a fourth-century Latin poem by Marcus Aurelius Prudentius. He was the greatest Christian poet of his time, and he gave up his prosperous life as a judge to serve the church in a monastic lifestyle. This poem is a confession of faith in Christ as Savior.

It is astounding when we connect our faith to ancient times. If we think about the reach of Christ's ministry, we find ourselves woven into the vast web of his kingdom spanning ages and generations. Our testimonies add to the great chorus of faithful ones through the centuries. May we be willing to share with those in our lives this powerful hope that does not begin or end with us.

Jehovah, you are the beginning and the end, and in you all things find their fulfillment. Broaden my perspective as I meditate on your power and mercy throughout history; meet me here with your Spirit.

Not One

A person of too many friends comes to ruin,
But there is a friend who sticks closer than a brother.

Proverbs 18:24 NASB

There's not a friend like the lowly Jesus—
No, not one! No, not one!
None else could heal all our soul's diseases—
No, not one! No, not one!

Jesus knows all about our struggles,
He will guide till the day is done;
There's not a friend like the lowly Jesus—
No, not one! No, not one!

There's not an hour that he is not near us—
No, not one! No, not one!
No night so dark but his love can cheer us—
No, not one! No, not one!

Was e'er a gift like the Savior given?
No, not one! No, not one!
Will he refuse us a home in heaven?
No, not one! No, not one!

Jesus is the friend who sticks closer than a brother. He does not leave in our time of need, and he does not require we do anything in our strength. When we need wisdom, he offers clarity. When we need provision, he meets our needs. When we don't know what to do or where to go, he illuminates the path. He is that good, and he is faithful to all who trust him.

Johnson Oatman (1856-1922) wrote over three thousand hymns in his lifetime, and many are in gospel song books. He did this while working as a businessman as well as a preacher in his hometown in New Jersey. He grew to love singing as a young boy listening to his father, and that love carried through his entire life. Take time to sing to the one who knows about all your loves and struggles. There is no other friend like him.

Jesus, it is my honor to know and be known by you.

JUNE 29

Tender Heart

The sacrifice you desire is a broken spirit.
You will not reject a broken and repentant heart, O God.
PSALM 51:17 NLT

Savior, while my heart is tender,
I would yield that heart to thee;
All my powers to thee surrender,
Thine and only thine to be.
Take me now; Lord Jesus, take me,
Let my youthful heart be thine;
Thy devoted servant make me,
Fill my soul with love divine.

Send me, Lord, where thou will send me,
Only do thou guide my way;
May thy grace through life attend me,
Gladly then shall I obey.
Let me do thy will, or bear it,
I would know no will but thine;
Shouldst thou take my life, or spare it,
I that life to thee resign.

John Burton wrote many hymns for children. He began contributing his hymns to publications in 1822, and he continued for many years. "Savior, While My Heart Is Tender" is a beautiful petition to the Lord for any age. When our hearts are tender, God can move in mighty ways.

It is a good practice to humble our hearts before the Lord. Sometimes, we are more receptive than others, but no matter what we feel in the moment, we can invite the Lord to make his home in us. He will lead us as we trust him, and he won't lead us astray. Is your heart tender today? Yield it to your Savior, for he is trustworthy and true.

Savior, I give you my heart. In all my questions, hopes, and disappointments, be King over them all. I am yours.

Fill My Life

I will praise the LORD at all times;
his praise is always on my lips.
PSALM 34:1 NCV

Fill thou my life, O Lord my God,
In ev'ry part with praise,
That my whole being may proclaim
Thy being and thy ways.
Not for the lip of praise alone,
Nor e'en the praising heart,
I ask, but for a life made up
Of praise in ev'ry part:

So shall each fear, each fret, each care
Be turned into a song,
And ev'ry winding of the way
The echo shall prolong.
So shall no part of day or night
From sacredness be free,
But all my life, in ev'ry step,
Be fellowship with thee.

Horatius Bonar was a famous Scottish preacher and poet. He penned this text and titled it "Life's Praise" in 1866. In every part of our lives, Christ can be honored. There is no distinction between the ordinary things of life and the holy aspects, for it all belongs to him. May we praise the Lord as much in the mundane as we do in the extraordinary.

Perhaps you already include the Lord as you go about your day. Maybe you pray while washing the dishes or meditate on his Word while you commute. Christ invites us to commit it all to him. You can praise him in how you treat others just as much as you do when you praise him in a church. Aim to praise him throughout your day no matter where you are or what you are doing.

Lord, may the details of my life become places of praise as I turn my heart and attention to you.

July

All creatures of our God and King,
Lift up your voice and with us sing Alleluia! Alleluia!
Thou burning sun with golden beam,
Thou silver moon with softer gleam,
O praise him, O praise him!
Alleluia! Alleluia! Alleluia!

All for Jesus

What things were gain to me,
these I have counted loss for Christ.

Philippians 3:7 NKJV

All for Jesus! All for Jesus!
All my being's ransomed pow'rs,
All my thoughts and words and doings,
All my days and all my hours.

Let my hands perform his bidding,
Let my feet run in his ways;
Let my eyes see Jesus only,
Let my lips speak forth his praise.

Worldlings prize their gems of beauty,
Cling to gilded toys of dust,
Boast of wealth and fame and pleasure;
Only Jesus will I trust.

Since my eyes were fixed on Jesus,
I've lost sight of all beside;
So enchained my spirit's vision,
Looking at the Crucified.

Mary James was not a prolific hymnist, but this hymn reflects her heart for the Lord. She was a leading figure in the holiness revival movement in New Jersey in the 1800s. One of the main values of this movement was fervent commitment of one's life to God: every area of it. This can clearly be seen in "All for Jesus."

It is a privilege to follow Christ and an honor know him. His love of participating in our lives as we yield our hearts to him is a beautiful mystery. As we offer him our lives, he fills us with his grace. No area is untouched by his mercy. He is Lord of our whole lives and not just Lord of our Sundays.

Lord, it is my joy to know you in the details of my day as much as in congregational time. Move in my life as I continually submit to your love and leadership.

Children of the Father

Better a day in your courts
than a thousand anywhere else.
I would rather stand at the threshold of the house of my God
than live in tents of wicked people.

Psalm 84:10 CSB

Children of the heav'nly Father
Safely in his bosom gather;
Nestling bird nor star in heaven
Such a refuge e'er was given.

God his own doth tend and nourish;
In his holy courts they flourish.
From all evil things he spares them;
In his mighty arms he bears them.

Neither life nor death shall ever
From the Lord his children sever;
Unto them his grace he showeth,
And their sorrows all he knoweth.

Though he giveth or he taketh,
God his children ne'er forsaketh;
His the loving purpose solely
To preserve them pure and holy.

This hymn was originally written in Swedish by Caroline Sandell (1823-1903) who was often referred to as the "Fanny Crosby of Sweden." She tragically witnessed her father drown, and it is said she wrote hymns to deal with that traumatic loss. Psalm 84 is a prophetic psalm about the beauty of God and the longing we feel for his presence. Even birds find rest in his sanctuary. How much more can we?

God cares for us even when we cannot make sense of the world's tragedies. Our hope is not in lives of affluence, or in a lack of suffering, but in the promise of Christ. He is our peace, defense, and true home. Rest in his presence today.

Father God, I long for you and your experiential, practical presence more than I can express. Move in me as I move toward you. I long to know you more.

Pilot Me

He shepherded them with a pure heart
and guided them with his skillful hands.
PSALM 78:72 CSB

Jesus, Savior, pilot me,
Over life's tempestuous sea:
Unknown waves before me roll,
Hiding rocks and treach'rous shoal;
Chart and compass come from thee—
Jesus, Savior, pilot me!

As a mother stills her child,
Thou canst hush the ocean wild;
Boist'rous waves obey thy will
When thou say'st to them, "Be still!"
Wondrous Sov'reign of the sea,
Jesus, Savior, pilot me!

When at last I near the shore,
And the fearful breakers roar
'Twixt me and the peaceful rest—
Then, while leaning on thy breast,
May I hear thee say to me,
"Fear not—I will pilot thee!"

Edward Hopper (1816-1888) was a reverend, author, and poet. Among the churches he served was the Church of Sea and Land in New York City which was a church for sailors. The theme of sailing and Jesus as a pilot reflects the audience to whom Hopper was writing when he penned this hymn.

Imagery is a great gift to our understanding. When we can contextualize how God might lead us through stormy seas as our Savior and pilot, his leadership becomes more concrete in our hearts and minds. How might you imagine God leading you through where you are now? Don't be afraid to be creative, for the one who stilled the seas created them. The one who spoke the stars into being speaks to your heart today. You were made to be creative and innovative just as he is.

Creator, thank you for the power of your leadership in my life. As I seek you, reveal yourself to me in new ways and in deeper understanding. Thank you.

God of the Ages

Praise be to the LORD, the God of our ancestors,
who has put it into the king's heart to bring honor
to the house of the LORD in Jerusalem in this way.

EZRA 7:27 NIV

God of the ages, whose almighty hand
leads forth in beauty all the starry band
of shining worlds in splendor through the skies,
our grateful songs before thy throne arise.

Thy love divine hath led us in the past;
in this free land with thee our lot is cast;
be thou our ruler, guardian, guide, and stay,
thy Word our law, thy paths our chosen way.

From war's alarms, from deadly pestilence,
be thy strong arm our ever sure defense;
thy true religion in our hearts increase;
thy bounteous goodness nourish us in peace.

Refresh thy people on their toilsome way;
lead us from night to never-ending day;
fill all our lives with love and grace divine,
and glory, laud, and praise be ever thine.

Daniel Roberts worte this hymn specifically for a Fourth of July celebration at his Vermont rectory in 1876. It was later used as the theme for the centennial celebration of the United States Constitution. Though a very patriotic hymn, this song can cross borders because God is God of the ages. He helps all who look to him.

On this day when Americans celebrate the declaration of their independence from Great Britain, may we recognize the even greater liberty we have in Christ. No matter our nationality, race, or creed, Christ breaks down every barrier and declares us liberated in his love.

Liberator, you set my heart free and allow me to live, move, and have my being without guilt or fear. Thank you for the power of your love which sets the captive free and calls us forth in peace.

I'm Coming Home

"He arose and came to his father.
But while he was still a long way off,
his father saw him and felt compassion,
and ran and embraced him and kissed him."

LUKE 15:20 ESV

I've wandered far away from God,
Now I'm coming home;
The paths of sin too long I've trod,
Lord, I'm coming home.

Coming home, coming home,
Nevermore to roam,
Open wide thine arms of love,
Lord, I'm coming home.

I've wasted many precious years,
Now I'm coming home;
I now repent with bitter tears,
Lord, I'm coming home.

My soul is sick, my heart is sore,
Now I'm coming home;
My strength renew, my hope restore,
Lord, I'm coming home.

The story of the prodigal son is popular for a reason. It reveals the generosity and kindness of the Father's heart toward his children. When we turn or return to him, he meets us with joy and offers everything he has as our own. He covers us in robes of mercy and restores us as his children.

William Kirkpatrick wrote this 1892 hymn based on the parable of the prodigal son. Though we wander from the Lord, we can come home to him at any moment. May we not neglect the time we have. Today is the day of salvation, for we have no control over what tomorrow will bring. Let's go to the Lord with our hearts wide open. He will receive us with tender kindness every time.

Loving Father, I often forget how wonderful you are. You are patient in love, gentle in kindness, and unrelenting in generosity. I come to you today.

Send the Light

Send out Your light and Your truth,
they shall lead me;
They shall bring me to Your holy hill
And to Your dwelling places.

PSALM 43:3 NASB

There's a call comes ringing o'er the
restless wave,
"Send the light! Send the light"
There are souls to rescue, there are souls
to save,
Send the light! Send the light!

Send the light, the blessed gospel light;
Let it shine from shore to shore!
Send the light the blessed gospel light;
Let it shine forevermore!

Let us pray that grace may ev'rywhere abound,
"Send the light! Send the light!"
And a Christ-like spirit ev'rywhere be found,
Send the light! Send the light!

Let us not grow weary in the work of love,
"Send the light! Send the light!"
Let us gather jewels for a crown above,
Send the light! Send the light!

Charles Gabriel wrote this hymn as a missionary song for an Easter service in 1890. It is believed to be based on Acts 16 where Paul had a vision of a man in Macedonia asking for help. When we ask that the light be sent, the Word of the Lord goes forth. His liberating love and foundational truth set us free.

Jesus commissioned his followers to go into the world and make disciples of all nations, and we should partner with that mission. We can do so in many ways, but let's not neglect the power of loving our neighbors, praying for the Lord's light to shine on those near and far, and living as Christ commanded us while teaching others to do the same. The Holy Spirit graciously helps us in all these things.

Christ Jesus, your light shines and diminishes the darkness. Thank you for the power of your Word which is as strong today as when you first spoke it. Send the light to the nations and use me in my corner of your world.

Deeper

I pray that your love will overflow more and more,
and that you will keep on growing
in knowledge and understanding.

PHILIPPIANS 1:9 NLT

Deeper, deeper in the love of Jesus
Daily let me go;
Higher, higher in the school of wisdom,
More of grace to know.

Oh, deeper yet, I pray,
And higher ev'ry day,
And wiser, blessed Lord,
In thy precious, holy Word.

Deeper, deeper! Blessed Holy Spirit,
Take me deeper still,
Till my life is wholly lost in Jesus,
And his perfect will.

Deeper, higher, ev'ry day in Jesus,
Till all conflict past,
Finds me conqu'ror, and in his own image
Perfected at last.

Charles Jones was one of America's first African American hymnists. He wrote "Deeper, Deeper" in 1900 while pastoring a Baptist church in Mississippi. He found himself unsatisfied with his limitations to do good. He committed to know Christ more, to believe him fully, and to go deeper in his walk with the Lord every day.

The Lord is constantly gracious with us. He reveals himself to those who seek him so hungry hearts will be filled. Let's not neglect the pangs of our souls longing for more of the Lord. The more we know him, the more we love him. The more we love him, the more we want to know him. On and on it goes, deeper and deeper, until we are face to face with him in glory.

Redeemer, thank you for the power of your love which breaks through my defenses. I want to walk in your power, live by your wisdom, and love like you. I want to go deeper.

Join to Sing

Let's come to him with thanksgiving.
Let's sing songs to him.
PSALM 95:2 NCV

Come, Christians, join to sing
Alleluia! Amen!
Loud praise to Christ our King;
Alleluia! Amen!
Let all, with heart and voice,
Before his throne rejoice;
Praise is his gracious choice:
Alleluia! Amen!

Come, lift your hearts on high,
Alleluia! Amen!
Let praises fill the sky;
Alleluia! Amen!
He is our guide and friend,
To us he'll condescend;
His love shall never end:
Alleluia! Amen!

"Come, Christians, Join to Sing" was originally titled, "Come, Children, Join to Sing." Many of the hymns we know, love, and sing today were written for children. Christian Bateman ministered in Scotland after studying in the Moravian church. He wrote many sacred songs for use in Sunday schools, and this 1843 hymn is one of them.

When we offer praise to God, it need not be eloquent. We don't need to have the right words, and we don't need angelic voices with perfect pitch. It is all beautiful to the Lord. When we lift an alleluia or a simple song of praise, God is as glorified as when we use grandiose phrases. As long as we bring him our authentic hearts, he is honored.

Glorious Lord, I offer you simple praises today from a genuine heart of gratitude. "Alleluia! Amen!"

Nothing Between

When Jesus heard these things, He said to him,
"You still lack one thing. Sell all that you have and distribute to the poor,
and you will have treasure in heaven; and come, follow Me."

Luke 18:22 NKJV

Nothing between my soul and the Savior,
Naught of this world's delusive dream:
I have renounced all sinful pleasure—
Jesus is mine! There's nothing between.

Nothing between my soul and the Savior,
So that his blessed face may be seen;
Nothing preventing the least of his favor:
Keep the way clear! Let nothing between.

Nothing between, like worldly pleasure:
Habits of life, though harmless they seem,
Must not my heart from him ever sever—
He is my all! There's nothing between.

Nothing between, like pride or station:
Self or friends shall not intervene;
Though it may cost me much tribulation,
I am resolved! There's nothing between.

Charles Tindley (1851-1933) was a pastor, theologian, writer, social activist, and hymnist among other things. Before he received his appointment as minister of a large church, he was a janitor for one. He knew humble beginnings, and he was no stranger to hardship. He was an African American in ministry in a time when that was especially complicated. Even so, his powerful sermons and thoughtful theology impacted many lives.

In Romans 8, we are told nothing can separate us from the love of God. Our souls have fellowship with Christ through his Spirit. As Tindley's hymn says, there is nothing between our souls and the Savior. Let's do our part to keep our hearts open before the Lord.

Jesus, my heart is yours. Make yourself at home even as I make room for you. Let nothing come between us; draw me closer to your heart.

JULY 10

One Day

When we die we will be face-to-face with Christ,
the One who experienced death once for all to bear the sins of many!
And now to those who eagerly await him, he will appear a second time;
not to deal with sin, but to bring us the fullness of salvation.

HEBREWS 9:28 TPT

One day when heaven was filled with his praises,
One day when sin was as black as could be,
Jesus came forth to be born of a virgin,
Dwelt among men, my example is he!

Living, he loved me; dying, he saved me;
Buried, he carried my sins far away;
Rising, he justified freely, forever;
One day he's coming: O glorious day!

One day they left him alone in the garden,
One day he rested, from suffering free;
Angels came down o'er his tomb to keep vigil;
Hope of the hopeless, my Savior is he!

One day the trumpet will sound for his coming,
One day the skies with his glory will shine;
Wonderful day, my beloved ones bringing;
Glorious Savior, this Jesus is mine!

John Wilbur Chapman wrote "One Day" in 1908. He was an evangelist who longed to share the message of the Gospel with as many as he could. This hymn refers to many of the "one days" Christ had, from his birth in a manger to his death on the cross, to the garden where he wrestled with grief, to his resurrection from the dead, and ultimately, to the one day we still await: his return.

Jesus lived the human experience, and he experienced even more we do not. We can trust him to do everything he said he would. As we wait for the fulfillment of God's timing, let's not grow discouraged. His presence is with us even now by the power of his Spirit. Take courage, friend, and hold on to hope.

Jesus, when the waiting grows long, encourage my heart in your presence. Wash over me with the purity and power of your love and lift my hope in you.

For All the Saints

It deceives those who live on the earth because of the signs that it is permitted to perform in the presence of the beast, telling those who live on the earth to make an image of the beast who was wounded by the sword and yet lived.

REVELATION 13:14 CSB

For all the saints who from their labors rest,
Who thee by faith before the world confessed,
Thy name, O Jesus, be forever blest.
Alleluia! Alleluia!

Thou wast their rock, their fortress, and their might;
Thou, Lord, their captain in the well-fought fight;
Thou, in the darkness drear, their one true light.
Alleluia! Alleluia!

Oh, may thy soldiers, faithful, true, and bold
Fight as the saints who nobly fought of old
And win with them the victor's crown of gold.
Alleluia! Alleluia!

Oh, blest communion, fellowship divine!
We feebly struggle, they in glory shine;
Yet all are one in thee, for all are thine.
Alleluia! Alleluia!

William Walsham How wrote this hymn in 1864. The Anglican bishop originally wrote eleven stanzas, but the verses included in hymnals vary. The heading and supposed theme are from Hebrews 12:1: "Therefore, since we also have such a large cloud of witnesses surrounding us… Let us run with endurance the race that lies before us."

It can be encouraging to know our experiences are neither uniquely awful nor uniquely wonderful. Our lives echo those of others, and we can relate to one another in our human experience. Let's draw encouragement from the solace of others as well as their victories. Jesus is the same yesterday, today, and forever, and we can always find rest in him.

Lord Jesus, thank you for the solidarity of the saints and for the encouragement of your mercy at work in each of us.

Give to the Winds

Wait for the LORD;
be strong and take heart
and wait for the LORD.

PSALM 27:14 NIV

Give to the winds thy fears,
Hope and be undismayed;
God hears thy sighs and counts thy tears;
God shall lift up thy head.

Through waves and clouds and storms,
He gently clears the way;
Wait thou his time, so shall this night
Soon end in joyous day.

Still heavy is thy heart,
Still sink thy spirits down?
Cast off the weight, let fear depart,
And ev'ry care be gone.

Far, far above thy thought
His counsel shall appear,
When fully he the work hath wrought,
That caused thy needless fear.

Paul Gerhardt was one of the most significant Lutheran hymn writers second only to Martin Luther himself. This hymn was published in 1656 while he was serving as pastor in a small village church. John Wesley translated it into Enlish from German in 1739. Its themes of letting go of our worries and trusting the Lord are a comfort to every generation.

How can you cast off your worries before the Lord today? Perhaps fears have kept you from moving ahead in areas where you desperately want to find freedom. Give your cares to the Lord; offer him the worries and anxieties you cannot shake. Follow the Lord where he leads you. He is a good shepherd.

Faithful Father, I don't want to be stuck in cycles of fear, shame, or disappointment. As I give you my worries, lead me in the light of your truth.

I Love Thy Kingdom

Even the sparrow finds a home,
and the swallow a nest for herself,
where she may lay her young,
at your altars, O Lord of hosts,
my King and my God.

Psalm 84:3 ESV

I love thy kingdom, Lord,
The house of thine abode,
The Church our blest Redeemer saved
With his own precious blood.

I love thy Church, O God:
Her walls before thee stand,
Dear as the apple of thine eye
And graven on thy hand.

For her my tears shall fall,
For her my prayers ascend;
To her my cares and toils be giv'n,
'Til toils and cares shall end.

Jesus, thou friend divine,
Our Savior and our King,
Thy hand from ev'ry snare and foe
Shall great deliv'rance bring.

Timothy Dwight (1752-1817) was one America's first hymnists. He graduated from Yale University, served as a chaplain under George Washington during the Revolutionary War, and went on to become well-accomplished in many areas. He was a minister, farmer, state legislator, and president of Yale. This hymn is one of many he based on psalms.

Though the church of our Savior has no nationality, Christ remains head over us all. God's kingdom crosses every boundary of class, ethnicity, language, and nation. As we follow Christ, we follow the ways of his kingdom and spread the foundation of his love wherever we go.

Savior, thank you for the power of your mercy and the trustworthy leadership you show. I choose to follow you, for you are great and greatly to be praised. Be glorified in your church as you are glorified in heaven.

Glorious Names

"It is no longer because of what you said that we believe, for we have heard for ourselves and know that this One truly is the Savior of the world."

JOHN 4:42 NASB

Join all the glorious names
Of wisdom, love, and pow'r,
That ever mortals knew,
That angels ever bore:
All are too poor to speak his worth,
Too poor to set my Savior forth.

Great Prophet of my God,
By tongue would bless thy name:
By thee the joyful news
Of our salvation came,
The joyful news of sins forgiv'n,
Of hell subdued and peace with heav'n.

My Savior and my Lord,
My conqu'ror and my King,
Thy scepter and thy sword,
Thy reigning grace, I sing:
Thine is the pow'r; behold I sit
In willing bonds beneath thy feet.

Our great God is not known by one name but many. Isaac Watts' hymn uses many titles to describe who Jesus is to him. In Scripture, God is described as a creator, shepherd, king, lord, counselor, guide, and comforter. These are only a few! He is Jehovah, provider, the beginning and end, and the Spirit. We can ascribe him many titles, for he is worthy of them all. He is faithful and kind, powerful and just. He is greater than we can describe or imagine.

Join all the glorious names you know and give God praise today. Consider your relationship with God and the things he has helped you through. Write down the many roles as he's filled for you and don't hold back from thanking him for each one.

Wonderful One, thank you for being more for me than I can describe. I will try to describe it today.

Look and Live

Let all the world look to me for salvation!
For I am God;
there is no other.
Isaiah 45:22 NLT

I've a message from the Lord, hallelujah!
The message unto you I'll give.
'Tis recorded in his Word, hallelujah!
It is only that you look and live.

Look and live, my brother, live.
Look to Jesus now and live.
'Tis recorded in his Word, hallelujah!
It is only that you look and live.

I've a message full of love, hallelujah!
A message, O my friend, for you.
'Tis a message from above, hallelujah!
Jesus said it, and I know 'tis true.

Life is offered unto you. Hallelujah!
Eternal life your soul shall have
If you'll only look to him. Hallelujah!
Look to Jesus, who alone can save.

"Look and Live" was inspired by a remarkable story from Numbers 21. God had sent poisonous snakes to punish the disobedient Hebrews. However, God told Moses that if someone was bitten by a snake, all they had to do was look at the bronze serpent Moses was to make and attach to a pole. All they had to do was "look and live." For all of us who look to our Savior hung on a cross, we can do the same. When we look to Jesus for our healing, we will live.

Whatever trials you face, you can find your healing in Christ. He takes away the sins of the world. He gives everlasting life. He is our salvation, and we come alive in his love.

Lord, I look to you today with intention. I raise my eyes to who you are. As I do, heal what needs to be made whole in me and let your Spirit renew my life.

Stand by Me

"I told you these things so that you can have peace in me.
In this world you will have trouble, but be brave!
I have defeated the world."

John 16:33 NCV

When the storms of life are raging,
Stand by me;
When the storms of life are raging,
Stand by me.
When the world is tossing me
Like a ship upon the sea,
Thou who rulest wind and water,
Stand by me.

In the midst of persecution,
Stand by me;
In the midst of persecution,
Stand by me.
When my foes in war array
Undertake to stop my way,
Thou who rescued Paul and Silas,
Stand by me.

Charles Tindley knew trials and tribulations. He was the son of an enslaved man and a free woman. He worked to support his family from a young age. He was a voracious learner and read thousands of books. Though he did not graduate from college or seminary, he received two honorary doctorates of divinity. He had a hungry mind and a hungry heart to know the Lord.

Though his 1905 hymn "Stand by Me" is simple, it is powerful. Whether we battle through storms or breeze through sunny days, the Lord is near. We can always lean on his strength and wisdom in our weakness. He is trustworthy, powerful, and ready to help us.

Lord, as I face this day, stand by me. Be close in all I do, everywhere I go, and in all I say. I want to know your nearness and friendship more with each passing day.

Not Denied

"Let Me go, for the day breaks." But he said,
"I will not let You go unless You bless me!"
GENESIS 32:26 NKJV

When pangs of death seized on my soul,
Unto the Lord I cried,
Till Jesus came and made me whole,
I would not be denied.

I would not be denied,
I would not be denied,
Till Jesus came and made me whole,
I would not be denied.

As Jacob in the days of old,
I wrestled with the Lord;
And instantly with a courage bold,
I stood upon his Word.

Old Satan said my Lord was gone
And would not hear my pray'r,
But praise the Lord the work is done,
And Christ the Lord is here.

Charles Price Jones (1865-1949) artfully used the story of Jacob wrestling with the angel of the Lord in Genesis to mirror his own tenacious spiritual hunger. Jones wanted a deeper experience of God's grace, and he spent three days fasting and praying for it. He felt a closeness with God after wrestling through that time. We don't know if this hymn was a direct result of that experience, but it transformed the focus of his ministry for the rest of his life.

When we go to God with a hunger in our hearts, let's not give up easily when we don't see breakthrough. He is close, and he has more to share with us than we could ask for. However, we still need to ask. Ask, seek, and knock today, for Christ is near.

Jesus Christ, I won't hesitate to ask you for what I really want, and I'm not afraid to hear your answer. Wrestle with me, Lord. I need you.

The Lord Is King

Be cheerful with joyous celebration
in every season of life.
Let your joy overflow!

Philippians 4:4 TPT

Rejoice, the Lord is King:
Your Lord and King adore!
Rejoice, give thanks and sing,
And triumph evermore.
Lift up your heart,
Lift up your voice!
Rejoice, again I say, rejoice!

Rejoice in glorious hope!
Our Lord and judge shall come
And take his servants up
To their eternal home:
Lift up your heart,
Lift up your voice!
Rejoice, again I say, rejoice!

Written by Charles Wesley for Easter and Ascension, this 1744 hymn celebrates the kingship of Christ. He rose from the grave; death was unable to keep him there because of the power of his resurrection life. What joy there is in our God who lives. He is not dead but is seated in the heavenly throne room, and he moves in the world by his Holy Spirit.

Rejoice, the Lord is King! Rejoice, give thanks and sing. There are many reasons to give thanks not the least of whom is your Savior. Come to Christ today, however long it has been, and receive his salvation and help. Rejoice in his fellowship, for the Spirit makes his home in you.

Christ my Savior, I can't thank you enough for all you've done for me and for all living creatures who come to you. I am yours. Receive me, empower me by your Spirit, and may your name be glorified in my life.

God Leads Us

"When you pass through the waters,
I will be with you, and the rivers will not overwhelm you.
When you walk through the fire,
you will not be scorched, and the flame will not burn you."

Isaiah 43:2 CSB

In shady, green pastures, so rich and so sweet,
God leads his dear children along;
Where the water's cool flow bathes the weary
one's feet,
God leads his dear children along.

Some through the waters, some through the
flood,
Some through the fire, but all through the
blood;
Some through great sorrow, but God gives
a song,
In the night season and all the day long.

Sometimes on the mount where the sun
shines so bright,
God leads his dear children along;
Sometimes in the valley, in darkest of night,
God leads his dear children along.

Away from the mire, and away from the clay,
God leads his dear children along;
Away up in glory, eternity's day,
God leads his dear children along.

George Young (dates unknown) was a man of humble means. He was a rural preacher and carpenter who struggled to support his family. Eventually, he was able to construct a home for them, but while he was away holding meetings, his house burned to the ground. It was tragic, but it did not deter his faith in God.

Through everything we face, be it waters, fire, sorrow, or flood, God is not just with us. He gives us a song in the night. Even in our greatest disappointments, we can know the peace, joy, and hope of our Lord, for he is our Redeemer and restorer.

Gracious God, thank you for your persistent presence in my life. I continue to follow you, for you are dearer to me than any other.

JULY 20

How Wonderful Thou Art

When I consider your heavens, the work of your fingers,
the moon and the stars, which you have set in place,
what is mankind that you are mindful of them,
human beings that you care for them?

Psalm 8:3-4 NIV

My God, how wonderful thou art,
Thy majesty how bright!
How beautiful thy mercy seat,
In depths of burning light!

Wondrous are thine eternal years,
O everlasting Lord,
By holy angels day and night
Unceasingly adored!

No earthly father loves like thee,
No mother half so mild
Bears and forbears, as thou hast done
With me, thy sinful child.

Father of Jesus, Love divine,
What rapture it will be,
Prostrate before thy throne to lie,
And gaze and gaze on thee!

Although Frederick Faber (1814-1863) was born into a strict Calvinist home, he eventually became ordained in the Roman Catholic Church. He wrote over a hundred hymns because he believed Catholics should be singing hymns with theological depth just as the Protestants were doing. "My God, How Wonderful Thou Art" is an anthem of God's glory. No matter our tradition, those who follow Christ can agree: He is wonderful and worthy to be praised.

In moments of glorious awareness of God's mercy and grace, we catch glimpses of what will one day be plain to see. God's marvelous beauty is found in who he is, and that never changes. Though we only see a muddied reflection of God's glory today, one day we will see it clearly.

Glorious One, I want to know you more today. Reveal yourself in ways I have not yet known. I want to catch a new glimpse of you.

Awakening Chorus

Awake, my glory!
Awake, O harp and lyre!
I will awake the dawn!
Psalm 57:8 ESV

Awake! Awake! And sing the blessed story;
Awake! Awake! And let your song of praise arise;
Awake! Awake! The earth is full of glory,
And light is beaming from the radiant skies;
The rocks and rills, the vales and hills resound with gladness,
All nature joins to sing the triumph song.

The Lord Jehovah reigns and sin is backward hurled!
Rejoice! rejoice! Lift heart and voice, Jehovah reigns!
Proclaim his sov'reign pow'r to all the world,
And let his glorious banner be unfurled!
Jehovah reigns! Rejoice! Rejoice! Rejoice!
Jehovah reigns!

Ring out! Ring out! O bells of joy and gladness;
Repeat, repeat anew the story o'er again,
Till all the earth shall lose its weight of sadness,
And shout anew the glorious refrain;
Ye angels in the heights, sing of the great Redeemer,
Who saves us from the pow'r of sin and death.

Echoing the psalms, the 1905 hymn "Awakening Chorus" by Charles Gabriel encourages us to take charge of our souls and direct them to God. We don't sing in vain to the one who holds the stars in their place. Our minds are prone to forgetfulness, and our memories are often swayed by inner narratives.

As we learn to be present in moments through the day, we can offer God our attention. As our souls awaken to the beauty he has placed in our lives and the gifts of his presence hidden in ordinary places, we can rejoice to the giver of good gifts. Awake, awake, and see that the earth is full of his glory.

Lord Jehovah, as I train my heart to turn toward you and look for the fingerprints of your mercy in the world, may the space for awe grow larger with each revelation. You are wonderful, and you are worthy of my praise

JULY 22

Jordan's Stormy Banks

There will be no night there—no need for lamps or sun—
for the Lord God will shine on them.
And they will reign forever and ever.

Revelation 22:5 NLT

On Jordan's stormy banks I stand,
And cast a wishful eye
To Canaan's fair and happy land,
Where my possessions lie.

I am bound for the promised land,
I am bound for the promised land;
Oh, who will come and go with me?
I am bound for the promised land.

O'er all those wide extended plains
Shines one eternal day;
There God the Son forever reigns,
And scatters night away.

When I shall reach that happy place,
I'll be forever blest,
For I shall see my Father's face,
And in his bosom rest.

This hymn is an adaptation from the original 1787 English version by Samuel Stennett. His title for the hymn was "Heaven Anticipated," which is a hopeful glimpse at what we have to look forward to in the promised land of Christ's eternal kingdom.

Everything we leave behind in this life, though not worthless to us, pales in comparison to what awaits in the abundance of God's kingdom. There is more ahead than anything we leave behind. Every moment of love and acceptance, every celebration and joy, is but a foretaste. It all counts, and it is all beautiful, yet it is just a morsel of an abundant feast we will experience.

Great God, I have hope in you and in the coming of your kingdom. I trust your goodness and faithfulness will continue to follow and keep me all the days of my life. When this life is over, I will stand in awe of all I could not have dreamed alone.

Where'er the Sun

Praise his glorious name forever.
Let his glory fill the whole world.
Amen and amen.

Psalm 72:19 NCV

Jesus shall reign where'er the sun
Does its successive journeys run,
His kingdom stretch from shore to shore,
Till moons shall wax and wane no more.

To him shall endless prayer be made,
And praises throng to crown his head.
His name like sweet perfume shall rise
With every morning sacrifice.

People and realms of every tongue
Dwell on his love with sweetest song,
And infant voices shall proclaim
Their early blessings on his name.

Let every creature rise and bring
The highest honors to our King,
Angels descend with songs again,
And earth repeat the loud amen.

This hymn was included in Isaac Watts' 1719 publication of his Psalms of David, Imitated. It was based on Psalm 72, and Watts positioned Christ as the king Solomon wrote about in his interpretation. Jesus is King of kings and Lord of lords. He is the ruler who will reign into eternity.

While we wait for Christ's kingdom to come in its fullness, we know who deserves our allegiance. He is the King of love who draws us to himself with kindness. He does not change his nature depending on when you approach him. He is always the same, and he can be trusted. Let's pray to him in ceaseless measure, for he loves when we reach out to him. Let's depend on him for wisdom, for he has every answer. Let's bring our honors to the King, for he is worthy.

King of kings, I will pray to you throughout my day and offer you my questions, hopes, and fears. I know you are near.

Think on Me

"I will not leave you orphans;
I will come to you."
JOHN 14:18 NKJV

Lord Jesus, think on me,
And purge away my sin;
From earth-born passions set me free,
And make me pure within.

Lord Jesus, think on me,
With care and woe oppressed,
Let me thy loving servant be,
And taste thy promised rest.

Lord Jesus, think on me,
Nor let me go astray;
Through darkness and perplexity
Point thou the heav'nly way.

Lord Jesus, think on me,
That, when the flood is past,
I may eternal brightness see,
And share thy joy at last.

This hymn was translated from an ancient text written by Synesius of Cyrene sometime in the fourth or fifth century. Allen Chatfield was a Greek scholar, and he translated many original hymns from ancient Greek into English. This particular hymn was published in a compilation in 1876. Reading through the text, we can see it is a prayer for Jesus to be near and to keep us in mind as we travel through this life.

God is not blind to our struggles, nor is he indifferent to them. Let's look to the Lord, our leader and Savior, for he promises rest to all who come to him. He will faithfully guide us into his goodness.

Lord my God, I trust you know me better than I account for. Guide me through the hills and valleys of this life, and above all, make your nearness known to me.

Sing to Jesus

"Because you were slaughtered for us,
you are worthy to take the scroll and open its seals.
Your blood was the price paid to redeem us.
You purchased us to bring us to God
out of every tribe, language, people group, and nation."

REVELATION 5:9 TPT

Alleluia! Sing to Jesus;
His the scepter, his the throne;
Alleluia! His the triumph,
His the victory alone.
Hark! The songs of peaceful Zion
Thunder like a mighty flood:
"Jesus, out of ev'ry nation
Has redeemed us by his blood."

Alleluia! Bread of heaven,
Here on earth our food, our stay;
Alleluia! Here the sinful
Flee to you from day to day.
Intercessor, friend of sinners,
Earth's Redeemer, hear our plea
Where the songs of all the sinless
Aweep across the crystal sea.

This hymn was originally titled "Redemption by the Precious Blood" by William Dix in 1866. There is a joyful tone throughout it as alleluias begin each stanza. We joyfully praise Jesus for what he has done, the victory he has won, and the redemption we find in him.

The implications of Christ's resurrection are many. He proved he was who he claimed to be: the Son of God. Death was disarmed in Christ's triumph over the grave. Salvation is not found in what we do; we can never earn it. We simply come to Christ, believing he is enough, and find ourselves loved to life in his presence.

Redeemer, thank you for the power of your life that gives me a hope and a future. I receive the mercy of your help, and I give up trying to earn it. You are so good to me, Lord.

We Praise Thy Name

One called to another:
Holy, holy, holy is the LORD of Armies;
his glory fills the whole earth.

ISAIAH 6:3 CSB

Holy God, we praise thy name.
God of all, we bow before thee.
All on earth your scepter claim;
All in heav'n above adore thee.
Infinite thy vast domain,
Everlasting is thy reign.

Hark, the loud celestial hymn,
Angel choirs above are raising.
Cherubim and seraphim,
In unceasing chorus praising,
Fill the heav'ns with sweet accord:
Holy, holy, holy Lord.

Lo! The apostolic train
Join thy sacred name to hallow.
Prophets swell the glad refrain,
And the blessed martyrs follow,
And, from morn till set of sun,
Through the church the song goes on.

This hymn text is based on an anonymous fourth-century Latin hymn: "Te Deum Laudamus." All traditions of Christianity have embraced this text through the ages, and it has been translated and creatively expressed in many languages and styles.

It is worthwhile to look up a more precise English translation of the original text to see what inspired so many iterations. It is a song of praise and acclamation, and it reads as a statement of faith. God, the one who is Creator, King, and Father of all, is worthy of our adoration. As we join with generations who have proclaimed Christ as King, we are unified with the angels and all creation in reverently bowing before him.

Great God, I praise you as my Lord and as the King over all creation. I am in awe of who you are and humbled by who I am to you. Be glorified and be near.

Gladsome Mind

Give thanks to the LORD,
for he is good;
his love endures forever.
PSALM 118:1 NIV

Let us, with a gladsome mind,
Praise the LORD, for he is kind:
For his mercies shall endure,
Ever faithful, ever sure.

Let us blaze his name abroad,
For of gods he is the God:
For his mercies shall endure,
Ever faithful, ever sure.

He his chosen race did bless
In the wasteful wilderness:
For his mercies shall endure,
Ever faithful, ever sure.

He hath with a pious eye
Looks upon our misery:
For his mercies shall endure,
Ever faithful, ever sure.

Though not a prolific hymn writer, John Milton was a famous poet and author. He wrote this text in 1623 when he was only fifteen years old. He wrote nineteen versions of different psalms, and this particular poem was based on Psalm 136. It was later set to music so we can sing the beauty of its meaning to the Lord.

How has the Lord been kind to you? How has he provided for you when you had no other help? May you offer the Lord your authentic gratitude for all you have, all he's done, and all he's yet to do. He will prove faithful time and time again.

Faithful Father, you are the one who steadies me when the world is shaking. I trust you as my Savior, provider, and Shepherd.

JULY 28

Sun of My Soul

To Him who made the great lights,
For His faithfulness is everlasting:
The sun to rule by day,
For His faithfulness is everlasting,
The moon and stars to rule by night.

Psalm 136:7-9 NASB

Sun of my soul, thou Savior dear,
It is not night if thou be near;
O, may no earthborn cloud arise,
To hide thee from thy servant's eyes.

When the soft dews of kindly sleep
My weary eyelids gently steep,
Be my last thought—how sweet to rest
Forever on my Savior's breast!

Abide with me from morn till eve,
For without thee I cannot live;
Abide with me when night is nigh,
For without thee I dare not die.

Be near to bless me when I wake
Ere through the world our way I take;
Abide with me till in thy love
I lose myself in heav'n above.

Reverend John Keble was a professor of poetry at Oxford University as well as a member of the high clergy in the Church of England. In 1827, he published a collection of sacred poetry entitled "The Christian Year," from which this hymn is taken from a longer work called "Evening."

The presence of Christ is a comfort to those going through a dark night of the soul. He is the light guiding us, the safe place holding us close, and our ever-present help. As we abide in Christ, we find he, too abides in us through his Spirit. What a wonderful reality to awaken to. Let's tune in to the presence of God here with us now: the sun of our souls, our Savior dear.

Comforter, be near in every waking moment and while I sleep. Watch over me even when I don't know I need it. I am yours, and I rely on you.

Comfort Ye My People

"Comfort, comfort my people,"
says your God.
Isaiah 40:1 ESV

"Comfort, comfort all my people;
Speak of peace," so says our God.
"Comfort those who sit in darkness,
Groaning from their sorrows' load.
Speak to all Jerusalem
Of the peace that waits for them;
Tell them that their sins I cover,
That their warfare now is over."

Then make straight the crooked highway;
Make the rougher places plain.
Let your hearts be true and humble,
Ready for his holy reign.
For the glory of the Lord
Now o'er earth is spread abroad,
And all flesh shall see the token
That his Word is never broken.

Isaiah 40 is a prophetic declaration of what is to come under Christ's leadership, and it is also a call to repentance which is how we prepare the way of the Lord. This song focuses on the first five verses of the chapter. Catherine Winkworth translated it in the nineteenth centry from the seventeeth-century German original by Johann Olearius.

There is peace in Christ now because he is the coming peace the Scriptures foretold. We no longer wait for that blessed hope, for he has already appeared. 2 Corinthians 6:2 says, "Behold, now is the favorable time; behold, now is the day of salvation." We do not have to wait a moment longer to know true acceptance, forgiveness, and restoration, for we have it in Christ.

Restorer, I have humbled my heart before you, for I long to know the power of your leading in my life. Heal, save, and lead me, for I am yours today and forever.

JULY 30

Lift Your Heads

Open up, ancient gates!
Open up, ancient doors,
and let the King of glory enter.

PSALM 24:7 NLT

Lift up your heads, ye mighty gates;
Behold, the King of glory waits;
The King of kings is drawing near;
The Savior of the world is here!

Fling wide the portals of your heart;
Make it a temple, set apart
From earthly use for heaven's employ,
Adorned with prayer and love and joy.

Redeemer, come, with us abide;
Our hearts to thee we open wide;
Let us thy inner presence feel;
Thy grace and love in us reveal.

Thy Holy Spirit lead us on
Until our glorious goal is won;
Eternal praise, eternal fame
Be offered, Savior, to thy name!

Georg Weissel (1590-1635) wrote the original text for this hymn in his native German. He based it on Psalm 24 and wrote it for the first Sunday of Advent, though it aptly declares the glory of God any time of year. David's psalm is entitled "The King of Glory" which is appropriate for describing the majesty and beauty of Jesus.

We are God's living gateways, for he enters the welcoming heart. We can awaken our inner gates and the portals of our hearts to the King of glory. What fellowship we have with the Spirit of glory, and what light and love we experience as he makes our hearts his dwelling place. It is almost too much to comprehend, yet it is our lived reality.

King of glory, there is no one like you who heals, restores, and saves all who come to you. I am yours, and I open the gates of my heart to you. Come in.

Sons and Daughters Sing

"Death, where is your victory?
Death, where is your pain?"
1 CORINTHIANS 15:55 NCV

O sons and daughters of the King,
Whom heavenly hosts in glory sing,
Today the grave has lost its sting.
Alleluia!

"My pierced side, O Thomas, see,
And look upon my hands, my feet;
Not faithless but believing be."
Alleluia!

No longer Thomas then denied;
He saw the feet, the hands, the side.
"You are my Lord and God!" he cried.
Alleluia!

How blest are they who have not seen
And yet whose faith has constant been,
For they eternal life shall win.
Alleluia!

This text was written by Franciscan monk Jean Tisserand in the fifteenth century and translated into English in the nineteenth century by John Neale. The hymn is a narrative telling of the Easter story from the women at the tomb to Thomas's doubting of Christ's resurrection. If we struggle with our doubt, the merciful kindness of Christ's presence can relieve all our fears.

Jesus did not rebuke Thomas' doubt, but he did say those who believe without seeing are blessed by their faith. Jesus appeared to his disciples; he did not leave them wondering. He offered Thomas to feel the wound in his side and touch the nail-scarred hands outstretched before him. He is kind to us even in our doubt. He never changes, and his faithfulness never fails.

Gentle Savior, I can't get over your kindness. You are gentle with us in our weakness. Even your correction is full of kindness and truth. Thank you.

All hail the power of Jesus' name!

Let angels prostrate fall.

Bring forth the royal diadem, and crown him Lord of all.

Bring forth the royal diadem, and crown him Lord of all!

Father of Mankind

O LORD, You are our Father;
We are the clay, and You our potter;
And all we are the work of Your hand.

ISAIAH 64:8 NKJV

Dear Lord and Father of mankind,
Forgive our foolish ways;
Reclothe us in our rightful mind,
In purer lives thy service find,
In deeper reverence, praise.

Drop thy still dews of quietness,
Till all our strivings cease;
Take from our souls the strain and stress,
And let our ordered lives confess
The beauty of thy peace.

Breathe through the heats of our desire
Thy coolness and thy balm;
Let sense be dumb, let flesh retire;
Speak through the earthquake, wind, and fire,
O still, small voice of calm!

John Greenleaf Whittier was an American Quaker poet who lived in the nineteenth century. Many of his poems were adapted and compiled into hymns including "Dear Lord and Father of Mankind." It was taken from a larger poem, "The Brewing of Soma," which critiques the use of various "intoxications" to grow closer to the Lord.

The Lord is forgiving of our foolishness. If he were not, none of us would stand a chance! No one has a full grasp of the Lord or his ways. He is easier on us than we are on others or ourselves. We receive his grace continually to remain humble and teachable before him.

Lord, forgive me of my foolishness and pride. Keep my heart in check when I judge others while overlooking my faults. Only you are perfect, and I choose to move in love even as you move in love toward me.

AUGUST 2

Heavenly Dove

"When the Father sends the Spirit of Holiness,
the One like me who sets you free,
he will teach you all things in my name.
And he will inspire you to remember every word that I've told you."

JOHN 14:26 TPT

Come, Holy Spirit, Heav'nly Dove,
With all thy quick'ning pow'rs;
Kindle a flame of sacred love
In these cold hearts of ours.

Look, how we grovel here below,
Fond of these earthly toys;
Our souls, how heavily they go,
To reach eternal joys.

In vain we tune our formal songs,
In vain we strive to rise;
Hosannas languish on our tongues,
And our devotion dies.

Father, and shall we ever live
At this poor dying rate,
Our love so faint, so cold to thee,
And thine to us so great?

Isaac Watts' hymn reveals tender devotion, hunger for the Lord and his help, and an admission of weakness. We are easily distracted as humans, and in a time of more opportunities for distraction than ever, it is necessary to build slow rhythms of rest and reliance. These rhythms are necessary to know God.

We need God's help to know him. We need his love to awaken our own. 1 John 4:19 says it this way: "Our love for others is our grateful response to the love God first demonstrated to us." Or, put another way, "We love because he first loved us" (CSB). He is our source, and his resources are abundant. He never runs out of mercy, kindness, or peace. Let's give up our vain pursuits of independent thriving and instead lean on the Lord's power to awaken our hearts with his Spirit at work in us.

Holy Spirit, I need you for healing, rest, vision, peace, and more. Fill my soul with the purity of your presence and awaken me in your love.

Crowded Life

When he saw the crowds,
he felt compassion for them,
because they were distressed and dejected,
like sheep without a shepherd.
MATTHEW 9:36 CSB

Where cross the crowded ways of life,
Where sound the cries of race and clan,
Above the noise of selfish strife,
We hear your voice, O Son of Man.

From tender childhood's helplessness,
From human grief and burdened toil,
From famished souls, from sorrow's stress,
Your heart has never known recoil.

The cup of water given for you
Still holds the freshness of your grace;
Yet long these multitudes to view
The sweet compassion of your face.

Till all the world shall learn your love,
And follow where your feet have trod;
Till glorious from your heaven above
Shall come the city of our God.

This hymn from 1905 was inspired by a challenge to write a hymn based on city missions and the words of Jesus: "Go then to where the roads exit the city and invite everyone you find to the banquet" (Matthew 22:9). Frank North's hymn focuses on the challenges of urban poverty and encourages those who would be the hands and feet of Christ to join with the heart of Christ in praying over cities and ministering to the poor.

True love is not displayed in speeches but in active service. We love through word and deed; they have to go together. Love follows through on its word, offers grace when we would rather give up, and is not bound by fear.

Christ, you are the Savior of the world and not of the affluent. May my heart remain humble and open in compassion. I want to partner with your love in practical ways.

Blessing Honor Glory Power

Since we have a great high priest who has ascended into heaven, Jesus the Son of God, let us hold firmly to the faith we profess.

HEBREWS 4:14 NIV

Blessing and honor and glory and pow'r,
Wisdom and riches and strength evermore
Give ye to him who our battle hath won,
Whose are the kingdom, the crown, and the throne.

Soundeth the heav'n of the heav'ns with his name;
Ringeth the earth with his glory and fame;
Ocean and mountain, stream, forest, and flow'r
Echo his praises and tell of his pow'r.

Ever ascendeth the song and the joy;
Ever descendeth the love from on high;
Blessing and honor and glory and praise—
This is the theme of the hymns that we raise.

Give we the glory and praise to the Lamb;
Take we the robe and the harp and the palm;
Sing we the song of the Lamb that was slain,
Dying in weakness, but rising to reign.

This hymn from 1858 is based on Revelation 5:13 where John recorded a vision of countless angels, living creatures, and elders surrounding the throne of God. "In a loud voice they were saying: 'Worthy is the Lamb, who was slain, to receive power and wealth and wisdom and strength and honor and glory and praise!'" Horatius Bonar's interpretation of this verse encourages us to envision what John saw.

What glory, honor, blessing, and power Christ deserves! He is already receiving the adoration and praise of those who dwell with him in heaven: the angels, elders, and all the living creatures around his throne. We can join their song today in faith and give him everything he is due.

Majestic One, you are worthy of my praise and adoration. You are worthy of praise and adoration from everyone, everywhere. I glorify and worship you; please meet me with your love and power.

Evening Hymn

When you lie down,
you will not be afraid;
When you lie down,
your sleep will be sweet.

PROVERBS 3:24 NASB

All praise to you, my God, this night,
For all the blessings of the light.
Keep me, O keep me, King of kings,
Beneath the shelter of your wings.

Forgive me, Lord, for this I pray,
The wrong that I have done this day.
May peace with God and neighbor be,
Before I sleep restored to me.

Lord, may I be at rest in you
And sweetly sleep the whole night thro'.
Refresh my strength, for your own sake,
So I may serve you when I wake.

Praise God, from whom all blessings flow;
Praise him all creatures here below;
Praise him above, ye heav'nly host;
Praise Father, Son, and Holy Ghost.

In the seventeenth century, Thomas Ken wrote this hymn within a trio of prayer-focused hymns for morning, evening, and midnight. The last verse may be the most memorable, for it is now a famous doxology. Intentionality is an important part of our daily spirituality. As we start the day, we can focus on today's opportunity rather than the need to let go at the end of the day.

Before you go to sleep tonight, read through this prayerful hymn. Offer God the blessings of goodness you encountered in your day as well as the failures and mistakes. Ask for the peace of God to rest on your heart and mind as you give God everything you cannot control. He is good, and he watches over you.

Lord, you are the God of my rising and the God of my rest. You are with me in my attentive focus and with me as I dream under your care. Thank you for the blessings and challenges of today.

AUGUST 6

Peace Like a River

The fruit of the Spirit is love, joy, peace, patience, kindness, goodness, faithfulness.

GALATIANS 5:22 ESV

I've got peace like a river,
I've got peace like a river,
I've got peace like a river in my soul.
I've got peace like a river,
I've got peace like a river,
I've got peace like a river in my soul.

I've got love like a river…
I've got joy like a river…

This simple song is a wonderful response to God's work within and among us. While its origin is unknown, we do know it is an African American spiritual. In Isaiah 66:12, the Lord says, "Behold, I will extend peace to her like a river." The fruit of the Spirit are many, but the first three described in Galatians 5 are love, joy, and peace. Put these two Scriptures together, and you have a hymn declaring the Spirit's work in our lives.

If you are in Christ, you have his Holy Spirit. If you have the Spirit, the seeds of his fruit will be evident in your heart and life. Don't be afraid to remind your soul by singing this hymn over your heart, life, and relationships. The Lord extends you his kindness through peace like a river.

Holy Spirit, thank you for the fruit you produce in my life. I am your vessel; move in me in greater waves of love, joy, and peace as I yield to your river's current.

O Gladsome Light

He alone can never die, and he lives in light so brilliant that no human can approach him. No human eye has ever seen him, nor ever will. All honor and power to him forever! Amen.

1 Timothy 6:16 NLT

O gladsome light, O grace
Of God the Father's face,
Th'eternal splendor wearing;
Celestial, holy, blest,
Our Savior Jesus Christ,
Joyful in thine appearing!

Now, as day fadeth quite,
We see the evening light,
Our wonted hymn outpouring;
Father of might unknown,
Thee, his incarnate Son,
And Holy Ghost adoring.

To thee of right belongs
All praise of holy songs,
O Son of God, life-giver;
Thee, therefore, O Most High,
The world does glorify
And shall exalt forever.

"O Gladsome Light" is a translation of an ancient Greek hymn whose author is unknown to us today. Twilight, which teeters between fading light and impending darkness, was an invitation to the early Christian to pray. As we notice the transition of light in our lives, we are also invited to turn our hearts to the Lord in prayer.

If you can, take some time to notice the sunset today. Allow it to be your call to prayer. God's gracious light shines as brightly in the night as it does in the day; it is only the point of our perspective, our place in the rotation of the earth, that makes it seem different. God reigns in light, and he will never dim.

Lord, as the transitions of the days and seasons give me pause, I will use those pauses to turn my attention to you in prayer. Meet me in those liminal spaces.

AUGUST 8

Bread of the World

"God's bread is the One who comes down from heaven and gives life to the world. I am the bread that gives life. Whoever comes to me will never be hungry, and whoever believes in me will never be thirsty."

John 6:33, 35 NCV

Bread of the world in mercy broken,
Wine of the soul in mercy shed,
By whom the words of life were spoken,
And in whose death our sins are dead.

Look on the heart by sorrow broken,
Look on the tears by sinners shed;
And be thy feast to us the token
That by thy grace our souls are fed.

This hymn wasn't published until 1827 after the death of the author, Reginald Heber. Heber was an Anglican bishop and hymnist, and his hymn is an apt accompaniment to taking the Lord's Supper. Jesus, whose body was broken, offers us the nourishment of his own being to bring us life. It's a marvelous mystery.

In some Christian traditions, the practice of confession is a normal part of the believer's life. In others, confession is often overlooked in the church setting. Confession, whether done privately or in a group setting, is a powerful tool of repentence. When we offer God the honesty of our lived experiences, while also making room for others, we can experience great love, acceptance, and empowered faith in Christ's forgiveness of our sins.

Bread of Life, I can trust you with my life. I will not hide the shame, fear, or sin entangling me. I humble myself before you and let you in.

Joy of Loving Hearts

"Through the tender mercy of our God,
With which the Dayspring from on high has visited us;
To give light to those who sit in darkness and the shadow of death,
To guide our feet into the way of peace."

LUKE 1:78-79 NKJV

O Jesus, joy of loving hearts,
Thou fount of life, thou light of men,
From fullest bliss that earth imparts
We turn unfilled to thee again.

Thy truth unchanged has ever stood,
Thou savest those that on thee call;
To them that seek thee, thou art good,
To them that find thee, all in all.

Our restless spirits yearn for thee,
Where'er our changeful lot is cast,
Glad that thy gracious smile we see,
Blest that our faith can hold thee fast.

O Jesus, ever with us stay,
Make all our moments calm and bright;
Chase the dark night of sin away,
Shed o'er the world thy holy light.

In the Middle Ages, Bernard of Clairveaux wrote a lengthy devotional poem based on the Song of Solomon. It is from this poem that this hymn was taken and formed by Ray Palmer, who translated it into English in 1858.

We find many blessings in Christ. He is the fount of life that brings joy and the light that shines bright. He is the saving truth. He is our living bread and water of life. He is our resting place and eternally present in our lives. Praise God for what we have in him! What a blessed hope, and what a present power that never leaves or forsakes us.

Jesus Christ, you bring satisfaction to my soul in more ways than I can thank you for. Move in me as I continue to yield to your love. I belong to you.

AUGUST 10

Sons of the Morning

Darkness will cover the earth,
and total darkness the peoples;
but the LORD will shine over you,
and his glory will appear over you.
ISAIAH 60:2 CSB

Brightest and best of the sons of the morning,
Dawn on our darkness and lend us your aid.
Star of the east, the horizon adorning,
Guide where our infant Redeemer is laid.

Cold on his cradle the dewdrops are shining;
Low lies his head with the beasts of the stall.
Angels adore him in slumber reclining,
Maker and monarch and Savior of all.

Shall we yield him in costly devotion
Rarest of fragrances, tribute divine,
Gems of the mountain and pearls of the
ocean,
Myrrh from the forest and gold from the mine?

Vainly we offer each ample oblation,
Vainly with gifts would his favor secure.
Richer by far is the heart's adoration,
Dearer to God are the prayers of the poor.

This hymn was originally written by bishop Reginald Heber in 1811 for the feast of Epiphany which, for those who practice it in Western traditions, primarily celebrates the visit of the Magi to the newborn Christ. It is typically celebrated at the beginning of January, but it is valuable to meditate on the powerful gift of Christ and the journey of the Magi any time of year.

The third verse asks, "Shall we yield him in costly devotion?" What have we to give? We can offer the best we have. As we devote our lives to him, we receive the richest treasure, for Christ is better than all the silver and gold the world holds.

Lord Jesus, I may not have endless resources, but what I have, I offer you. It is my joy and honor to bring you all I am.

Come Ye Sinners

"The Son of Man has come to seek out
and to give life to those who are lost."
LUKE 19:10 TPT

Come, ye sinners, poor and needy,
Weak and wounded, sick and sore;
Jesus ready stands to save you,
Full of pity, love, and power.

Come, ye thirsty, come and welcome,
God's free bounty glorify;
True belief and true repentance,
Ev'ry grace that brings you nigh.

Let not conscience make you linger,
Nor of fitness fondly dream;
All the fitness he requireth
Is to feel your need of him.

Come, ye weary, heavy laden,
Lost and ruined by the fall;
If you tarry till you're better,
You will never come at all.

Joseph Hart's hymn has undergone many text and tune changes since the original was written in 1759. It is a classic hymn where the Lord invites us to turn from our sinful ways and receive the grace of God in fellowship with him. God is mighty to save, and it is by grace that we are saved, not by any work of our own (Ephesians 2:8-9).

Everyone is welcome in the kingdom of Christ. He waits with open arms. He does not discriminate against anyone, and he is not impressed by power, prestige, or how put-together we may seem. He welcomes the weak, the poor, and the sick. Whatever reasons you have to stay away from him, none actually deter him. Come to your gracious Savior and find yourself loved to life in his embrace.

Jesus Christ, I believe you are the way, the truth, and the life. I lay down all my excuses and come to you just as I am today to receive your grace.

AUGUST 12

Priceless Treasure

I consider everything a loss because of the surpassing worth of knowing Christ Jesus my Lord, for whose sake I have lost all things. I consider them garbage, that I may gain Christ.

PHILIPPIANS 3:8 NIV

Jesus, priceless treasure,
Source of purest pleasure,
Friend most sure and true:
Long my heart was burning,
Fainting much and yearning,
Thirsting, Lord, for you.
Yours I am, O spotless Lamb,
So will I let nothing hide you,
Seek no joy beside you!

Catherine Winkworth translated this 1653 hymn from German to English. It relates the power of what we value and the fulfillment we can find in Christ. He fills our needs, calms our fears, sticks close in our weakness, and offers us pervasive peace.

Jesus told us clearly, "Where your treasure is, there your heart will be also" (Matthew 6:21). If our treasure is in Christ, then our hearts are with him, and the hope we have cannot be broken by our circumstances. Let's cling to him through good and bad, for his grace strengthens us in our weakness, and his Spirit comforts us in our grief.

Priceless Jesus, fill me with your joy as I lean into your presence with me. I want to know peace that passes all understanding as you wash over me.

Take Up Thy Cross

"Whoever does not carry his own cross
and come after Me cannot be My disciple."

LUKE 14:27 NASB

Take up your cross, the Savior said,
If you would my disciple be;
Deny yourself, the world forsake,
And humbly follow after me.

Take up your cross, be not ashamed!
Let not disgrace your spirit fill!
For God himself endured to die
Upon a cross, on Calvary's hill.

Take up your cross, which gives you strength,
Which makes your trembling spirit brave:
'Twill guide you to a better home
And lead to vict'ry o'er the grave.

Take up your cross, and follow Christ,
Nor think till death to lay it down;
For only they who bear the cross
May hope to wear the glorious crown.

Charles Everest (1814-1877) wrote this as a poem titled "Visions of Death." It's based on Matthew 16 where Jesus says that whoever wants to live for him must deny themselves, take up their cross, and follow him. The poem was edited for and included in many hymnals. Christ's invitation reminds us that there is sacrifice of self—even death to self—in following his ways.

When we choose to follow the law of God's love in Christ's footsteps, it requires us to step outside our comfort zones mentally, emotionally, and physically. He leads us in truth and does not ask anything of us that he does not first do himself. He is trustworthy. Take up your cross and follow him.

Savior, I trust you will not lead me into confusion as you lead me on your path of sacrificial love. You always know what you're doing.

AUGUST 14

Raise the Strain

Jesus met them and said, "Greetings!"
And they came up and took hold of his feet and worshiped him.

MATTHEW 28:9 ESV

Come, you faithful, raise the strain
Of triumphant gladness!
God has brought his Israel
Into joy from sadness,
Loosed from Pharaoh's bitter yoke
Jacob's sons and daughters,
Led them with unmoistened foot
Through the Red Sea waters.

Now the queen of seasons, bright
With the day of splendor,
With the royal feast of feasts,
Comes its joy to render;
Comes to gladden faithful hearts
Which with true affection
Welcome in unwearied strains
Jesus' resurrection!

John of Damascus was an eighth-century Greek poet. He wrote this resurrection hymn to be sung the Sunday after Easter. It was based on "The Song of Moses" from Exodus 15. The major theme ringing through this text is deliverance. The same God who delivered his people from their captors in Egypt delivers all who take refuge in his Son.

God is a master at restoring what was lost, redeeming that which seems too fargone, and healing our brokenness. He is our hope, and that is no small thing. The hope we have in his power is not in vain. He continues to deliver us from our fears, liberate us in his love, and comfort us in our pain. He really is that good.

Faithful One, you are my deliverer and hope. Turn my circumstances around as I put my trust in you. You are wonderful in your restoration.

God Is So Good

Give thanks to the Lord, for he is good!
His faithful love endures forever.
1 Chronicles 16:34 NLT

God is so good,
God is so good,
God is so good,
He's so good to me.

He cares for me,
He cares for me,
He cares for me,
He's so good to me.

God answers prayer,
God answers prayer,
God answers prayer,
He's so good to me.

I praise his name,
I praise his name,
I praise his name,
He's so good to me.

This popular song is a traditional hymn from Africa. Zambian hymn writer Paul Makai is credited with the original, and it spread throughout the continent as a popular praise song. It was translated into English in 1970 by missionary Marilyn Foulkes, and the popular refrain still makes its mark in music today as it is incorporated into new songs.

The truth of "God Is So Good" never gets old. He is faithful, just, and true. He is a good father, kind shepherd, and reliable caregiver. Think about how God has been good to you through your life. Where can you pinpoint the fingerprints of his mercy through answered prayers, relieved fears, and plentiful provision?

Good God, you are so good to me! What a wonderful father you are. I come to you with gratitude. I trust you to continue to care for me.

AUGUST 16

At Thy Word

"The same thing is true of the words I speak.
They will not return to me empty.
They make the things happen that I want to happen,
and they succeed in doing what I send them to do."

Isaiah 55:11 NCV

Blessed Jesus, at your Word
We are gathered all to hear you.
Let our hearts and souls be stirred
Now to seek and love and fear you.
By your gospel pure and holy,
Teach us, Lord, to love you solely.

All our knowledge, sense, and sight
Lie in deepest darkness shrouded,
Till your Spirit breaks our night
With your beams of truth unclouded.
You alone to God can win us;
You must work all good within us.

Glorious Lord, yourself impart;
Light of Light, from God proceeding,
Open lips and ears and heart;
Help us by your Spirit's leading.
Hear the cry your church now raises;
Lord, accept our prayers and praises.

Tobias Clausnitzer's prayerful hymn from the seventeeth century invites the Lord to illuminate our hearts and minds with the truth of Jesus. We need the power of his Word to penetrate our hearts. As we acknowledge our dependence on the Holy Spirit to reveal the mysteries of God, we can also claim the promise of Christ that the Spirit will do these things (John 14:26).

When we come to the Lord, we can prepare our hearts by asking for his help in opening us to receive. We do not accept anything from him that he is not already willing to do. It is good for us to recognize how much we need the Lord, and he is faithful to teach us as we look to him.

Holy Spirit, open my heart to receive the truth you speak. Open the eyes of my soul and the ears of my spirit to understand the greatness of God.

Gates of Beauty

When Jacob awoke from his sleep, he said,
"Surely the LORD is in this place, and I did not know it."
He was afraid and said, "What an awesome place this is!
This is none other than the house of God.
This is the gate of heaven."

GENESIS 28:16-17 CSB

Open now thy gates of beauty,
Zion, let me enter there,
Where my soul in joyful duty
Waits for him who answers prayer.
Oh, how blessed is this place,
Filled with solace, light, and grace!

Here thy praise is gladly chanted,
Here thy seed is duly sown;
Let my soul, where it is planted,
Bring forth precious sheaves alone,
So that all I hear may be
Fruitful unto life in me.

Thou my faith increase and quicken,
Let me keep thy gift divine,
Howsoe'er temptations thicken;
May thy Word still o'er me shine
As my guiding star through life,
As my comfort in all strife.

This hymn was written by 1704 by German preacher Benjamin Schmolck and later translated into English by Catherine Winkworth. The first verse echoes Jacob's experience encountering the Lord where he slept in Genesis 28. As we awake from our slumber and become aware of the glory of God dwelling with us, joy, awe, and peace overtake us.

The Lord speaks to those who take time to listen. Make some room in your day to ask the Lord to speak to your heart. You don't have to sit still to hear from him; he will meet you in the minutiae of your day. Only keep your heart open and ask him to speak. We have a resting place in his presence. It is our fountain of life and the balm for every sorrow.

Spirit, speak to me today. Will you open my eyes and ears to see where you are and what you're doing? I long to know you more.

AUGUST 18

Descend on My Heart

Likewise the Spirit also helps in our weaknesses.
For we do not know what we should pray for as we ought,
but the Spirit Himself makes intercession for us
with groanings which cannot be uttered.

ROMANS 8:26 NKJV

Spirit of God, who dwells within my heart,
Wean it from sin, through all its pulses move.
Stoop to my weakness, mighty as you are,
And make me love you as I ought to love.

Did you not bid us love you, God and King,
Love you with all our heart and strength
and mind?
I see the cross there teach my heart to cling.
O let me seek you and O let me find!

Teach me to feel that you are always nigh;
Teach me the struggles of the soul to bear,
To check the rising doubt, the rebel sigh;
Teach me the patience of unceasing prayer.

Teach me to love you as your angels love,
One holy passion filling all my frame:
The fullness of the heaven-descended Dove;
My heart an altar, and your love the flame.

In our walk with the Lord, there will be times when we are desperate for the renewal work of the Holy Spirit within us. Not every season is light and happy, nor are they all dark and dreary. Sometimes in the midst of the mundane, we need a burst of renewed hope, joy, and love. In these times, this hymn is a great song to set ourselves before the Lord.

Whole-hearted devotion to the Lord is not something we achieve. It's not something we can strive for. We need the Spirit's help to rest in the sufficiency of Christ. We also need his grace to empower us. George Croly (1780-1860) wrote this hymn based on Galatians 5:25, which says, "If we live in the Spirit, let us also walk in the Spirit." Today, let's do as Paul said and walk in the Spirit with his help.

Spirit, increase my love and awareness of your goodness. Do what only you can do within my heart. I love you because you first loved me—what a notion!

Giving to God

Every time you give to the poor you make a loan to the Lord.
Don't worry—you'll be repaid in full for all the good you've done.

Proverbs 19:17 TPT

We give thee but thine own,
Whate'er the gift may be;
All that we have is thine alone,
A trust, O Lord, from thee.

May we thy bounties thus
As stewards true receive
And gladly, as thou blessest us,
To thee our first fruits give.

Bishop William How included a reference to Proverbs 19:17 when he wrote this hymn in 1858. Whatever we offer to others, we offer to the Lord. Since everything we have originated with Christ, our offering it back to him through service to others is a reflection of his generous kingdom.

When we stubbornly withhold what we could easily give to others, we do ourselves a disservice. We were created to participate in the world with our unique gifts. We do not give endlessly without receiving anything in return; that is not how reciprocity works. No, we give of what we have and find our needs met as we do.

Lord, I don't want to be consumeristic or stingy. May I live with generosity of heart, mind, resources, and talents because you are generous with us. It is a privilege to partner with your heart by offering my gifts to others.

AUGUST 20

Glory Be

Ascribe to the LORD the glory due his name;
bring an offering and come before him.
Worship the LORD in the splendor of his holiness.

1 CHRONICLES 16:29 NIV

Glory be to God the Father,
Glory be to God the Son,
Glory be to God the Spirit:
Great Jehovah, Three in One!
Glory, glory while eternal ages run!

Glory be to him who loved us,
Washed us from each spot and stain;
Glory be to him who bought us,
Made us kings with him to reign!
Glory, glory to the Lamb that once was slain!

Glory, blessing, praise eternal!
Thus the choir of angels sings;
Honor, riches, pow'r, dominion!
Thus its praise creation brings.
Glory, glory to the King of kings!

Horatius Bonar's acclamation of praise was published in a collection of Hymns of Faith and Hope in 1866. What glory can we offer the one who loved us and washed us from each spot and stain? What does that actually look like? What does glory even mean? When we take great pleasure in something, we can glory in it. When we recognize great beauty or magnificence, we acknowledge its glory. When we achieve high renown or honor by our notable acts, we receive glory.

As you meditate on what glory means, how can you relate it to the triune God? How do you recognize it in your life or in the world? In the end, all glory, honor, and praise are God's. May we offer him the honor of our hearts and glorify his name.

Glorious One, I want to honor you in the way I live my life. Be glorified in me!

Spirit Divine

He would grant you, according to the riches of His glory,
to be strengthened with power through His Spirit in the inner self.
EPHESIANS 3:16 NASB

Spirit divine, attend our prayer,
And make this house your home;
Descend with all your gracious pow'r;
O come, great Spirit, come!

Come as the light; to us reveal
Our emptiness and woe,
And lead us in those paths of life
Where all the righteous go.

Come as the fire and purge our hearts
Like sacrificial flame;
Let our whole soul an off'ring be
To our Redeemer's name.

Come as the dove, and spread your wings,
The wings of peaceful love;
And let your Church on earth become
Blest as the Church above.

Written by Andrew Reed in the nineteenth century, this hymn was first published anonymously in 1829. It is directed to the Holy Spirit, and it is a prayerful invitation for God to work in our hearts. With requests for God to "come as the light… come as the fire… [and] come as the dove," Reed describes many of the descriptions of the Spirit in Scripture.

As we pray for God's help and look to him for what only he can do, let us not forget who he is. He is the light that shines on our minds, the fire that consumes the offering of our hearts, and the dove that rests on us in peace. The power of God is present in the Spirit of God, and he is all we need.

Holy Spirit, come and move in me in powerful ways as I present myself before you today. Let your presence permeate my being.

AUGUST 22

O King of Peace

He shall judge between many peoples,
and shall decide disputes for strong nations far away;
and they shall beat their swords into plowshares,
and their spears into pruning hooks; nation shall not lift up
sword against nation, neither shall they learn war anymore.

MICAH 4:3 ESV

O God of love, O King of peace,
Make wars throughout the world to cease;
Our greed and violent ways restrain.
Give peace, O God, give peace again.

Remember, Lord, your works of old,
The wonders that your people told;
Remember not our sins' deep stain.
Give peace, O God, give peace again.

Whom shall we trust but you, O Lord?
Where rest but on your faithful Word?
None ever called on you in vain.
Give peace, O God, give peace again.

Where saints and angels dwell above
All hearts are joined in holy love;
Oh, bind us in that heav'nly chain.
Give peace, O God, give peace again.

This world has not known universal peace since Adam and Eve were in the garden. There are wars and rumors of wars. Jesus told us we should not be afraid of these things (Matthew 24:6). Still, we long for the peace only he can bring. He is king of love and peace, and in him alone will the nations find their rest.

Just because something is the norm does not mean we should settle for it. Let's not be quick to war against others; Jesus told his disciple to put away his sword when he cut off a guard's ear trying to protect his friend. Instead of fighting, let's be peacemakers. He will rule the nations. It is not our role to force others into his kingdom; rather, to be the light of his reflection on earth.

King of Peace, I don't want to encourage quarrels. Help me to follow your peaceful lead and not my desire to be right.

Sure Foundation

"Didn't you ever read this in the Scriptures?
'The stone that the builders rejected
has now become the cornerstone.'"

MARK 12:10 NLT

Christ is made the sure foundation,
Christ, our head and cornerstone,
Chosen of the Lord and precious,
Binding all the Church in one;
Holy Zion's help forever
And our confidence alone.

Grant, we pray, to all your faithful
All the gifts they ask to gain;
What they gain from you forever
With the blessed to retain;
And hereafter in your glory
Evermore with you to reign.

Praise and honor to the Father,
Praise and honor to the Son,
Praise and honor to the Spirit,
Ever three and ever one:
One in might and one in glory
While unending ages run!

John Neale (1818-1866) translated many texts, especially Medieval hymns, into English. He also translated ancient Greek and Latin texts and adapted them for modern singing. This particular hymn was originally written for the dedication of a church. We know Christ is the sure foundation of his church, and we, his people, are his living dwellings.

Have you ever dedicated a space to the Lord? It is a powerful practice to not only dedicate sacred sanctuaries but also our homes to honoring the Lord. When we dedicate them, we invite his presence to dwell as if it were his own home. More than that, our very bodies are temples of the Spirit. Let's not forget to make Christ the foundation of our living temples.

Lord, I want every part of my life, every space I inhabit, to be dedicated to you.

AUGUST 24

O Splendor Bright

Whatever work you do, do your best,
because you are going to the grave,
where there is no working, no planning,
no knowledge, and no wisdom.

ECCLESIASTES 9:10 NCV

O Splendor of God's glory bright,
From light eternal bringing light,
O Light, of light the fountain-spring,
O Day, all days illumining.

Come, very Sun of truth and love,
Pour down your radiance from above,
And shed the Holy Spirit's ray
On all we think or do today.

Teach us to work with all our might,
Put Satan's fierce assaults to flight;
Turn all to good that seems most ill,
Help us our calling to fulfill.

All praise to God the Father be,
All praise to Christ eternally,
Whom with the Spirit we adore
Forever and forevermore.

Saint Ambrose wrote this hymn in the fourth century. He was instrumental in changing church music, and his numerous compositions reflect that. It was Ambrose who led Augustine, one of the most prominent church figures of all time, to the Lord.

As you read, sing, or listen to this hymn today, offer it as a prayer to God. "Teach us to work with all our might" is a fitting prayer for us to do our best with what we have. This work does not earn us favor with the Lord, but as we partner with him, we join with him in a way that won't be necessary in the age to come. Let's not waste the opportunity we have to serve him with sacrificial joy and offerings of praise.

Lord, I don't want to wake up one day and feel as if I've wasted my life. Give me purpose and vision; meet me in necessary, mundane work. I believe you're in it all.

O'er the Tumult

As he was walking along the Sea of Galilee, he saw two brothers, Simon (who is called Peter), and his brother Andrew. They were casting a net into the sea—for they were fishermen. "Follow me," he told them, "and I will make you fish for people."

MATTHEW 4:18-19 CSB

Jesus calls us o'er the tumult
Of our life's wild, restless sea;
Day by day his voice invites me,
Saying "Christian, follow me!"

As the first disciples heard it
By the Galilean lake,
Turned from home and toil and kindred,
Leaving all for his dear sake.

Jesus calls us from the worship
Of the vain world's golden store,
From each idol that would keep us,
Saying "Christian, love me more."

Jesus calls us! In your mercy,
Savior, help us hear your call;
Give our hearts to your obedience,
Serve and love you best of all!

Irish writer Cecil Alexander wrote this hymn in 1852 for a church service on St. Andrew's Day. The reading for that particular Sunday was from Matthew 4. On the banks of the Sea of Galilee, Jesus called Simon Peter and Andrew to follow him.

Jesus calls each of us by name, and he speaks to us differently. Peter and Andrew were fishermen, and Jesus used that in his call for them to follow him. He said he would make them fishers of men. Don't overlook how God relates to you. He is so good at knowing exactly how to speak to you in a way you understand. Listen for his voice and follow his leading when he calls you.

Lord, I want to follow you with wholehearted devotion. Speak to me today; I am listening.

Every Corner Sing

You are my King, O God;
Command victories for Jacob.

PSALM 44:4 NKJV

Let all the world in ev'ry corner sing,
"My God and King!"
The heav'ns are not too high,
God's praise may thither fly;
The earth is not too low,
God's praises there may grow.
Let all the world in ev'ry corner sing,
"My God and King!"

Let all the world in ev'ry corner sing,
"My God and King!"
The Church with psalms must shout:
No door can keep them out.
But, more than all, the heart
Must bear the longest part.
Let all the world in ev'ry corner sing,
"My God and King!"

A contemporary of Shakespeare, George Herbert was an English poet who lived a short life. He focused on the heart, and many of his hymns were reflections of intimacy with the Lord. This particular hymn, however, expands its vision worldwide and echoes the expansion of the British Empire in the seventeenth century.

The kingdom of God is a global kingdom. It surpasses borders, political affiliations, and languages. Christ opens the gates of his kingdom to all, and he does not deceive or control his people. He is our great liberator. We have reason to join with those around the world and sing, "My God and King!"

Father, you are the King of creation, and I am your child. Be honored to the ends of the earth. May every heart that knows you come alive in your love.

I Have Promised

You are my satisfaction, Lord,
and all that I need,
so I'm determined to do
everything you say.
PSALM 119:57 TPT

O Jesus, I have promised
To serve thee to the end;
Be thou forever near me,
My master and my friend;
I shall not fear the battle
If thou art by my side,
Nor wander from the pathway
If thou wilt be my guide.

O let me hear thee speaking
In accents clear and still,
Above the storms of passion,
The murmurs of self-will.
O speak to reassure me,
To hasten or control;
O speak, and make me listen,
Thou guardian of my soul.

John Ernest Bode wrote this hymn for the confirmation service of his children in 1866. Filled with important messages he wanted his children to remember, this personal hymn was published a couple years later for wider use. Supposedly, it was used so regularly for confirmations that clergy begged their musicians to use anything else. Songs become popular for a reason, though, and whether or not we grow tired of them, we can appreciate the power they have to connect to the listener.

As you read this hymn, which important messages stand out to you? Remember whose you are, child of the King; serving God begins with knowing him and following his leadership. He is good, and he is always with you. Turn to him today, for he is the guardian of your soul.

King Jesus, I humble my life before you time and again.

AUGUST 28

Praise God and King

The trumpeters and musicians joined in unison
to give praise and thanks to the LORD.
Accompanied by trumpets, cymbals and other instruments,
the singers raised their voices in praise to the LORD and sang:
"He is good; his love endures forever."

2 CHRONICLES 5:13 NIV

Praise, O praise our God and King;
Hymns of adoration sing:

For his mercies still endure
Ever faithful, ever sure.

Praise him that he made the sun
Day by day his course to run:

And the silver moon by night,
Shining with her gentle light:

Praise him that he gave the rain
To mature the swelling grain:

Glory to our bounteous King;
Glory let creation sing:
Glory to the Father, Son,
And blest Spirit, Three in One.

This hymn is adapted from a poem on Psalm 136 by John Milton who wrote it in the seventeenth century. Sir Henry Baker wrote the adaption two centuries later as a song of thanks and praise. The theme of God's faithfulness and constant mercy speak to hearts of every generation and age.

As we join our adoration with creation's reverence to the King over all, we offer praise to the one who was, is, and is to come. Let's take every opportunity we have to give thanks to the Lord. Every seemingly insignificant thing counts: the air in our lungs, the sun shining overhead, the hug of a loved one. Every movement of gratitude leads us to look at the present gifts all around us. May God's name be praised for it all.

Worthy One, I am grateful for your fresh mercies. As I tune in to the gifts already present in my life, will you expand my heart in wonder of your goodness?

Word of God Incarnate

In the beginning was the Word,
and the Word was with God,
and the Word was God.

JOHN 1:1 NASB

O Word of God incarnate,
O wisdom from on high,
O truth unchanged, unchanging,
O light of our dark sky,
We praise thee for the radiance
That from the hallowed page,
A lantern to our footsteps,
Shines on from age to age.

O make your Church, dear Savior,
A lamp of purest gold
To bear before the nations
Your true light, as of old.
O teach your wand'ring pilgrims
By this their path to trace
Till, clouds and darkness ended,
They see you face to face.

When "O Word of God Incarnate" was first published in 1867, William How included a subheading quoting Proverbs 6:23 under his hymn's title: "For the commandment is a lamp: and the law is light; and reproofs of instruction are the way of life" (KJV). The theme of this hymn is God being the light illuminating our path.

When you are confused about what direction to go or which steps to take, you can go to the living Word for wisdom. He lights up shadows and offers clarity for your confusion. He is full of wisdom for any circumstance and question. Go to him, nurture the fellowhsip you have with him, and follow his directives. He is a good and perfect leader.

Light of the World, you speak to my heart in clear ways. I'm grateful you do not confuse your children. I trust your leadership as I take your hand.

AUGUST 30

Day of Resurrection

"You have sorrow now, but I will see you again,
and your hearts will rejoice,
and no one will take your joy from you."
JOHN 16:22 ESV

The day of resurrection!
Earth, tell it out abroad;
The passover of gladness,
The passover of God.
From death to life eternal,
From earth unto the sky,
Our Christ hath brought us over,
With hymns of victory.

Now let the heavens be joyful!
Let earth the song begin!
Let the round world keep triumph,
And all that is therein!
Let all things seen and unseen
Their notes in gladness blend,
For Christ the Lord hath risen,
Our joy that hath no end.

Even in our sorrow, we have hope. Death deals heavy blows to our hearts, but Christ has overcome the grip of the grave. The power and promise of his resurrection is our hope, and we can rely on his promise of redemption and restoration.

Taken from the eighth-century canon by John of Damascus, one of the Greek Church fathers, this hymn is a popular Easter hymn in the Orthodox church. The power of Christ's resurrection should not be relegated only to the Easter season, for by this power, we are alive in Christ today. Thank God that his victory is ours! We have reason to rejoice even in our pain and grief. There is always hope in him.

Redeemer, your victory over the grave is my overwhelming hope. Minister to me in my sorrow and bolster my heart with courage and comfort.

Beneath the Cross

It was necessary for him to be made in every respect like us,
his brothers and sisters, so that he could be
our merciful and faithful High Priest before God.
Then he could offer a sacrifice that would take away the sins of the people.

HEBREWS 2:17 NLT

Beneath the cross of Jesus
I fain would take my stand,
The shadow of a mighty rock
Within a weary land;
A home within the wilderness,
A rest upon the way,
From the burning of the noontide heat
And the burden of the day.

Upon the cross of Jesus
Mine eye at times can see
The very dying form of one
Who suffered there for me:
And from my stricken heart with tears
Two wonders I confess,
The wonders of redeeming love
And my unworthiness.

Elizabeth Clephane only lived to be thirty-nine. While in frail health for most of that time, she did not stay isolated in her struggles. She and her sister found ways to help the poor and sick in their small Scottish town and gavetheir extra funds to charity. Her writings were only shared after her death in 1869, and this poem was turned into a hymn.

Clephane must have found respite and hope in the fellowship of Christ. We can know this comfort too. As we "take, O cross, thy shadow for [our] abiding place," we can know the light of God's presence as our constant help. We humble ourselves before him, and he lifts us up (James 4:9).

Savior, I come to the foot of your cross today. I humble myself before you and rely on the light of your countenance to shine on me. Please be near to me today.

September

Blessed assurance, Jesus is mine!
Oh, what a foretaste of glory divine!
Heir of salvation, purchase of God,
Born of his Spirit, washed in his blood.

When I Need Him

My God will use his wonderful riches in Christ Jesus
to give you everything you need.
PHILIPPIANS 4:19 NCV

Just when I need him, Jesus is near,
Just when I falter, just when I fear;
Ready to help me, ready to cheer,
Just when I need him most.

Just when I need him most,
Just when I need him most,
Jesus is near to comfort and cheer,
Just when I need him most.

Just when I need him, Jesus is true,
Never forsaking, all the way through;
Giving for burdens pleasures anew,
Just when I need him most.

Just when I need him, he is my all,
Answering when upon him I call;
Tenderly watching lest I should fall,
Just when I need him most.

Who is without need in this world? Part of the human experience is suffering. We cannot avoid loss or change. What is startling to our souls is not suprising to the Lord, and we can trust him to help in our times of need. Instead of trying to power through, let's look to Jesus who is always near.

There is no such thing as too much need. When we need him the most, when all our plans and provisions have failed, Jesus remains faithful. William Poole's 1907 hymn is a welcome reminder that we all have needs, we all falter, and we all are weak. We can rely on Christ through every transition. He is there "to comfort and cheer, just when [we] need him most."

Jesus, thank you for meeting me in my need and for leading me in love every step. I ask for your help today.

SEPTEMBER 2

Lead Me to Calvary

Calling the crowd along with his disciples, he said to them, "If anyone wants to follow after me, let him deny himself, take up his cross, and follow me."

MARK 8:34 CSB

King of my life I crown thee now—
Thine shall the glory be;
Lest I forget thy thorn-crowned brow,
Lead me to Calvary.

Lest I forget Gethsemane,
Lest I forget thine agony,
Lest I forget thy love for me,
Lead me to Calvary.

Show me the tomb where thou wast laid,
Tenderly mourned and wept;
Angels in robes of light arrayed
Guarded thee whilst thou slept.

May I be willing, Lord, to bear
Daily my cross for thee;
Even thy cup of grief to share—
Thou hast borne all for me.

Jennie Evelyn Hussey (1874-1958) started writing poetic verses when she was just a child. Her first poems were published at the age of thirteen. She grew up in a Quaker home but chose to be baptized into the Baptist Church later in life. Though she dealt with rheumatoid arthritis for all her life, she found reason to still give praise to God.

As we ask the Lord to help us follow him, he answers our cries. We come to him with open hearts and lives, and he fills them with his presence. This doesn't make our lives pain-free, but we know his peace, comfort, love, and joy even in hard times. May we be willing, as Hussey prayed, to bear our daily cross for the Lord, for he gave everything for us.

Lord Jesus, lead me to your cross to remember the cost of your love. Thank you for choosing to move in mercy in everything you did and still do.

Almost Persuaded

Then Agrippa said to Paul,
"You almost persuade me to become a Christian."
And Paul said, "I would to God that not only you,
but also all who hear me today, might become both almost
and altogether such as I am, except for these chains."

Acts 26:28-29 NKJV

Almost persuaded now to believe;
Almost persuaded Christ to receive;
Seems now some soul to say,
Go, Spirit, go thy way;
Some more convenient day
On thee I'll call.

Almost persuaded, come, come today;
Almost persuaded, turn not away;
Jesus invites you here,
Angels are lingering near,
Prayers rise from hearts so dear;
O wanderer, come.

Almost persuaded harvest is past!
Almost persuaded doom comes at last!
Almost cannot avail;
Almost is but to fail!
Sad, sad, that bitter wail,
Almost but lost!

Philip Bliss (1838-1876) was inspired to write this hymn by a sermon he heard from a man named Brundage. The preacher had said the act of almost believing in Christ as Son of God was to almost be saved, but the "almost" lent to them being entirely lost. Are there any areas of your life you are "almost persuaded" to do something about?

2 Corinthians 6:2 says, "Behold, now is the accepted time; behold, now is the day of salvation." Today is all we are promised. We cannot control what will happen tomorrow, but we can choose how we will live this day. Jesus invites us to come to him and be liberated in his love. Let's not linger at the doorway of his lordship any longer. His mercy is powerful; dive into it today.

Lord, help me surrender what needs to be surrendered and to trust you with my whole heart. I turn my almosts over to you today and choose to follow you.

SEPTEMBER 4

Make Me Captive

I can do all things through
him who strengthens me.

Philippians 4:13 ESV

Make me a captive, Lord,
And then I shall be free.
Force me to render up my sword
And I shall conqueror be.
I sink in life's alarms
When by myself I stand;
Imprison me within thine arms,
And strong shall be my hand.

My pow'r is faint and low
Till I have learned to serve;
It lacks the needed fire to glow,
It lacks the breeze to nerve.
It cannot drive the world
Until itself be driv'n;
Its flag can only be unfurled
When thou shalt breathe from heav'n.

Jesus presented many paradoxes to the people as he taught them the ways of God's kingdom. Whoever wants to be first must be last and whoever wants to be great must be a servant are two prime examples. When we are weak, God's power is made perfect in us. Therefore, any hardship is not a reason to despair but to delight.

When we ask the Lord to make us captive to him, it means we will rely on him for all we need. He is our sustenance and strength, and he is incredibly good. In serving him, we find ourselves completely liberated in his love. George Matheson (1842-1906), the writer of this hymn, was completely blind by the age of eighteen. He relied on others, especially his sisters, for research, reading, and writing, but in his weakness, the Lord's power was made strong.

Lord Jesus, I submit my life to you. You are my Lord, and I am your servant. Take care of me and teach me as I serve for your kingdom.

Christ for the World

He said to them,
"But who do you yourselves say that I am?"
Simon Peter answered,
"You are the Christ, the Son of the living God."
MATTHEW 16:15-16 NASB

Christ for the world we sing;
The world to Christ we bring
With loving zeal:
The poor and them that mourn,
The faint and overborne,
Sin-sick and sorrow worn,
Whom Christ doth heal.

Christ for the world we sing;
The world to Christ we bring
With joyful song:
The newborn souls whose days,
Reclaimed from error's ways,
Inspired with hope and praise,
To Christ belong.

Samuel Wolcott (1813-1886) spent two years as a missionary in Syria after graduation from seminary. When he returned to the States, he pastored various churches though his heart for missions remained strong. He wrote this hymn after noticing a Young Men's Christian Association banner at a service he attended with the motto, "Christ for the World, and the World for Christ." He was so inspired, he wrote the hymn that evening on his way home from the service.

Christ's power and message are not reserved for an elite few. Jesus commissioned his disciples to go into all the world and spread the good news of his life-giving message. Join with the heart of God and break down the barriers of religion by living out loud the love Christ has shown you.

Jesus, your good news is still good news today. Use me in my community and beyond. I am yours.

SEPTEMBER 6

Cleansing Wave

If we keep living in the pure light that surrounds him,
we share unbroken fellowship with one another,
and the blood of Jesus, his Son, continually cleanses us from all sin.

1 John 1:7 TPT

Oh, now I see the crimson wave!
The fountain deep and wide;
Jesus, my Lord, mighty to save,
Points to his wounded side.

The cleansing stream I see, I see!
I plunge, and, oh, it cleanseth me!
Oh, praise the Lord, it cleanseth me!
It cleanseth me, yes, cleanseth me.

I rise to walk in heav'n's own light,
Above the world and sin,
With heart made pure and garments white,
And Christ enthroned within.

Amazing grace! 'Tis heav'n below
To feel the blood applied,
And Jesus, only Jesus know,
My Jesus crucified.

Phoebe Palmer (1807-1874) wrote this hymn celebrating the sanctifying power of Jesus' blood with her daughter, Phoebe Knapp, who composed the music. They were active in the holiness movement that erupted in the nineteenth century, and this song was used in many camp meetings.

No matter how we feel about ourselves, when we yield our lives to Christ, we find complete purification in him. His sacrifice is powerful enough to cleanse us from every sin so we stand completely clean before God. We find true freedom and acceptance in him. We will be loved to life in his presence as we remember the power of his blood in our lives.

Christ Jesus, you are the way, the truth, and the life, and I stand redeemed and pure in your sacrifice. Thank you.

If It Were Today

"You also must be ready all the time,
for the Son of Man will come when least expected."
MATTHEW 24:44 NLT

Jesus is coming to earth again—
What if it were today?
Coming in power and love to reign—
What if it were today?
Coming to claim his chosen Bride,
All the redeemed and purified,
Over this whole earth scattered wide—
What if it were today?

Glory, glory!
Joy to my heart 'twill bring;
Glory, glory!
When we shall crown him King.
Glory, glory!
Haste to prepare the way;
Glory, glory!
Jesus will come someday.

Leila Morris's 1912 hymn asks, "What if Christ were to return today?" Would we be ready to receive him? Would we have regrets? Just as we do not know when the end of our lives will be, so we do not know when he will return. It's important to live with intention, surrender, and love as the banner over our lives. Consider what important things you want to be true of your life and make them a priority today.

It is valuable to put our priorities in order on a regular basis. We shouldn't wait until a diagnosis, job transition, or family change to consider whether the lives we are living are the lives we want. Let's keep Christ in our sights, for his presence can transform us. What if we were to see him today?

Lord Jesus, I don't want to waste my life on things that don't matter. I want to live true to who you are. You are my joy, and you bring satisfaction to my soul in the simplest of ways.

Swing Low Sweet Chariot

As they were walking and talking,
a chariot and horses of fire appeared
and separated Elijah from Elisha.
Then Elijah went up to heaven in a whirlwind.

2 Kings 2:11 NCV

Swing low, sweet chariot,
Coming for to carry me home.
Swing low, sweet chariot,
Coming for to carry me home.

I looked over Jordan, and what did I see,
Coming for to carry me home.
A band of angels coming after me,
Coming for to carry me home. Oh.

If you get there before I do,
Coming for to carry me home.
Tell all my friends I'm coming too,
Coming for to carry me home. Oh.

Though its author is unknown, this African American spiritual is one of the best-known of its kind. It approaches death as an occasion to come home to glory and leave the troubles of this world behind. Though many are afraid of death, may we look to the hope we have in Christ as our grounding peace.

We can find comfort in what awaits us in the everlasting kingdom of Christ. Even in times of transition when we leave what we know behind, we can ground ourselves in our true home in Christ. Hebrews 11:16 says of the prophets of old, "they were waiting for a better country—a heavenly country. So God is not ashamed to be called their God, because he has prepared a city for them." Wait for that heavenly country while living by faith.

Father God, your kingdom is where my true hope lies. I want to be found in you all the days of my life. Increase my faith as I live for you.

Jesus I Come

Grace and peace to you from God our Father and the Lord Jesus Christ, who gave himself for our sins to rescue us from the present evil age, according to the will of our God and Father.

GALATIANS 1:3-4 NIV

Out of my bondage, sorrow and night,
Jesus, I come, Jesus, I come;
Into thy freedom, gladness, and light,
Jesus, I come to thee.
Out of my sickness into thy health,
Out of my want and into thy wealth,
Out of my sin and into thyself,
Jesus, I come to thee.

Out of my shameful failure and loss,
Jesus, I come, Jesus, I come;
Into the glorious gain of thy cross,
Jesus, I come to thee.
Out of earth's sorrows into thy balm,
Out of life's storms and into thy calm,
Out of distress to jubilant psalm,
Jesus, I come to thee.

William Sleeper (1819-1904) worked in home missions in Massachusetts and Maine in his ministry. He wrote hymns part-time as well. This hymn is his best known, and it showcases the power of Christ over our adverse circumstances.

In return for all we offer Jesus, we get his peace, love, joy, and hope. The trade is more than in our favor! He is such a gracious savior, and he does not hesitate to shower us with his gracious presence. We need not hold back anything from him today, for he can be trusted to give us far more than we can imagine.

Lord, I'm tired of holding on to things. I choose to surrender to you today knowing that what you offer is far greater. I rest in you, and I trust your power to redeem, restore, and rebuild what seems lost to me.

Saved by Grace

You are saved by grace through faith,
and this is not from yourselves;
it is God's gift.

EPHESIANS 2:8 CSB

Some day the silver cord will break,
And I no more as now shall sing;
But oh, the joy when I shall wake
Within the palace of the King!

And I shall see him face to face,
And tell the story—Saved by grace;
And I shall see him face to face,
And tell the story—Saved by grace.

Some day, when fades the golden sun
Beneath the rosy-tinted west,
My blessed Lord will say, "Well done!"
And I shall enter into rest.

Some day: till then I'll watch and wait,
My lamp all trimmed and burning bright,
That when my Savior opens the gate,
My soul to him may take its flight.

Though our bodies age, our health fails, and our hearts are tried, the reality of God's glorious kingdom awaits. We shall see him face to face as Fanny Crosby's song reminds us. We are saved by grace and not by anything we do or don't do. It is a gracious gift from a generous God.

It is not wrong to look at our mortality. We won't live forever in these failing bodies, but our souls will live on. There is more joy than we can imagine waiting in the courts of our King. We can live for him today and hold on to the power of his resurrection life that points us to the hope of our own.

Redeemer, I long for the day when I will see you face to face with nothing between us. Until that day, keep me close to your heart and covered in your love.

On the Lord's Side

You shall also be a crown of glory
In the hand of the LORD,
And a royal diadem
In the hand of your God.
ISAIAH 62:3 NKJV

Who is on the Lord's side? Who will serve
the King?
Who will be his helpers, other lives to bring?
Who will leave the world's side? Who will face
the foe?
Who is on the Lord's side? Who for him
will go?
By thy call of mercy, by thy grace divine,
We are on the Lord's side—Savior, we are
thine!

Not for weight of glory, nor for crown
and palm,
Enter we the army, raise the warrior psalm;
But for love that claimeth lives for whom
he died:
He whom Jesus saveth marches on his side.
By thy love constraining, by thy grace divine,
We are on the Lord's side—Savior, we are
thine!

Frances Havergal was a nineteenth-century English poet and hymn writer. Her hymn is a challenge to our souls. Are we on the Lord's side? If we belong to the Savior, doing the work of our Father, then our lives will show it. How we treat others is a large part of this. If we create division rather than sow seeds of peace, we may want to look again at the life Christ called us to as his followers.

The truth of Christ's ministry is not diminished by time. It stands firm forever. Let's not be quick to excuse our lack of love when he has called us to love our enemies just as well as we love our friends. We must keep our hearts humble and teachable as we follow his lead. None of us know better than God, so let's allow his Word to penetrate our hearts and correct us when we need it.

Faithful One, you are the only one perfectly pure, true, and faithful. I want to reflect those values in my choices and relationships. Help me, for I am yours.

The Lord Will Provide

Abraham called the name of that place,
"The LORD will provide";
as it is said to this day,
"On the mount of the LORD it shall be provided."
GENESIS 22:14 ESV

In some way or other the Lord will provide,
It may not be my way,
It may not be thy way,
And yet in his own way, the Lord will provide.

At some time or other the Lord will provide;
It may not be my time,
It may not be thy time,
And yet in his own time, the Lord will provide.

Despond then no longer, the Lord will provide;
And this be the token
No word he hath spoken
Was ever yet broken; the Lord will provide.

March on, then, right boldly; the sea shall
divide;
The path shall be glorious;
With shoutings victorious
We'll join in the chorus; the Lord will provide.

Though this nineteenth-century hymn has fallen into obscurity, its message is poignant. Though we may have ideas about how God should provide, he knows better than we do. "It may not be my way, it may not be thy way" says the hymnist, Martha Cook, "and yet in his own way, 'the Lord will provide.'" Do we truly trust him to do so?

The Lord is faithful to provide for his children. He did so for the Israelites, he did for Jesus, and he does so for us today. Perhaps if we let go of what the provision had to look like, our faith could expand as he meets our needs in ways we don't anticipate. "Despond then no longer, the Lord will provide."

Provider, thank you for the reminder of your faithfulness and the reminder that your provision doesn't always look how I expect it to. Your nature is more constant than my expectations, and I delight in trusting you.

Haven of Rest

Then they were glad because they were quiet,
So He guided them to their desired harbor.
PSALM 107:30 NASB

My soul in sad exile was out on life's sea,
So burdened with sin, and distressed,
Till I heard a sweet voice saying,
"Make me your choice,"
And I entered the haven of rest.

I've anchored my soul in the haven of rest,
I'll sail the wide seas no more;
The tempest may sweep
o'er the wild stormy deep,
In Jesus I'm safe evermore.

I yielded myself to his tender embrace,
And faith taking hold of the Word,
My fetters fell off, and I anchored my soul:
The haven of rest is my Lord.

Oh, come to the Savior, he patiently waits
To save by his power divine;
Come, anchor your soul in the haven of rest,
And say, "My beloved is mine."

We rarely appreciate the calm as poignantly as we do right after a fierce storm. When waves crash, winds howl, and chaos rages, we feel the fragility of life. Though we cannot escape the storms of life, we can know the peace of Christ, a haven and safe harbor, in the midst of them.

As Jesus calms the storms of our souls and speaks peace to the waves, we experience a haven of rest in his presence. We are never without him. May we yield ourselves to Christ's tender embrace, as Henry Gilmour so eloquently put it in this hymn from 1885. As we do, our souls are anchored in his limitless love.

Prince of Peace, you are my stronghold when the world is shaking. I trust you as my safe place and haven of rest. Flood me with your peace today as I yield to your embrace.

SEPTEMBER 14

The Higher Rock

From the ends of the earth,
I cry to you for help
when my heart is overwhelmed.
Lead me to the towering rock of safety.

Psalm 61:2 NLT

O sometimes the shadows are deep,
And rough seems the path to the goal,
And sorrows, sometimes how they sweep
Like tempests down over the soul!

O then to the rock let me fly,
To the rock that is higher than I;
O then to the rock let me fly,
To the rock that is higher than I!

O sometimes how long seems the day,
And sometimes how weary my feet;
But toiling in life's dusty way,
The rock's blessed shadow, how sweet!

O near to the rock let me keep
If blessings or sorrow prevail,
Or climbing the mountain way steep,
Or walking the shadowy vale.

Erastus Johnson wrote this hymn while attending a Young Men's Christian Association convention in 1871. While at the conference, news came through of a financial panic. Many banks failed, leading many who had money with them to lose their funds. In light of the common feeling of despair that settled over the conference, Johnson wrote the text and gave it to one of the musicians. At that very convention, it was sung many times.

When we are rocked by life-changing news, we may feel the same desparation many of those men felt. What can we do? We can always run to the rock that is higher than we are. He is not shaken even when our lives are turned upside down. We can find our footing in the shelter of the Most High, for he will take care of us.

Rock of Ages, I take comfort that you are not discouraged by what discourages me. You are the rock that is higher than I, and I run to you.

Take the Name

"Jesus is the only One who can save people.
No one else in the world is able to save us."

Acts 4:12 NCV

Take the name of Jesus with you,
Child of sorrow and of woe.
It will joy and comfort give you,
Take it then where'er you go.

Precious name, O how sweet!
Hope of earth and joy of heaven;
Precious name, O how sweet!
Hope of earth and joy of heaven.

Take the name of Jesus ever
As protection ev'rywhere.
If temptations 'round you gather,
Breathe that holy name in prayer.

At the name of Jesus bowing,
When in heaven we shall meet,
King of kings, we'll gladly crown him
When our journey is complete.

First published in 1870, Lydia Baxter's hymn reminds us to carry Jesus throughout our days and lives. He is a faithful companion as close as his name is on our lips. Like an urging from a dear friend, "Take the Name of Jesus with You" is wisdom for all who will take it.

As we go about our lives, as we interact with loved ones, acquaintances, and strangers, Jesus' presence is with us. We can call on his name no matter where we are or what we are facing. He is a faithful helper, and he will not leave us without the strength of his grace. He is more than we can imagine, and he is always available to us. Let's not take this for granted, but even if we do, we can choose to turn around at any point.

Jesus, your presence is life, strength, and joy to my soul. You empower me by your Spirit. I will take your name with me everywhere I go.

Living Spirit

"Afterward, I will pour out my Spirit on all people.
Your sons and daughters will prophesy,
your old men will dream dreams,
your young men will see visions."

JOEL 2:28 NIV

O Spirit of the living God,
In all the fullness of your grace,
Wherever human feet have trod,
Descend upon our fallen race.

Give tongues of fire and hearts of love
To preach the reconciling Word;
Anoint with power from heaven above
Whenever gospel truth is heard.

Let darkness turn to radiant light,
Confusion vanish from your path;
Those who are weak inspire with might:
Let mercy triumph over wrath!

Baptize the nations; far and near
The triumphs of the cross record;
Till Christ in glory shall appear
And every race declare him Lord! Amen.

The Spirit of God is not often given the address of an entire hymn. However, we know no parts of the Trinity are better than others; Father, Son, and Spirit are one. They are God. We should not hesitate to entreat the Spirit of God just as we do the Father or Jesus. The Spirit is as divine as our Heavenly Father and the Son of God.

James Montgomery wrote this as a mission song in 1823 to be sung at a meeting of the Auxiliary Missionary Society. Each of us, whether we are in ministry or not, need the Spirit's work in our lives. He continues to teach us the ways of Christ, bring deeper understanding, comfort us in our sorrow, prepare our hearts to receive him, and lead us into the throne room of our God. There is nothing God's Spirit cannot do.

Holy Spirit, thank you for your work in my life. I am yielded to you. Have your way and move through me.

Banner of the Cross

You have given a signal flag
to those who fear you,
so that they can flee before the archers.
Selah.

Psalm 60:4 CSB

There's a royal banner given for display
To the soldiers of the King;
As an ensign fair we lift it up today,
While as ransomed ones we sing.

Marching on, marching on,
For Christ count ev'rything but loss!
And to crown him King,
toil and sing 'neath the banner of the cross!

Though the foe may rage and gather as the
flood,
Let the standard be displayed;
And beneath its folds, as soldiers of the Lord,
For the truth be not dismayed!

When the glory dawns 'tis drawing very near—
It is hast'ning day by day;
Then before our King the foe shall disappear,
And the cross the world shall sway!

Major Daniel Whittle was a soldier in the Civil War who rose through the ranks. After the war, he moved to Chicago to work for a clock company but left that work to go into full-time ministry with Dwight L. Moody. He wrote many hymns, and "The Banner of the Cross" is one. Perhaps drawing from his military background, the theme of God's banner raised over the "soldiers of the King" reminds us we do not labor for ourselves. Everything we do is under the banner of Christ's cross.

When life feels like more of a battleground than a calm field, look to the one who leads his people well. His banner over you is love. Trust he will not let you down or leave you to fight on your own.

King Jesus, you have my allegiance. May your name and nature be glorified in my life.

SEPTEMBER 18

Song in the Air

Suddenly there was with the angel
a multitude of the heavenly host praising God.

LUKE 2:13 NKJV

There's a song in the air!
There's a star in the sky!
There's a mother's deep prayer
And a baby's low cry!
And the star rains its fire
While the beautiful sing,
For the manger of Bethlehem
Cradles a King!

There's a tumult of joy
O'er the wonderful birth,
For the virgin's sweet boy
Is the Lord of the earth.
Ay! The star rains its fire
While the beautiful sing,
For the manger of Bethlehem
Cradles a King!

Although this song from 1872 is a lesser-known Christmas carol by Josiah Holland, its message is just as poignant in the transition of seasons. The star over Bethlehm pointed the Magi to the Messiah. The stars still speak of his wonders and point our hearts to their Creator.

If you listen, you will hear a song in the air today. It speaks of Christ's coming and of his death and resurrection. It sings of his unceasing wonders and points to his coming again. Rejoice in the light, for it shines brightly today.

Messiah, thank you for the way nature points toward you. I join with creation's song to praise your glory. Open my eyes so I may see more of you today.

Circle Be Unbroken

You are not foreigners or guests,
but rather you are the children of the city of the holy ones,
with all the rights as family members of the household of God.

Ephesians 2:19 TPT

There are loved ones in the glory
Whose dear forms you often miss,
When you close your earthly story
Will you join them in their bliss?

Will the circle be unbroken
by and by, yes, by and by?
In a better home awaiting
In the sky, in the sky?

In the joyous days of childhood,
Oft they told of wondrous love,
Pointed to the dying Savior,
Now they dwell with him above.

One by one their seats were empty,
One by one they went away,
Now the fam'ly is parted,
Will it be complete one day?

This hymn is a gospel lament about our mortality and the question of whether we will be united with our loved ones as our mortal bodies fail. Ada Habershon (1861-1918) was an English hymnist, Bible teacher, and author, and her song "Will the Circle Be Unbroken" remains a standard to this day.

It is a tender, painful moment when someone we love passes from this world. Their place in our lives cannot be replaced. As we feel the sting of their absence, let us hope in Christ who is God over all and God over us. Let's lean on his comfort and the sweet embrace of his love. Our story is not finished yet, and the love of our dear ones lives on in us until we see them again.

Lord, I believe there will be a great reunion in your kingdom. I long for it, but I also know there is goodness to be had here and now. Be near in comfort.

SEPTEMBER 20

Lord Our Righteousness

No one has ever seen God;
the only God, who is at the Father's side,
he has made him known.

JOHN 1:18 ESV

Jesus, your blood and righteousness
My beauty are, my glorious dress;
Mid flaming worlds, in these arrayed,
With joy shall I lift up my head.

Bold shall I stand in that great day;
Who can a word against me say?
Fully absolved through these I am
From sin and fear, from guilt and shame.

Lord, I believe your precious blood,
Which at the very throne of God
Pleads for the captives' liberty,
Was also shed in love for me.

Jesus, be worshiped endlessly!
Your boundless mercy has for me,
For me and all your hands have made,
An everlasting ransom paid.

Nicolaus Ludwig Zinzendorf was a noble count in eighteenth-century Germany. He had all the wealth he could dream of, yet he resigned from all public duties in 1731 and devoted himself to missionary work. He was the founder of the Moravian religious community in Herrnhut, Germany. His hymn, "The Lord our Righteousness," reads as a beautiful statement of faith.

As you read through the hymn today, which stanza speaks to you the most? Consider carrying it with you the rest of the day. The Lord our righteousness goes with us, and when we turn our attention to him, our hearts join with his presence and acknowledge the power of his mercy in our lives.

Lord, as I go about my day, help me meditate on the truth of your righteousness and mercy. What you are is more than enough for me.

Whispering Hope

This hope we have as an anchor of the soul,
a hope both sure and reliable
and one which enters within the veil.

Hebrews 6:19 NASB

Soft as the voice of an angel,
Breathing a lesson unheard,
Hope with a gentle persuasion
Whispers her comforting word:
Wait till the darkness is over,
Wait till the tempest is done,
Hope for the sunshine tomorrow,
After the shower is gone.

Whispering hope, oh, how welcome thy voice,
Making my heart in its sorrow rejoice.

Septimus Winner composed this hymn and published it under the pseudonym Alice Hawthorne in 1868. He wrote many popular secular songs, and it is said he never intended "Whispering Hope" to be a sacred hymn. Still, as we read its lyrics, it's hard to imagine it as anything but.

In our sorrow, we can still learn to rejoice in hope. That whispering hope breathes life into our hearts. Hope is an anchor to our souls as both this hymn and Scriptures say. It keeps us grounded in the truth of Christ's love which never leaves or forsakes us. May we each know the incredible relief a whisper of hope brings as we allow Christ's presence to wash over us.

God of my hope, there isn't a moment I am without your presence, and that brings me peace. Whisper to me as I turn my attention to you.

Yield Not to Temptation

Humble yourselves before God.
Resist the devil, and he will flee from you.
JAMES 4:7 NLT

Yield not to temptation,
For yielding is sin;
Each vict'ry will help you,
Some other to win;
Fight valiantly onward,
Evil passions subdue;
Look ever to Jesus,
He will carry you through.

Ask the Savior to help you,
Comfort, strengthen and keep you;
He is willing to aid you,
He will carry you through.

H.R. Palmer (1834-1907) wrote this hymn in while working on one area of his expertise: music theory. The idea came to him quickly, so he laid aside the theoretical work and composed the lyrics and melody to "Yield Not to Temptation." With its roots in Scripture, this hymn is a reminder that temptation is not in itself a sin. When we yield to it, then we are compromised.

1 Corinthians 10:13 says, "No temptation has overtaken you except what is common… and God is faithful… when you are tempted, he will also provide a way out so that you can endure it" (NIV). God helps us in our temptation as this hymn reminds us. Do not afraid to ask your Savior for help when you need it.

Savior, you were tempted to a great many things when you walked this earth, yet you didn't sin. Fill me with the law of your love and give me grace and strength to follow in your footsteps. I need you.

Little Brown Church

Lord, I love the Temple where you live,
where your glory is.
Psalm 26:8 NCV

There's a church in the valley by the wildwood,
No lovelier spot in the dale;
No place is so dear to my childhood
As the little brown church in the vale.

Come to the church in the wildwood,
Oh, come to the church in the vale;
No spot is so dear to my childhood
As the little brown church in the vale.

How sweet on a clear Sunday morning,
To list to the clear ringing bell;
Its tones so sweetly are calling,
Oh, come to the church in the vale.

From the church in the valley by the wildwood,
When day fades away into might,
I would fain from this spot of my childhood
Wing my way to the mansions of light.

It is said that William Pitts' hymn was a prophetic poem. On a trip to visit his future wife, he had to wait for the stagecoach to change, and he saw a perfect little spot for a church. He wrote the poem "Church in the Wildwood" based on it. Years later, he taught this song to his students who would sing it at the dedication of the very church he had envisioned but never shared with anyone.

These happy accidents are wonderful gifts. The Lord loves to surprise us, and how encouraging to know we are connected in some way to each other and to the King of heaven. As you read through this hymn, consider how you have been surprised by a dream come to life.

Lord, you are infinitely wise and wonderful. Your hand is at work in this world and in my life. Encourage my heart in hope today.

Land of Pure Delight

Your eyes will see the king in his beauty
and view a land that stretches afar.

ISAIAH 33:17 NIV

There is a land of pure delight,
Where saints immortal reign;
Infinite day excludes the night,
And pleasures banish pain.

There everlasting spring abides,
And never-withering flowers;
Death, like a narrow sea, divides
That heavenly land from ours.

But timorous mortals start and shrink
To cross the narrow sea,
And linger shivering on the brink,
And fear to launch away.

O could we make our doubts remove,
Those gloomy doubts that rise,
And see the Canaan that we love
With unbeclouded eyes.

This is another hymn from one of the greatest hymn writers in history, Isaac Watts (1674-1748). The poem likens the "land of pure delight" to heaven. The Israelites were looking forward to their promised land which they found in Canaan. We find our eternal promised land in the kingdom of Christ where we will join him as we cross the shores from this life into the next.

Remember: this short life is not the end. That is not to say we shouldn't enjoy it while we have it, but there are far greater things in the abundant land of God's kingdom of heaven. We will find our fullness there. Let's not despair when the days are hard, for we have a promised land full of peace, plenty, and endless delight.

King of Heaven, keep my perspective fixed on you and your everlasting kingdom. This temporary home is not the only goodness I will know. I trust your unfailing love to guide me to your promised land of peace.

Saved

He is able to save completely
those who come to God through him,
since he always lives to intercede for them.
HEBREWS 7:25 CSB

I've found a friend who is all to me,
His love is ever true;
I love to tell how he lifted me,
And what his grace can do for you.

Saved by his pow'r, by his pow'r divine,
Saved to new life, to new life sublime!
Life now is sweet and my joy is complete,
For I'm saved, saved, saved.

He saves me from ev'ry sin and harm,
Secures my soul each day;
I'm leaning strong on his mighty arm—
I know he'll guide me all the way.

When poor and needy and all alone,
In love he said to me,
"Come unto me and I'll lead you home
To live with me eternally."

Packed with the joy of salvation, this hymn was inspired by an outburst in a meeting Jack Scholfield (1882-1972) attended. The evangelist, Mordecai Ham, was preaching on Christ as our refuge when a man who had murdered several men in his past jumped up and shouted, "Saved! Saved! Saved!" Scholfield composed both the words and music the next day, and it was sung that evening.

What joy there is in knowing that, no matter what we have done, the Lord redeems us as we yield our lives to him. We can shout it from the rooftops: we are saved by his power! Thank God our salvation is not dependent on our works, for all of us fall short of the glory of God. Through Christ, we come alive in the liberty of his love where all our sins are washed away.

Savior, I can't begin to thank you for the power of your salvation in my life. I am free in you! Thank you.

Ninety and Nine

"What man of you, having a hundred sheep,
if he loses one of them,
does not leave the ninety-nine in the wilderness,
and go after the one which is lost until he finds it?"

LUKE 15:4 NKJV

There were ninety and nine that safely lay
In the shelter of the fold,
But one was out on the hills away,
Far off from the gates of gold,
Away on the mountains wild and bare,
Away from the tender Shepherd's care.

"Lord, thou hast here thy ninety and nine:
Are they not enough for thee?"
But the Shepherd made answer,
"This of mine has wandered away from me,
And although the road be rough and steep,
I go to the desert to find my sheep."

And all through the mountains, thunder-riven,
And up from the rocky steep,
There rose a glad cry to the gate of heaven,
"Rejoice! I have found my sheep!"
And the angels echoed around the throne,
"Rejoice, for the Lord brings back his own."

Elizabeth Clephane wrote this beautiful poem in the late nineteenth century. It was first published in 1868 in a small children's magazine. It was then included in a series of her hymns. It picked up popularity when a Mr. Sankey set it to music and sang it at gospel meetings he held.

The power of the prose is in the development of Jesus' words in Luke 15. The third verse poignantly paints a picture of the journey the shepherd took to find the one sheep who wandered away. Our God is strong to save and goes to any length to bring us back to the safety of his care. He pursues us relentlessly in kindness. How could we not be grateful?

Good Shepherd, thank you for making the power of this story sink deeper into my understanding. You are good, and I am grateful.

Precious to Me

Beloved, we are God's children now,
and what we will be has not yet appeared;
but we know that when he appears we shall be like him,
because we shall see him as he is.

1 John 3:2 ESV

So precious is Jesus, my Savior, my King,
His praise all the day long with rapture I sing;
To him in my weakness for strength I can cling,
For he is so precious to me.

For he is so precious to me,
For he is so precious to me;
'Tis heaven below, my Redeemer to know,
For he is so precious to me.

He stood at my heart's door in sunshine and rain
And patiently waited an entrance to gain;
What shame that so long he entreated in vain,
For he is so precious to me.

I stand on the mountain of blessing at last,
No cloud in the heavens a shadow to cast;
His smile is upon me, the valley is past,
For he is so precious to me.

When we call something precious, it is of great value to us. When Charles Gabriel, the writer of this 1902 hymn, declares, "He is so precious to me," the tenderness and value of his relationship with Christ ring through the lyrics. Have you known Jesus as a faithful friend and powerful savior? Sing this song to him directly and allow it to express the depths of your gratitude.

There are wonderful treasures in fellowship with the living God and his Spirit. No matter how long it takes someone to come to him, Jesus stands at the door of the heart and knocks. Let's answer his call by making time and room for him in our day. He is precious to those who know him.

Jesus, you are the most precious gift I have. I will not neglect your Spirit who draws me nearer to your heart today.

SEPTEMBER 28

Light of the World

The one who is the true light,
who gives light to everyone,
was coming into the world.
JOHN 1:9 NLT

The whole world was lost in the darkness of sin,
The Light of the World is Jesus!
Like sunshine at noonday, his glory shone in;
The Light of the World is Jesus!

Come to the light, 'tis shining for thee;
Sweetly the light has dawned upon me;
Once I was blind, but now I can see:
The Light of the World is Jesus!

No darkness have we who in Jesus abide;
The Light of the World is Jesus!
We walk in the light when we follow our guide!
The Light of the World is Jesus!

No need of the sunlight in heaven we're told;
The Light of the World is Jesus!
The Lamb is the light in the city of gold,
The Light of the World is Jesus!

Jesus is the Light of the World as he himself stated in John 8:12. As we embrace Christ and his life-giving light, we are promised we will never walk in darkness. Philip Bliss wrote this hymn in the nineteenth century, and its invitation is still open. "Come to the light… shining for thee."

Take some time to come into the light of God's presence. He has clarity for your confusion, peace for your chaos, and wisdom for your questions. He is faithful to lead you step by step in his glorious goodness. Follow your heavenly guide and rest in the light of his presence today.

Light of the World, you light the path in front of me. Draw near to me as I draw near to you. I rely on you.

The Cross Leads Home

"I am the way, and the truth, and the life;
no one comes to the Father except through Me."
John 14:6 NASB

I must needs go home by the way of the cross,
There's no other way but this;
I shall ne'er get sight of the gates of light,
If the way of the cross I miss.

The way of the cross leads home,
The way of the cross leads home;
It is sweet to know as I onward go,
The way of cross leads home.

I must needs go on in the blood sprinkled way,
The path that the Savior trod,
If I ever climb to the heights sublime,
Where the soul is at home with God.

Then I bid farewell to the way of the world,
To walk in it nevermore;
For the Lord says, "Come," and I seek my home
Where he waits at the open door.

Jessie Brown Pounds wrote this hymn in 1906 to emphasize that following Christ does not mean following the path of least resistance. When we choose to follow Christ, we have to continually die to ourselves and put the law of his love above our preferences. Fortunately, the way of his cross always leads us home.

Jesus is the way, the truth, and the life. We come to the Father of creation through him. We are liberated in his love poured out on the cross, and we come alive in the power of his resurrection life. Let's humble ourselves before God as often as we think of it, for his ways are not our ways, and his thoughts are higher than ours.

Lord Jesus, I follow the path of your love not knowing exactly where it will lead me. I only know it will lead me home. You are my leader and my companion, and I trust you.

SEPTEMBER 30

To Be Like Thee

God knew his people in advance,
and he chose them to become like his Son,
so that his Son would be the firstborn
among many brothers and sisters.

ROMANS 8:29 NLT

Oh! To be like thee, blessed Redeemer,
This is my constant longing and prayer;
Gladly I'll forfeit all of earth's treasures,
Jesus, thy perfect likeness to wear.

Oh! To be like thee, Oh! To be like thee,
Blessed Redeemer, pure as thou art;
Come in thy sweetness, come in thy fullness;
Stamp thine own image deep on my heart.

Oh! To be like thee, lowly in spirit,
Holy and harmless, patient and brave;
Meekly enduring cruel reproaches,
Willing to suffer, others to save.

Oh! To be like thee, while I am pleading,
Pour out thy Spirit, fill with thy love,
Make me a temple meet for thy dwelling,
Fit me for life and heaven above.

Published in 1897, Thomas Chisholm's hymn is a prayer to be like our glorious Redeemer. Jesus Christ—full of compassion, helping the helpless, pursuing the wanderer, and forgiving all who yield to his love—is the greatest standard to reach for. He empowers us by his Spirit, and he transforms our hearts as we surrender to his mercy.

We don't become like Jesus by accident. We don't wake up one day and unconsiously choose the law of his love rather than self-protection, pride, and exclusion. As we submit to his leadership, follow his wisdom, and put his truth into practice, we take steps to becoming more like him. We don't do this to earn our salvation, for we are saved by grace alone.

Perfect One, while I am weak, you are strong. I don't want to rely on my goodness to get me through. I lean on your love, for it is life to me.

October

To God be the glory, great things he hath done;
So loved he the world that he gave us his Son,
Who yielded his life an atonement for sin,
And opened the life gate that all may go in.

OCTOBER 1

Ring the Bells

"There is joy in the presence of the angels of God
when one sinner changes his heart and life."
LUKE 15:10 NCV

Ring the bells of heaven!
There is joy today,
For a soul, returning from the wild!
See, the Father meets him out upon the way,
Welcoming his weary, wandering child.

Glory! Glory! How the angels sing:
Glory! Glory! How the loud harps ring!
'Tis the ransomed army, like a mighty sea,
Pealing forth the anthem of the free.

Ring the bells of heaven!
There is joy today,
For the wanderer now is reconciled;
Yes, a soul is rescued from his sinful way,
And is born anew, a ransomed child.

William Cushing's nineteenth-century hymn is one of triumphant joy over each soul saved and set free in Christ. Scripture tells us there is rejoicing over even one soul who surrenders to the Lord and comes home in him. In times of great celebration past and present, the tolling of bells is a key element. What do you think when you hear church bells ring?

The next time you hear the chime of bells, whether it be in a city center or rural community, remember this hymn. God pursues us with loyal love all the days of our lives. As we yield our hearts to him, there is great rejoicing. Let's celebrate the significance of such things. There is joy in the restoration of a lost soul.

Loving Father, you know how to celebrate better than anyone. I look forward to eternally rejoicing with you. For now, please show me your joy in the little things.

Trusting Jesus

Commit your way to the LORD;
trust in him and he will do this.
PSALM 37:5 NIV

Simply trusting every day,
Trusting through a stormy way;
Even when my faith is small,
Trusting Jesus, that is all.

Trusting as the moments fly,
Trusting as the days go by;
Trusting him whate'er befall,
Trusting Jesus, that is all.

Brightly doth his Spirit shine
Into this poor heart of mine;
While he leads I cannot fall;
Trusting Jesus, that is all.

Singing if my way is clear,
Praying if the path be drear;
If in danger for him call;
Trusting Jesus, that is all.

Edward Page Stites wrote this poem in 1876. It first appeared in the newspaper, and when it came into the hands of evangelist Dwight L. Moody, he passed it along to his song leader, Ira Sankey, to set it to music. Its simple message is timeless, and we can bolser our hearts in hope as we simply trust Jesus every day.

As you go through your day, consider how you can deepen your trust in Christ. When an unexpected crisis emerges, offer him the weight of it and ask for his wisdom. When you don't know what to do, pray for his help and trust him to come through. He is faithful to help all who call on his name. May your trust deepen as you witness his faithfulness time and time again.

Faithful God, I need your help in more ways than I can express. Thank you for your loyal love that never leaves me. Help me trust you with my whole heart.

OCTOBER 3

Wondering Soul

I did not hide your righteousness in my heart;
I spoke about your faithfulness and salvation;
I did not conceal your constant love and truth
from the great assembly.

Psalm 40:10 CSB

Where shall my wondering soul begin?
How shall I all to heaven aspire?
A slave redeemed from death and sin,
A brand plucked from eternal fire,
How shall I equal triumphs raise,
Or sing my great deliverer's praise?

And shall I slight my Father's love,
Or basely fear his gifts to own?
Unmindful of his favors prove,
Shall I, the hallowed cross to shun,
Refuse his righteousness to impart,
By hiding it within my heart?

Outcasts of men, to you I call,
Harlots, and publicans, and thieves;
He spreads his arms to embrace you all,
Sinners alone his grace receive.
No need of him the righteous have;
He came the lost to seek and save.

Charles Wesley wrote this hymn in the same timeframe as his famous hymn, "And Can It Be That I Should Gain?" in 1738. Together, they are a wonderful testimony of a time when Wesley went through a spiritual transformation. Though this hymn is the lesser known of the pair, it is still powerful.

Consider your testimony of coming to the Lord. Let your wondering soul begin where it will. Each of us has a unique story to tell about how the Lord has transformed our lives, and the details of those stories become our testimony. Let's not hold back from digging in to our history with God, for we will find the treasure of his mercies as we do.

Savior, thank you for the power of your mercy at work in my life. Remind me of what felt so powerful at first and widen my heart in awe of who you are and what you have done.

Ye Heavens Adore

Praise the Lord!
Praise the Lord from the heavens;
Praise Him in the heights!

Psalm 148:1 NKJV

Praise the Lord! Ye heav'ns adore him;
Praise him angels, in the height;
Sun and moon, rejoice before him;
Praise him, all ye stars of light.
Praise the Lord! For he has spoken;
Worlds his mighty voice obeyed;
Laws which never shall be broken
For their guidance he has made.

Praise the Lord! For he is glorious;
Never shall his promise fail;
God has made his saints victorious;
Sin and death shall not prevail.
Praise the God of our salvation!
Hosts on high his pow'r proclaim;
Heav'n, and earth, and all creation,
Laud and magnify his name.

Originally, the first two verses of this hymn were printed in a four-page tract at the end of some copies of a popular hymnal at the end of the eighteenth century. A third verse was later added, but the hymn has been used both with and without this addition. Either way, the call to praise is directly from the Word of God.

How will you offfer worship, honor, glory, and blessing to the Lord today? Will you bow your heart before him in adoration? He is at work in your life, and he will not leave you to carry your burdens alone. Trust in him, rely on him, and offer him what you cannot and need not shoulder. He is your ever-present help and glorious Redeemer.

Glorious One, there is no one like you in all the universe. I offer you the praise you are due, and as I do, increase my awareness of who you are.

Into Your Heart

"Behold, I stand at the door and knock.
If anyone hears my voice and opens the door,
I will come in to him and eat with him, and he with me."

REVELATION 3:20 ESV

If you are tired of the load of your sin,
Let Jesus come into your heart;
If you desire a new life to begin,
Let Jesus come into your heart.

Just now your doubtings give o'er;
Just now reject him no more;
Just now throw open the door;
Let Jesus come into your heart.

If 'tis for purity now that you sigh,
Let Jesus come into your heart;
Fountains for cleansing are flowing near by,
Let Jesus come into your heart.

If you would join the glad songs of the blest,
Let Jesus come into your heart;
If you would enter the mansions of rest,
Let Jesus come into your heart.

Lelia Morris was active in her local church and in camp meetings in the area. She wrote hymns and gospel songs beginning in the 1890s. The story of this particular hymn is from a set of meetings she atttended in 1898. A refined woman went forward to respond to the altar call, and Lelia went to encourage her. The woman had doubts, and Lelia told her to give her doubts to Jesus. Afterward, Lelia remembered her words and composed them into a hymn.

Jesus can handle our doubts. He doesn't require that we do not have them; he only wants them not to hinder us from walking through the door of his love. As we open our hearts to him, he comes into our hearts and makes us his home.

Jesus, my heart is yours. I offer you my doubts, and I don't resist your mercy. Come in, minister to me, and make your home in me.

My Title Clear

I will rejoice greatly in the LORD, My soul will be joyful in my God;
For He has clothed me with garments of salvation,
He has wrapped me with a robe of righteousness,
As a groom puts on a turban,
And as a bride adorns herself with her jewels.

ISAIAH 61:10 NASB

When I can read my title clear
To mansions in the skies,
I'll bid farewell to every fear,
And wipe my weeping eyes.

I'm goin' to trust in the Lord,
I'm goin' to trust in the Lord,
I'm goin' to trust in the Lord till I die.

Should earth against my soul engage,
And fiery darts be hurled,
Then I can smile at Satan's rage,
And face a frowning world.

There shall I bathe my weary soul
In seas of heavenly rest,
And not a wave of trouble roll
Across my peaceful breast.

Isaac Watts originally titled this hymn, "The Hope of Heaven Our Support under Trials on Earth" when he included it in a collection of his hymns in 1707. This puts the rest of the hymn in context. It was never meant to put our salvation under question; it was meant as an encouragement until we stand before Christ.

As we rely on the Lord and trust him every day, our hope remains strong. May we be intentional with connecting to the God of ages who meets with us. Until we are face to face with him in glory, let's do as Isaac Watts encouraged in this hymn and choose to trust the Lord.

Jesus, I put my trust in you. No matter what comes, no matter what hurdles I must jump or messes I must wade through, help me trust you every step of the way.

Not Skilled to Understand

The healed man replied,
"I have no idea what kind of man he is.
All I know is that I was blind and now I can see
for the first time in my life!"

JOHN 9:25 TPT

I am not skilled to understand
What God hath willed, what God hath planned;
I only know at his right hand
Is one who is my Savior!

I take him at his word indeed:
"Christ died for sinners," this I read;
And in my heart I find a need
Of him to be my Savior!

That he should leave his place on high
And come for sinful man to die,
You count it strange? So once did I,
Before I knew my Savior!

Yes, living, dying, let me bring
My strength, my solace from this spring;
That he who lives to be my King
Once died to be my Savior!

Dora Greenwell was a nineteenth-century English poet. Her poem was set to music by William Kirkpatrick, and it became a beloved hymn. Greenwell's poetry reveals the questions she wrestled with in her own challenges and the struggles of the suffering children she worked with. Instead of dwelling on unknowable things, however, she allowed the unanswered questions to simply be while trusting that God is faithful through it all.

Each of us can relate to struggling to make sense of God's nature in a world full of pain and suffering. As we offer him our questions, can we receive the comfort of his presence at the same time? Can we be okay in the liminal space of not knowing and still trust him? Let's take him at his word, for he is our faithful God.

Jesus, I bring you all my questions knowing you don't turn me away. Where there are no sufficient answers, settle my heart in your peace. I choose to trust you still.

I Love to Proclaim

You know that God paid a ransom to save you
from the empty life you inherited from your ancestors.
And it was not paid with mere gold or silver, which lose their value.
It was the precious blood of Christ, the sinless, spotless Lamb of God.

1 Peter 1:18-19 NLT

Redeemed, how I love to proclaim it!
Redeemed by the blood of the Lamb;
Redeemed through his infinite mercy,
His child, and forever, I am.

Redeemed, redeemed,
Redeemed by the blood of the Lamb;
Redeemed, how I love to proclaim it!
His child, and forever, I am.

I think of my blessed Redeemer,
I think of him all the day long;
I sing, for I cannot be silent;
His love is the theme of my song.

I know I shall see in his beauty
The King in whose law I delight,
Who lovingly guardeth my footsteps,
And giveth me songs in the night.

Written as a reflection of the joy of her salvation experience, Fanny Crosby published this hymn in 1882. Her numerous hymns are still sung today. If this one is less familiar, take some time to read through it or listen to it. "Redeemed, How I Love to Proclaim It!" is an anthem of how we've been embraced by the love of God and liberated in the power of his sacrifice for us. We forever belong to him.

If we have lost the conviction with which we once knew our redemption, we have only to ask the Lord for a fresh encounter with his mercy. Don't hold anything back from him. He is faithful to redeem and restore, and he will not ignore the cries of his children.

Redeemer, thank you for saving me by the power of your love. I humble myself before you again. Meet me, lift my face to see your glory, and reveal the power of your mercy that still meets me in fresh waves.

OCTOBER 9

I Must Tell Jesus

He can help those who are tempted,
because he himself suffered and was tempted.

HEBREWS 2:18 NCV

I must tell Jesus all of my trials;
I cannot bear these burdens alone;
In my distress he kindly will help me;
He ever loves and cares for his own.

I must tell Jesus!
I must tell Jesus!
I cannot bear my burdens alone;
I must tell Jesus!
I must tell Jesus!
Jesus can help me, Jesus alone.

I must tell Jesus all of my troubles;
He is a kind, compassionate friend;
If I but ask him, he will deliver,
Make of my troubles quickly an end.

O how the world to evil allures me!
O how my heart is tempted to sin!
I must tell Jesus, and he will help me
Over the world the vict'ry to win.

Elisha Hoffman wrote this hymn in 1894. Among the thousands of hymns he wrote, this one stands the test of time because its message reminds us we can always throw our cares on Jesus. His friendship weathers every storm and trial, and his presence never recedes.

The Lord understands our struggles, for he faced temptations, trials, and suffering in his life on earth. He is able to help and empower us; we need never bear our burdens alone. As soon as our minds start to race and the weight of worry covers our chests, we can to turn our burdens over to Christ. He will help us with every one.

Jesus, thank you for your friendship. Help me as I bring you my cares and problems. I need you.

All I Need

It is because of him that you are in Christ Jesus,
who has become for us wisdom from God—
that is, our righteousness, holiness and redemption.

1 Corinthians 1:30 NIV

Jesus Christ is made to me,
All I need, all I need,
He alone, is all my plea,
He is all I need.

Wisdom, righteousness and pow'r,
Holiness forevermore,
My redemption full and sure,
He is all I need.

He's the treasure of my soul,
All I need, all I need,
He hath cleansed and made me whole,
He is all I need.

Glory, glory to the Lamb,
All I need, all I need,
By his Spirit sealed I am,
He is all I need.

Charles Price Jones wrote this hymn in 1908, and it is a timely reminder whenever it is sung. Jesus Christ is all we need no matter the time, place, or circumstance. His sacrifice was enough for once and for all. Christ's victory is our own, and we find our fullness in him.

Throughout the day, remember this age-old truth: "He is all I need." Through storms and times of peace, he is all we need. In our weakness, he is all we need. Our redemption is not in question; he remains all we need. This is not an excuse to ignore the needs of others but rather to press us closer to the presence of God who empowers us to help in love. He is all we need.

All in All, you are the source of everything I need. Please meet my weakness with your strength, my confusion with your wisdom, and my chaos with your peace.

OCTOBER 11

Clouds Descending

"Then the sign of the Son of Man will appear in the sky,
and then all the peoples of the earth will mourn;
and they will see the Son of Man coming on the clouds of heaven
with power and great glory."

MATTHEW 24:30 CSB

Lo! He comes with clouds descending,
Once for ev'ry sinner slain;
Thousand, thousand saints attending
Swell the triumph of his train:
Alleluia, alleluia, alleluia!
Christ reveals his endless reign.

Ev'ry eye shall now behold him
Robed in glorious majesty;
Those who set at naught and sold him,
Pierced and nailed him to the tree,
Deeply wailing, deeply wailing, deeply wailing,
Shall their true Messiah see.

Yea, amen, let all adore thee
High on thine eternal throne;
Savior, take the pow'r and glory,
Claim the kingdom as thine own.
Alleluia, alleluia, alleluia!
Thou shalt reign, and thou alone!

This hymn by Charles Wesley was taken from an earlier hymn John Cennick published as "Lo! He Cometh, Countless Trumpets." Wesley heavily revised the text, and it became the hymn we now know. Based on the second coming of Christ in Revelation and the glory we await in that day, this hymn directs our hearts in hope to that blessed day.

Most hymns are based on what Christ already accomplished and not on the impending glory of what he has yet to do, but not this one. It looks ahead with joy. Our hearts will swell with hope as we fix our eyes on Christ who was, who is, and who is still to come.

Savior, creation longs and waits for your second coming. Oh, that you would rend the heavens and come down to rule and reign forever! Come quickly, Lord, and be near as we wait.

The Lord Is King

The LORD reigns, He is clothed with majesty;
The LORD is clothed,
He has girded Himself with strength.
Surely the world is established,
so that it cannot be moved.

PSALM 93:1 NKJV

The Lord is King! Lift up thy voice,
O earth, and all ye heavens, rejoice;
From world to world the joy shall ring,
"The Lord omnipotent is King!"

The Lord is King! Who then shall dare
Resist his will, distrust his care,
Or murmur at his wise decrees,
Or doubt his royal promises?

He reigns! Ye saints, exalt your strains;
Your God is King, your Father reigns;
And he is at the Father's side,
The Man of love, the Crucified.

One Lord one empire all secures;
He reigns, and life and death are yours;
Through earth and heaven one song shall ring,
"The Lord omnipotent is King!"

Josiah Conder was an editor in nineteenth-century London, a writer of poems and hymns, and an abolitionist. Though we do not know the exact circumstances of the writing of this hymn, we do know Conder drew inspiration from various psalms. Psalm 10:16 declares, "The Lord is King forever and ever." Many other psalms speak of God's rule over the world and the majesty adorning him.

The Lord omnipotent—all powerful and able to do absolutely anything—is King above all. Let's remember his power and strength as we remain rooted in the present world. He alone rules, and there is nothing he cannot do. Let's raise our expectations to Christ, who can do all things, and refuse to be weighed down by worry.

Omnipotent King, you are more than able to do anything I could imagine and more. I trust you to faithfully fulfill your promises.

OCTOBER 13

The Grace of Christ

The grace of our Lord Jesus Christ
be with you all.
2 THESSALONIANS 3:18 ESV

May the grace of Christ our Savior
And the Father's boundless love
With the Holy Spirit's favor
Rest upon us from above.
Thus may we abide in union
With each other and the Lord,
And possess in sweet communion
Joys which earth cannot afford.

John Newton (1725-1807) was a contemporary of John Wilberforce and became an ardent abolitionist after giving up the slave trade. Previously, he was captain of a slave ship. He eventually left that life behind once convicted by the values of his faith.

Among the many hymns he penned, this simple doxology is a paraphrase of 2 Corinthians 13:14: "The grace of the Lord Jesus Christ and the love of God and the fellowship of the Holy Spirit be with you all." It is often used to close out services. In our gatherings with other believers, let's not lose sight of the power of blessing one another. It is a practice the apostles used to close out their letters, and we can benefit from using it in our interactions. Before you go on with your day, read this hymn once more, and receive it as the prayer it is. "May the grace of Christ..."

Christ Jesus, thank you for the boundless love you show. Keep me abiding in you and in unity with your children until I am standing before you in glory.

Sands of Time

"Then suddenly, in the middle of the night,
they were awakened by the shout
'Get up! The bridegroom is here!
Come out and have an encounter with him!'"

MATTHEW 25:6 TPT

The sands of time are sinking,
The dawn of heaven breaks,
The summer morn I've sighed for,
The fair sweet morn awakes;
Dark, dark hath been the midnight,
But dayspring is at hand,
And glory, glory dwelleth
In Emmanuel's land.

The King there in his beauty
Without a veil is seen;
It were a well-spent journey,
Though sev'n deaths lay between:
The Lamb with his fair army
Doth on Mount Zion stand,
And glory, glory dwelleth
In Emmanuel's land.

Ann Cousin wrote this hymn based on the letters and ministry of seventeeth-century Scottish pastor Samuel Rutherford. The hymn was first published in two centuries later in 1865. It's a poetic expression of the coming glory of Christ's return as well as the magnificence of his everlasting kingdom.

Picture an hourglass. The sands of time truly are sinking through the glass, and every moment brings us closer to the fulfillment of his promises and the restoration of all things. What a glory that shall be!

Eternal King, thank you for the promise of your faithful return. Keep my heart entrenched in your mercy and my focus fixed on you, my King and my God.

A Story for the Nations

"You, child, also will be called the prophet of the Most High;
For you will go on before the Lord to prepare His ways."

LUKE 1:76 NASB

We've a story to tell to the nations,
That shall turn their hearts to the right,
A story of truth and mercy,
A story of peace and light.

For the darkness shall turn to dawning,
And the dawning to noonday bright,
And Christ's great kingdom shall come on earth,
The kingdom of love and light.

We've a song to be sung to the nations,
That shall lift their hearts to the Lord,
A song that shall conquer evil,
And shatter the spear and sword.

We've a Savior to show to the nations,
Who the path of sorrow has trod,
That all of the world's great peoples
May come to the truth of God!

Henry Ernest Nichol wrote this popular children's hymn in 1896. Nearly all the hymns Nichol wrote were for children. Though he first studied to be an engineer, he changed his focus to music early on in his schooling and graduated from Oxford with a bachelor's degree in music.

What a story we have to tell the nations! What a story both children and adults alike can tell of Christ's kingdom. It is good news for all people everywhere. As you read, sing, or listen to this hymn today, remember the good news of your salvation. Whom can you share this wonderful news with today?

Lord Jesus, your gospel is profound and powerful. Your love exceeds all expectations. Continue to transform me in your mercy and move through me as I partner with you in telling others of your goodness.

All Things Are Possible

"What do you mean, 'If I can'?" Jesus asked.
"Anything is possible if a person believes."
MARK 9:23 NLT

All things are possible to him
That can in Jesus' name believe;
Lord, I no mote thy truth blaspheme,
Thy truth I lovingly receive;
I can, I do believe in thee;
All things are possible to me.

Though earth and hell the word gainsay,
The Word of God can never fail;
The Lamb shall take my sins away,
'Tis certain, though impossible;
The thing impossible shall be,
All things are possible to me.

When thou the work of faith hast wrought,
I here shall in thine image shine,
Nor sin in deed or word or thought;
Let men exclaim and fiends repine,
They cannot break the firm decree;
All things are possible to me.

The Word of God makes it clear: all things are possible with God. Charles Wesley's hymn also promotes this timeless truth. It was first published in 1749 in his collection Hymns for Those That Wait for Full Redemption. As we wait for the full redemption of the earth, we can hold on to the truth that nothing is impossible for God.

Not only are all things possible with God, but Jesus also said this is true for the person who believes (Mark 9:23). With our faith rooted in Christ, we are encouraged to take him at his Word. Let's lean on the everlasting goodness and limitless power of our God as we wait for the redemption of all things.

Redeemer, I believe every wrong will be made right one day. Help me to press on in faith and trust your timing until this truth comes to bear.

OCTOBER 17

Done All Things Well

They were completely amazed and said,
"Jesus does everything well. He makes the deaf hear!
And those who can't talk he makes able to speak."

Mark 7:37 NCV

Now in a song of grateful praise,
To thee, O Lord, my voice I'll raise:
With all thy saints I'll join to tell,
My Jesus has done all things well.

And above the rest this note shall swell,
This note shall swell, this note shall swell,
And above the rest this note shall swell,
My Jesus has done all things well.

How sov'reign, wonderful, and free
Has been thy love to sinful me!
Thou sav'dst me from the jaws of hell;
My Jesus has done all things well.

Since e'er my soul has known his love,
What mercies he has made me prove!
Mercies which do all praise excel!
My Jesus has done all things well.

This hymn was very popular in the early nineteenth century, but it has been obscured by the passage of time. Samuel Medley (1738-1799) continually pointed back to the theme of this song by ending each verse and refrain with "My Jesus has done all things well."

As you look back over your life, can you see the goodness of Jesus? Pray for the Spirit to open your eyes to the details time has caused you to overlook; see how he has done all things well. You don't have to prove his goodness to yourself. Simply ask for his help to see it, and when you do, praise him with a grateful heart.

Faithful One, remind me of the power of your mercy in my life and open my eyes to understand what I could not before. You are good to me, and I believe I will continue to see your goodness as long as I am in the land of the living.

The Cross Is Not Greater

The law was brought in so that the trespass might increase.
But where sin increased, grace increased all the more.

Romans 5:20 NIV

The cross that he gave may be heavy,
But it ne'er outweighs his grace;
The storm that I feared may surround me,
But it ne'er excludes his face.

The cross is not greater than his grace,
The storm cannot hide his blessed face;
I am satisfied to know
That with Jesus here below,
I can conquer ev'ry foe. Amen.

The thorns in my path are not sharper
Than composed his crown for me;
The cup which I drink not more bitter
Than he drank in Gethsemane.

Ballington Booth (1857-1940) was the son of William Booth, the man who founded the Salvation Army. When he grew up, he joined the ministry, preached, and performed music. He eventually traveled from England to Australia and then to North America. After disagreements with his father and brother about where he should live, he and his wife began their own ministry in the U.S. called Volunteers of America.

Booth knew disappointment and struggle. However, as this hymn reminds us, whatever burdens we have in this life, none are greater than the grace of God. Whatever sorrows or weakness we have, the grace of God is more abundant than these things. His generous grace meets us in these places and compensates for our inability to stand alone. The grace of God is poignant, practical, and always near.

Gracious God, thank you for never leaving me in my troubles. I rely on your grace which far outweighs the weight of the crosses I bear in this life.

A Stranger Here

We are aliens and temporary residents
in your presence as were all our ancestors.
Our days on earth are like a shadow, without hope.

1 Chronicles 29:15 CSB

I'm but a stranger here,
Heaven is my home;
Earth is a desert drear;
Heaven is my home:
Danger and sorrow stand
Round me on every hand;
Heaven is my fatherland,
Heaven is my home.

There at my Savior's side,
Heaven is my home;
I shall be glorified,
Heaven is my home.
There are the good and blest,
Those I love most and best;
And there I too shall rest,
Heaven is my home.

Written during his last illness, this hymn by Thomas Rawson Taylor is all about setting our hearts on our eternal home. This hymn was published with others a year after his death in 1835 at the young age of twenty-eight. Perhaps his illness propelled Taylor to fixate on heaven as his home. No matter how long we have on this earth, we all face mortality. Does our hope lie beyond our little lives?

As you spend time reading through "I'm but a Stranger Here," allow the question of your hope and faith in Christ to bubble to the surface. Hard realitites are not something to ignore but rather something to explore. Christ the Lord is a safe landing place for our wrestling, and he offers peace that surpasses any we can achieve alone.

Jesus, the brevity of life, though it seems so harsh, is not our end. I believe there is more beyond the veil of death. My hope is built on you, Lord.

Roll Call

We must all appear before the judgment seat of Christ,
that each one may receive the things done in the body,
according to what he has done, whether good or bad.

2 Corinthians 5:10 NKJV

When the trumpet of the Lord shall sound and
time shall be no more,
And the morning breaks, eternal, bright and fair;
When the saved of earth shall gather over on
the other shore,
And the roll is called up yonder, I'll be there.

When the roll is called up yonder,
When the roll is called up yonder,
When the roll is called up yonder,
When the roll is called up yonder, I'll be there.

On that bright and cloudless morning when
the dead in Christ shall rise,
And the glory of his resurrection share;
When his chosen ones shall gather to their
home beyond the skies,
And the roll is called up yonder, I'll be there.

Let us labor for the master from the dawn
till setting sun;
Let us talk of all his wondrous love and care.
Then when all of life is over and our work
on earth is done,
And the roll is called up yonder, I'll be there.

The turning of the seasons can signal us to reflect on the passing of time. For those entering the winter of their lives, take hope in the fellowship of your Savior who never changes. How has the firm foundation of his love kept you grounded? The one who has been faithful will continue even to the end.

James Milton Black's "When the Roll Is Called Up Yonder" was written for his youth Sunday School class, and it was published in 1893. It is never too early or late to think about when we will stand before the Lord. Do our lives reflect the values of his kingdom? We can yield to his ways, for he is trustworthy and true. He will not fail us.

Faithful Lord, I don't want to strive for your attention, and I trust I don't have to. Help me rest in the salvation of my soul found only in you. Encounter me with the power of your love as I live for the glory of your name.

OCTOBER 21

Deliverance Will Come

Moses said to Hobab the son of Reuel the Midianite, Moses' father-in-law,
"We are setting out for the place of which the LORD said,
'I will give it to you.'
Come with us, and we will do good to you,
for the LORD has promised good to Israel."

NUMBERS 10:29 ESV

I saw a wayworn trav'ler
In tatter'd garments clad,
His back was laden heavy,
His strength was almost gone,
And struggling up the mountain
It seem'd that he was sad;
Yet he shouted as he journeyed,
Deliverance will come.

I heard the song of triumph
They sang upon that shore,
Saying, Jesus has redeemed us
To suffer nevermore;
Then, casting his eyes backward
On the race which he had run,
He shouted loud, "Hosanna,
Deliverance has come!"

The authorship of this hymn is sometimes attributed to Reverend John Matthias in 1836 though he had no history of song-writing. Without much documentation, the question remains up in the air, but it has been attributed to no other author. Also known as "Palms of Victory" and "The Way-Worn Traveler," this hymn follows the arc of a specific story.

It is a song of perseverance and echoes the journey each of our lives takes. "Onward" is the cry that keeps us going. Let's keep our eyes fixed on the author of our faith, Jesus Christ, who goes with us and redeems, delivers, and saves us in full.

Deliverer, my hope is set on you. As I journey through this life, I need your steady hand and wisdom to guide and strengthen me along the way. Help me keep going and follow your every step.

Give of Your Best

Glorify God with all your wealth,
honoring him with your firstfruits,
with every increase that comes to you.

PROVERBS 3:9 TPT

Give of your best to the master;
Give of the strength of your youth;
Throw your soul's fresh, glowing ardor
Into the battle for truth.
Jesus has set the example,
Dauntless was he, young and brave;
Give him your loyal devotion;
Give him the best that you have.

Give of your best to the master;
Give of the strength of your youth;
Clad in salvation's full armor,
Join in the battle for truth.

Colossians 3:23 encourages us, "Whatever you do, work at it with all your heart, as working for the Lord" (NIV). No matter what kind of work we do, when we give our best, we honor the Lord with our offering. Howard Grose (1851-1939) worked in ministry for the majority of his adult life, and this hymn reflects a heart longing to serve the Lord well and encourage others to do the same.

It is no small gift to do the necessary but mundane things of this life as if we are offering them to the Lord. Others may notice the work we put into cleaning, caring for our loved ones, or building a business, but none to the extent the Lord does. Even if our service goes overlooked by others, the Lord sees every movement of faithfulness and love. Offer it all to him.

Lord, thank you for seeing my efforts. I offer you my best, and when that has run out, I offer you the rest. May your acknowledgment matter the most to me.

OCTOBER 23

Praying for You

If you also join in helping us through your prayers,
so that thanks may be given by many persons in our behalf
for the favor granted to us through the prayers of many.

2 Corinthians 1:11 NASB

I have a Savior, he's pleading in glory,
A dear, loving Savior, though earth-friends
be few;
And now he is watching in tenderness o'er me,
But O, that my Savior were your Savior, too!

For you I am praying,
For you I am praying,
For you I am praying,
I'm praying for you.

I have a Father; to me he has given
A hope for eternity, blessed and true;
And soon will he call me to meet him in
heaven,
But O, that he'd let me bring you with
me, too!

When he has found you, tell others the story,
That my loving Savior is your Savior, too;
Then pray that your Savior may bring them to
glory,
And prayer will be answered—'twas answered
for you!

The writer of this hymn was an Irish pastor named Samuel Cluff (1837-1910). When Ira Sankey, traveling with Dwight L. Moody, found this text written on a leaflet in London, he composed music to accompany it. It then spread through many nations and was sung the world over.

Prayer is powerful. It moves our hearts to connect to the divine, let go of what we cannot control, and ask for what we need. Even Jesus participates in prayer. God's Word says Jesus lives to make intercession for us; he is praying for us even now. Let's join with his heart and pray for those around us especially when we are at a loss for what to do.

Savior, it is almost too much to know you pray for me. It takes the weight of responsibility to be perfect off my mind. Lord, I choose to partner with you and pray for all I encounter today. Please move through my prayers and answer them.

Safe to the Rock

Turn your ear to listen to me;
rescue me quickly.
Be my rock of protection,
a fortress where I will be safe.

Psalm 31:2 NLT

O safe to the rock that is higher than I,
My soul in its conflicts and sorrows would fly.
So sinful, so weary, thine, thine would I be;
Thou blest Rock of Ages, I'm hiding in thee.

Hiding in thee, hiding in thee,
Thou blest Rock of Ages, I'm hiding in thee.

How oft in the conflict, when pressed by
the foe,
I have fled to my refuge and breathed out
my woe.
How often when trials like sea billows roll
Have I hidden in thee, O thou rock of my soul.

William Cushing wrote this hymn in 1876 after Ira Sankey requested something to help him in his gospel work. This hymn was born out of Cushing's own battles throughout his life. The imagery of God as a solid rock and refuge is used at least fifty times in the Bible. In that rock, we can hide anytime and anywhere.

When our hearts are wrestling with sorrow and questions, God is a safe place to run to. He can handle our messes, and he hides us in the shadow of his wings. We can run to him in times of trouble whether they be soul troubles, physical ones, or a mix of both. Hiding ourselves in him is not escaping this life but rather being rooted in the peace of his presence in the midst of it.

Almighty God, thank you for accepting me as I come to you. You do not force me to be happy, perfect, or uncomplicated. I run to you, just as I am, knowing you receive me. I hide myself in you, and there I find rest and come alive.

Kindly Light

The LORD guards you.
The LORD is the shade that protects you from the sun.
The LORD will guard you as you come and go,
both now and forever.

PSALM 121:5, 8 NCV

Lead, kindly light, amid the gloom of evening.
Lord, lead me on! Lord, lead me on!
On through the night! On to your radiance!
Lead, kindly light!
Lead, kindly light, kindly light!

The night is dark, and I am far from home,
Direct my feet; I do not ask to see
The distant scene; one step enough for me.
So lead me onward, Lord, and hear my plea.

Not always thus, I seldom looked for you,
I loved to choose and seek my path alone.
In spite of fear, my pride controlled my will,
Remember not my past, but lead me still.

So long your pow'r has blest me on the way,
And still it leads, past hill and storm and night!
And with the morn, those angel faces smile,
Which I have loved long since, and lost a
while.

John Henry Newman (1801-1890) penned this text while traveling by boat from Italy to France. He was recovering from a serious illness, and the seeming desperation of the refrain reveals what he must have felt at the time. Much like many of the psalms, this song is from a place of sheer helplessness the author felt when reaching out to the God whom he trusted.

No matter where we are in our lives, we can reach out to God for help. Call on his leadership and his grace to empower you in your weakness. He is faithful to help all who cry out to him.

Faithful One, thank you for your leadership in my life. You are the light illuminating the darkness around me, and you bring me peace. Lead me on, kindly Light; lead me on.

Heavenly Love Abiding

"As the Father has loved me,
so have I loved you.
Now remain in my love."

John 15:9 NIV

In heavenly love abiding,
No change my heart shall fear;
And safe is such confiding,
For nothing changes here:
The storm may roar without me,
My heart may low be laid;
But God is round about me,
And can I be dismayed?

Green pastures are before me,
Which yet I have not seen;
Bright skies will soon be o'er me,
Where darkest clouds have been;
My hope I cannot measure,
My path to life is free;
My Savior has my treasure,
And he will walk with me.

The writer of this hymn, Anna Waring (1823-1910), included Psalm 23:4 as an accompaniment when she penned it. That verse reads, "Even though I walk through the darkest valley, I will fear no evil, for you are with me; your rod and your staff, they comfort me."

As we learn to abide in the love of Christ, we can trust his leadership as he guides us through the twists and turns of this life. He is a faithful provider at every step. He does not require us to make our own way; we follow his. Though that path may look different for each of us, the fruit of his Spirit remains the same.

Lord, lead me with your Spirit and settle my heart in your confident presence. You are my courage, shield, and strength.

Lead Me Gently Home

My steps are on your paths;
my feet have not slipped.
PSALM 17:5 CSB

Lead me gently home, Father,
Lead me gently home,
When life's toils are ended,
And parting days have come,
Sin no more shall tempt me,
Ne'er from thee I'll roam,
If thou'lt only lead me, Father,
Lead me gently home.

Lead me gently home, Father,
Lead me gently,
Lest I fall upon the wayside,
Lead me gently home.

For Will Lamartine Thompson, music was a huge part of life. He studied music at various conservatories, and he formed his own publishing firm in Chicago in the late nineteenth century. Of his many hymns, two of the most well-known are "Jesus Is All the World to Me" and "Softly and Tenderly Jesus Is Calling." The tone of his hymns, including this one, reveals a child of God who knows the tender love of his Father.

As we yield our hearts to the Lord, his love leads us. Though some people want to go out with a bang, others find a gentle release more appealing. Whatever way we go, may we follow the tender lead of the Lord who draws us in with loving kindness and leads us in gracious mercy.

Father, I do not take for granted the power and pleasure of a simple life lived with you by my side. When all is said and done, lead me gently home.

Majestic Sweetness

All bore witness to Him, and marveled at the gracious words which proceeded out of His mouth. And they said, "Is this not Joseph's son?"

Luke 4:22 NKJV

Majestic sweetness sits enthroned
Upon the Savior's brow;
His head with radiant glories crowned,
His lips with grace o'erflow.

No mortal can with him compare,
Among the sons of men;
Fairer is he than all the fair
Who fill the heav'nly train.

He saw me plunged in deep distress,
And flew to my relief;
For me he bore the shameful cross,
And carried all my grief.

To him I owe my life and breath,
And all the joys I have;
He makes me triumph over death,
and saves me from the grave.

Originally published in 1782, Samuel Stennett's hymn was accompanied by the title, "Chief among ten thousand." This praise hymn uplifts the character and providence of Christ. He is not only clothed in majesty but also with sweetness. Christ, our living Word, is sweeter than honey to our mouths.

Take some time today to meditate on the glory of God as described in Scripture. If it helps, consider the works of his hands which point to his wisdom, power, and strength. Don't forget how kind and considerate he is. Don't neglect the delight of his heart for his children. He is too wonderful for words.

Living Word, expand my understanding of your greatness and goodness as I meditate on who you are. Reveal the power of your being and refresh my heart in the reality of your beauty.

Still, Still with Thee

How precious to me are your thoughts, O God!
How vast is the sum of them!
If I would count them, they are more than the sand.
I awake, and I am still with you.

Psalm 139:17-18 ESV

Still, still with thee, when purple morning
breaketh,
When the bird waketh, and the shadows flee;
Fairer than morning, lovelier than daylight,
Dawns the sweet consciousness I am
with thee.

Alone with thee amid the mystic shadows,
The solemn hush of nature newly born;
Alone with thee in breathless adoration,
In the calm dew and freshness of the morn.

Still, still with thee! As to each newborn
morning
A fresh and solemn splendor still is given,
So does this blessed consciousness, awaking,
Breathe each day nearness unto thee and
heaven.

So shall it be at last, in that bright morning,
When the soul waketh, and life's shadows flee;
O in that hour, fairer than daylight dawning,
Shall rise the glorious thought, I am with thee.

Harriet Beecher Stowe was an author, and she is best known for her novel Uncle Tom's Cabin. Though most of her hymns have not remained in common use, this one is a notable exception. She wrote this after a morning walk with the Lord, which she reportedly did every morning, in 1853. The poetic frame of the hymn, as well as the stark imagery of early morning, evokes an almost tangible world in which we can set ourselves.

As you read through this hymn, imagine yourself in a quiet wooded area at the break of morning. As we walk with the Lord through life, he meets us in mundane moments. The ordinary becomes extraordinary as we become aware of his glory. What a sweet communion it is to walk with the Lord.

Lord, I want to know you in the stillness and the chaos. Speak to me in quiet morning hours and above the din of the waking world. I want to know you more.

Matchless Worth

Who in the skies is comparable to the LORD?
Who among the sons of the mighty is like the LORD?

PSALM 89:6 NASB

O could I speak the matchless worth,
O could I sound the glories forth
Which in my Savior shine,
I'd soar and touch the heavenly strings,
And vie with Gabriel while he sings
In notes almost divine,
In notes almost divine.

I'd sing the characters he bears,
And all the forms of love he wears,
Exalted on his throne.
In loftiest songs of sweetest praise,
I would to everlasting days
Make all his glories known,
Make all his glories known.

Reflecting the gratitude of his salvation, Samuel Medley's 1878 hymn tells of the matchless worth of Christ. Whether or not our salvation story is dramatic, the person of Christ remains the same. His glory is matchless, and the love he pours out on us is always abundant.

Think about how the Lord has transformed your life as you've followed him. What kind of treasures has he hidden in the imprints of his mercy on your life? Allow your heart to reach out to your Savior, for he is near, and he is still working. Nothing is impossible for him, and he has not finished writing your story.

Lord, how can I describe the effect you've had on me? I am yours, and I humble myself before you. Remind me of the power of your practical and abundant mercy at work in my life. I praise you, for you have been good to me.

OCTOBER 31

Met to Worship

The LORD said to Moses,
"I will cause food to fall like rain from the sky for all of you.
Every day the people must go out
and gather what they need for that day.
I want to see if the people will do what I teach them."
EXODUS 16:4 NCV

Brethren, we have met to worship
And adore the Lord our God;
Will you pray with all your power,
While we try to preach the Word?
All is vain unless the Spirit
Of the Holy One comes down;
Brethren, pray, and holy manna
Will be showered all around.

Brethren, see poor sinners round you
Slumb'ring on the brink of woe;
Death is coming, hell is moving,
Can you bear to let them go?
See our fathers and our mothers,
And our children sinking down;
Brethren, pray and holy manna
Will be showered all around.

Not much is known of the Methodist minister who penned this hymn in the early nineteenth century including his name. It was either George Askins or George Atkins, distinct persons who shared many similarities. While the use of "brethren" may seem outdated, there is also the inclusion of "sisters" in verse three. The family of God is not divided by gender, and we can honor that as we remember we are brothers and sisters in the kingdom of Christ.

As we come to the Lord, he provides what we need. We pray, and he answers. Just as God showered down manna for the Israelites in the desert, literally providing their daily bread, so we can trust our Father provides what we need. Let us remember to pray as Christ did: "Give us this day our daily bread."

Lord God, you are a good father, and I trust you to provide for my needs.

November

When I survey the wondrous cross
On which the Prince of Glory died,
My richest gain I count but loss,
And pour contempt on all my pride.

NOVEMBER 1

Thank We Our God

Listen to this, Job.
Stop and consider God's wonders.

Job 37:14 CSB

Now thank we all our God
With heart and hands and voices,
Who wondrous things has done,
In whom his world rejoices;
Who from our mothers' arms
Has blessed us on our way
With countless gifts of love,
And still is ours today.

O may this bounteous God
Through all our life be near us,
With ever joyful hearts
And blessed peace to cheer us,
To keep us in his grace,
And guide us when perplexed,
And free us from all ills
Of this world in the next.

A simple prayer of thanksgiving, this hymn has ministered to us hundreds of years after its composition. Martin Rinkart (1536-1649) ministered in the city of Eilenburg during the Thirty Years War. He officiated over four thousand funerals during that time and sometimes up to fifty a day.

Has God's nearness been a comfort to you? Has the provision of your daily bread caused your faith in him to grow? Take some time to thank God for all the little ways he shows up in your day. He is so good, and he is always near. There are hints of his mercy hidden all around us from the birds above us to the love of a friend.

Faithful Provider, even when we go through hard times, you are near. Your blessings are present. Open my eyes to see where you are working in mercy and faithfulness.

Plow the Fields

"While the earth remains,
Seedtime and harvest,
Cold and heat, Winter and summer,
And day and night
Shall not cease."

GENESIS 8:22 NKJV

We plow the fields and scatter
The good seed on the land,
But it is fed and watered
By God's almighty hand.
God sends the snow in winter,
The warmth to swell the grain,
The breezes, and the sunshine,
And soft refreshing rain.

All good gifts around us are sent from heav'n
above.
We thank you, God, we thank you, God, for
all your love.

Matthias Claudius (1740-1815) grew up in a Lutheran home, but he wandered from his faith in his twenties and thirties. A serious illness brought him back to his roots of faith. He went on to write many devotional poems, but this is the only one in common use today as a hymn.

God is practical. He partners with our efforts to increase their effectiveness. We may put our hands to sowing seeds, plowing fields, and other necessary work, but God sends the rain and the sun to produce a harvest. As followers of Christ, we recognize our dependence on him even as we partner with him.

Jesus, your empowering grace is the strength of my life. I choose to follow you and to do my work. Even so, I rely on your hand of mercy to increase my efforts.

Break Bread Together

I will cry out to you,
the God of the highest heaven,
the mighty God,
who performs all these wonders for me.
PSALM 57:2 TPT

Let us break bread together on our knees.
Let us break bread together on our knees.

When I fall on my knees with my face to the rising sun,
O Lord have mercy on me.

Let us drink wine together on our knees.
Let us drink wine together on our knees.

Let us praise God together on our knees.
Let us praise God together on our knees.

This African American spiritual cannot be traced, but it probably dates back to the eighteenth century. Stanzas have been added throughout the years by oral tradition. This hymn may have been used as a signal song among enslaved people to communicate with one another. When we recognize "rising sun" as a metaphor for God, we can see why it is used in communion services especially with the themes of breaking bread, drinking wine, and humbling ourselves in worship.

As we humble ourselves before the Lord today, whether together with others or in our personal time with him, we can pray for God to have mercy on us. He surely will. Christ is our help, hope, and Savior.

Lord Jesus, I know the practice of communion recognizes the power of your sacrifice and the freedom of your resurrection life. I will take time to honor you as I break the bread and drink the cup in remembrance of your sacrifice.

O Love How Deep

I pray that you, being rooted and established in love,
may have power, together with all the Lord's holy people,
to grasp how wide and long and high and deep is the love of Christ.

EPHESIANS 3:17-18 NIV

O love, how deep, how broad, how high,
Beyond all thought and fantasy,
That God, the Son of God, should take
Our mortal form for mortals' sake!

He sent no angel to our race,
Of higher or of lower place,
But wore the robe of human frame,
And to this world himself he came.

For us baptized, for us he bore
His holy fast and hungered sore;
For us temptation sharp he knew,
For us the tempter overthrew.

All glory to our Lord and God
For love so deep, so high, so broad,
The Trinity whom we adore
Forever and forevermore.

The scope of this text is the whole life of Christ from birth to ascension. It comes from an anonymous Latin text from the fifteenth century, and it was translated to English by Benjamin Webb in the nineteenth century. As we meditate on Christ's life, we can see the beauty of his humanity. He chose to come to earth as a vulnerable baby and live within the confines of flesh and bones so we might know what God the Father is truly like.

Perhaps you hold on to ideas about who God is that Jesus came to shift. Take some time in the gospels and read his teachings. Ask the Holy Spirit to reveal mindsets you hold that simply are not true. God is merciful, patient, and kind. He is fierce in love, unashamed in truth, and available to all who come to him.

Lord God, I want to know you in spirit and truth. Reveal the truth of who you are and shift my false perspectives. I want to know you more.

Rejoice Pure in Heart

Be glad in the LORD and rejoice,
you righteous ones;
And shout for joy,
all you who are upright in heart.
PSALM 32:11 NASB

Rejoice, O pure in heart,
Rejoice, give thanks, and sing;
Your festal banner wave on high,
The cross of Christ your King.

Rejoice, rejoice, rejoice, give thanks, and sing!

Bright youth and snow-crowned age,
Both men and women, raise
On high your free, exulting song,
Declare God's wondrous praise.

Praise God, who reigns on high,
The Lord whom we adore:
The Father, Son, and Holy Ghost,
One God forevermore.

Edward Plumptre wrote this hymn as a processional in 1865. It was based on Philippians 4:4 which states, "Rejoice in the Lord always; again I will say, rejoice!" In sickness and health, in joy and sorrow, we can choose to rejoice in the Lord in every season of the soul.

In this world, there are harsh realities we cannot escape. We were not meant to ignore them, but we can still allow room for joy. Christ is not some vain hope. He is the Son of God, the living Word, our Savior and friend. His love is not a myth but the very substance the universe was created with, for God himself is love. Let's lift our hearts to him and give thanks for all he is while holding on to the hope of his goodness as he draws us to himself.

Great God, you are my joy. Fill me with your presence and lift the weariness I can't shake as I come to you. I choose to rejoice in you, for you are always good.

Day Is Ended

From the rising of the sun to its setting,
the name of the LORD is to be praised!

PSALM 113:3 ESV

The day you gave us, Lord, is ended,
The darkness falls at your request;
To you our morning hymns ascended,
Your praise shall sanctify our rest.

We thank you that your Church, unsleeping
While earth rolls onward into light,
Through all the world her watch is keeping
And never rests by day or night.

As over continent and island
Each dawn leads to another day,
The voice of prayer is never silent,
Nor do the praises die away.

So be it, Lord! Your throne shall never,
Like earth's proud empires, pass away;
Your kingdom stands and grows forever
Until there dawns your glorious day.

In many traditional churches in history, there were set times throughout the day to give thanks to God. One of those times was in the evening, a liminal space where one could offer both thanks for the day and protection for the looming night.. John Ellerton's "The Day Thou Gavest" from 1870 is called an evening hymn.

Before you lay your head on your pillow tonight, consider reading or singing this hymn. Even if you don't, take the principle to heart, give thanks for what the day held, and let go of what you cannot control. Ask the Lord to watch over you and take care of what you cannot. Rest in his peace. He never sleeps, and he is a trustworthy watchman.

Lord, I get so caught up in the busyness of my day that sometimes I forget to turn to you. Remind me to turn my heart toward you in prayer. Thank you.

NOVEMBER 7

The Lord's Prayer

"You fathers—if your children ask for a fish,
do you give them a snake instead?"
LUKE 11:11 NLT

Our Father, who art in heaven,
Hallowed be thy name.
Thy kingdom come, thy will be done
On earth as it is in heaven.

Give us this day our daily bread,
And forgive us our sins,
As we forgive them that sin against us.

And lead us not into temptation,
But deliver us from evil,
For thine is the kingdom, and the power,
And the glory forever.
Amen.

This hymn is the Lord's Prayer set to song. There have been many settings used throughout the ages, though one of the most recognizable is Albert Hay Malotte's. Putting Scripture to music is a powerful way to memorize it and to sink its meaning deeper into our hearts.

The Lord's Prayer is one of the most powerful tools Jesus gave his followers. We don't have to have eloquent words or repeat ourselves to be heard by God. He hears the words of our hearts, and he answers the prayers of his people. Keep things simple today and lay your heart before the Lord as you pray as Jesus taught. It is enough.

Jesus, you are the wisest teacher. I choose to rest in all you are knowing you are enough for me. So, as you taught us to pray, "Our Father..."

Lead On King Eternal

Be strong in the Lord
and in his great power.
EPHESIANS 6:10 NCV

Lead on, O King eternal,
The day of march has come;
Henceforth in fields of conquest
Your tents will be our home.
Through days of preparation
Your grace has made us strong;
And now, O King eternal,
We lift our battle song.

Lead on, O King eternal;
We follow, not with fears,
For gladness breaks like morning
Where'er your face appears.
Your cross is lifted o'er us,
We journey in its light;
The crown awaits the conquest;
Lead on, O God of might.

The 1887 hymn "Lead On, O King Eternal" is not a battle cry for physical war. It is a call for us to go forward in following the Lord as our King and commander. He who calls us to his kingdom leads us in wisdom and strength. He often leads us where we do not expect, but we can trust him to guide us in mercy and faithfulness.

As Ernest Shurtleff's hymn encourages, we follow our King eternal with joy. We don't need to fear where he will lead us, for he is with us every step of the way. No matter what we face, he is our present help and capable guide.

Eternal King, I choose to follow you and trust your leadership in my life. Lead me on in your love and give me your grace to strengthen my steps.

NOVEMBER 9

Glorious Things Are Spoken

Glorious things are said about you, city of God.
Selah.
PSALM 87:3 CSB

Glorious things of you are spoken,
Zion, city of our God;
He whose word cannot be broken
Formed you for his own abode.
On the Rock of Ages founded,
What can shake your sure repose?
With salvation's walls surrounded,
You may smile at all your foes.

See, the streams of living waters,
Springing from eternal love,
Well supply your sons and daughters
And all fear of want remove.
Who can faint while such a river
Ever will their thirst assuage?
Grace which, like the Lord, the giver,
Never fails from age to age.

John Newton (1725-1807) wrote this hymn based on Isaiah 33:20-21 which focuses on Zion, the Lord's city. Zion signifies the kingdom of our God and Savior. Though we look ahead to the fullness we will find in the physical kingdom of Christ, it is important to remember we experience Christ when he meets us with the glory of his goodness.

We have a glorious hope ahead, and we also have the generous grace of God moving in us now. It's a beautiful and powerful mystery. The same God who appeared as a cloud by day and a pillar of fire by night is with us in power and peace today. Lean into his presence; there, we garner graceful strength, peace for our souls, and bright hope for tomorrow.

Mighty One, I long for your kingdom to come in fullness, but as I wait, I have the goodness of your presence. Move in me and transform me from the inside out.

Servants of God

"Salvation belongs to our God
who sits on the throne,
and to the Lamb!"

Revelation 7:10 NKJV

You servants of God, your master proclaim,
And publish abroad his wonderful name;
The name all-victorious of Jesus extol;
His kingdom is glorious and rules over all.

God rules in the height, almighty to save;
Though hid from our sight, his presence
we have;
The great congregation his triumph shall sing,
Ascribing salvation to Jesus our King.

"Salvation to God, who sits on the throne!"
Let all cry aloud, and honor the Son;
The praises of Jesus the angels proclaim,
Fall down on their faces and worship
the Lamb.

Then let us adore and give him his right:
All glory and power, all wisdom and might,
All honor and blessing with angels above
And thanks never ceasing for infinite love.

Charles Wesley wrote this hymn in 1744 for his collection Hymns for Times of Trouble and Persecution. It was under a section titled, "Hymns to Be Sung in Tumult." We have all known tumultuous times. In these unsettling moments, we are never without God, so we are never without hope.

When all feels unsettled and shaky, we can rest on the foundation of who God is. He never changes. He is good to everything he has made. He is merciful and powerful to save. He is a good father, a defender of the weak, and a safe shelter in the storms of life. Whatever you are facing today, join in proclaiming the goodness of God who never leaves or forsakes you.

Faithful One, thank you for your constant presence in my life. I trust you more than I trust anyone. Your love never fails; your goodness never leaves me. I am yours, and I hide myself in you.

NOVEMBER 11

Balm in Gilead

"I will restore you to health
and heal your wounds,"
declares the LORD.

JEREMIAH 30:17 NIV

There is a balm in Gilead
To make the wounded whole,
There is a balm in Gilead
To heal the sin-sick soul.

Sometimes I feel discouraged
And think my work's in vain,
But then the Holy Spirit
Revives my soul again.

If you cannot preach like Peter,
If you cannot pray like Paul,
You can tell the love of Jesus
And say, "He died for all."

In the mountainous region known as Gilead, east of the Jordan River, skillful physicians applied an ointment made from the gum of a local tree to administer healing. This balm is spoken of in the Old Testament, and though it could heal the body, it could not heal the soul. Jesus became our balm of Gilead and brought miraculous restoration to our souls through his sacrifice. In him, we find true and lasting healing.

No matter how weak we feel, God is our strength. The one who brings restoration to our souls is the one who offers us grace in our weakness. We don't have to be highly skilled to glorify the name of Christ. The truth of who he is is powerful enough.

God, you are my healing, strength, and vision. Encourage my heart in hope today as I receive the grace of your empowering presence. I need you more than anything else.

Walking with God

Pursue peace with all people, and the holiness without which no one will see the Lord.

HEBREWS 12:14 NASB

O for a closer walk with God,
A calm and heav'nly frame,
A light to shine upon the road
That leads me to the Lamb!

Where is the blessedness I knew
When first I sought the Lord?
Where is the soul refreshing view
Of Jesus and his Word?

What peaceful hours I then enjoyed!
How sweet their mem'ry still!
But they have left an aching void
The world can never fill.

The dearest idol I have known,
Whate'er that idol be,
Help me to tear it from thy throne
and worship only thee.

William Cowper wrote this text in 1769 during the illness of a long-time friend. He was personally troubled and affected by her health struggle. Many of us, even if we remain in good health, know this same kind of trouble. When our loved ones deal with major diagnoses or chronic illnesses, we feel their weight.

Instead of wallowing in the burden we may feel, let's do as Cowper did and direct our hearts to the Lord. As we walk with him, his comfort will cover us. Even as we wrestle through the questions, worry, and the unknown of tomorrow, we can know the peace of Christ that passes all understanding.

Prince of Peace, I hold on to you in the hardships of life. Hold even tighter to me, Lord. As I offer you all my worries and cares, fill me with your presence and keep me at rest in you.

NOVEMBER 13

Sing Praise to God

I will proclaim the name of the LORD;
ascribe greatness to our God!
DEUTERONOMY 32:3 ESV

Sing praise to God who reigns above,
The God of all creation,
The God of power, the God of love,
The God of our salvation.
With healing balm my soul is filled
And every faithless murmur stilled:
To God all praise and glory.

Thus all my toilsome way along,
I sing aloud thy praises,
That earth may hear the grateful song
My voice unwearied raises.
Be joyful in the Lord, my heart,
Both soul and body bear your part:
To God all praise and glory.

God's loving care for his people is evident in Scripture. We need look no further than the life and ministry of Christ. He cares for us so much, he gave his Son so we might know him as he truly is: a good father and powerful redeemer.

This hymn comes from the German original by Johann Jakob Schütz published in 1675. It is a hymn of praise to the one who reigns above our circumstances: above creation, time, and space. He is not bound by the things that bind us. He is above all, but he is also present with us. He is never far away, or as the hymnist puts it, "an ever present help and stay." Let's give him glory, for he is worthy no matter what we are going through.

Great God, you are worthy of praise in both my suffering and my celebration. I choose to offer you all I am and look to you as you are: holy one, patient Father, and everlasting King.

God of Abraham

God replied to Moses,
"I AM WHO I AM.
Say this to the people of Israel:
I AM has sent me to you."
Exodus 3:14 NLT

The God of Abraham praise,
Who reigns enthroned above;
Ancient of everlasting days,
and God of love;
Jehovah, great I AM!
By earth and heaven confessed;
I bow and bless the sacred name
Forever blest.

The heavenly land I see,
With peace and plenty blest;
A land of sacred liberty,
And endless rest.
There milk and honey flow,
And oil and wine abound,
And trees of life forever grow
With mercy crowned.

The roots of this hymn go back to a traditional Jewish creed. In 1770, Thomas Olivers made a translation of it to incorporate Christ, and that version brings us this hymn. It directs our focus to God's power and guidance and encourages us to praise God for his incomparable nature.

Echoing the Yigdal, the creed on which this hymn is based, the text starts by praising God for his sovereignty and for his faithfulness toward his people. The God of Abraham is the same God who guides us today. We can trust him with everything we face, for he is the great I AM, and there are no mysteries to him.

Jehovah, you reign above everything. I give you honor and praise, for you are greater than I can fathom. Be glorified in my life and in this world.

Onward Christian Soldiers

Although we live in the natural realm, we don't wage a military campaign employing human weapons, using manipulation to achieve our aims. Instead, our spiritual weapons are energizedwith divine power to effectively dismantle the defenses behind which people hide.

2 Corinthians 10:3-4 TPT

Onward, Christian soldiers,
Marching as to war,
With the cross of Jesus
Going on before!
Christ, the royal master,
Leads against the foe;
Forward into battle,
See his banner go!

Onward, Christian soldiers,
Marching as to war,
With the cross of Jesus
Going on before!

There is a difference between physical battles and spiritual ones. We must be careful not to confuse the two lest we find excuses to wage war against others when Christ calls us to lay down our lives in love. We need to remember the armor of God is also partnered with the fruit of the Spirit. If it is not, we have lost sight of what Christ came to teach.

We can read Sabine Baring-Gould's nineteenth-century hymn while remembering our call to fight the forces of evil and not people. Our battle is not against flesh and blood but against the powers of this dark world. We can fight the fight of faith without personally attacking those who are different than us.

Christ, you are the King I follow into battle. Help me not get caught up in struggles of power, prestige, and control. Give me your perspective.

Sweet Hour of Prayer

Early the next morning, while it was still dark,
Jesus woke and left the house.
He went to a lonely place, where he prayed.
MARK 1:35 NCV

Sweet hour of prayer! Sweet hour of prayer!
That calls me from a world of care,
And bids me at my Father's throne
Make all my wants and wishes known.
In seasons of distress and grief,
My soul has often found relief,
And oft escaped the tempter's snare
By thy return, sweet hour of prayer!

Sweet hour of prayer! Sweet hour of prayer!
Thy wings shall my petition bear
To him whose truth and faithfulness
Engage the waiting soul to bless.
And since he bids me seek his face,
Believe his Word, and trust his grace,
I'll cast on him my every care,
And wait for thee, sweet hour of prayer!

Jesus took time to withdraw to quiet, secluded places to pray. He not only took time away from the crowds but also from his friends. Sometimes we need to do the same. An stolen hour can be enough to refresh our souls. Though we do not know for certain who the author of this hymn was, we do know William Bradbury (1816-1868) composed the music. It is a soft and lilting melody that nicely accompanies the words.

Take some time away from others today. Even if it is before anyone wakes or after everyone else is asleep, don't neglect the needs of your soul. Jesus needed solitary prayer time, and if he did, we certainly do too.

Lord, as I spend time alone, I lift my heart in prayer to you. Meet me here.

That Will Be Glory

When Christ, who is your life, appears,
then you also will appear with him in glory.

Colossians 3:4 CSB

When all my labors and trials are o'er,
And I am safe on that beautiful shore,
Just to be near the dear Lord I adore
Will through the ages be glory for me.

O that will be glory for me,
Glory for me, glory for me;
When by his grace I shall look at his face,
That will be glory, be glory for me.

When by the gift of his infinite grace,
I am accorded in heaven a place,
Just to be there and to look on his face
Will through the ages be glory for me.

Friends will be there I have loved long ago;
Joy like a river around me will flow;
Yet just a smile from my Savior, I know,
Will through the ages be glory for me.

Charles Gabriel (1856-1932) was inspired by his friend Ed Card when writing this song. Card would end his prayers with references to heaven and then punctuate it with, "and that will be glory for me." "O That Will Be Glory" helps us lift our thoughts from our temporal problems and pain and remember what awaits us in the glorious kingdom of our God and Savior.

Ask the Lord for greater revelation of what heaven holds as you read his Word. The Spirit teaches us all things, and heaven's hope is included in this promise. If we catch even a glimpse, our hearts will soar with hope. "When by His grace I shall look at His face, That will be glory, be glory for me."

Christ, I can't wait to behold the full glory of your face as I stand before you. Please expand my awareness and understanding of what it will be like.

Walk with Thee

"He who finds his life will lose it,
and he who loses his life for My sake will find it."
MATTHEW 10:39 NKJV

O Master, let me walk with thee
In lowly paths of service free;
Tell me thy secret, help me bear
The strain of toil, the fret of care.

Help me the slow of heart to move
By some clear, winning word of love;
Teach me the wayward feet to stay,
And guide them in the homeward way.

Teach me thy patience; still with thee
In closer, dearer company,
In work that keeps faith sweet and strong,
In trust that triumphs over wrong.

In hope that sends a shining ray
Far down the future's broad'ning way,
In peace that only thou canst give,
With thee, O Master, let me live.

Washington Gladden wrote this text in the late nineteenth century during a pivotal time in post-Civil War America. Gladden was a minister and social activist, and he emphasized applying the gospel to life in America throughout his ministry. This was one of a few hymns Gladden wrote and the only one to come into popular use.

As we walk with Christ in intimate fellowship, we can partner with him in service. This is emphasized in the opening line of the hymn: "Let me walk with thee in lowly paths of service free." As we serve others, we follow the lead of the Lord who showed us how to serve. Through fellowhship with Christ, he teaches us to rely on him and also offer what we have to others.

Lord, I don't face anything alone, and I partner with your purposes and serving others in love. Help me nurture the fruit of your Spirit: your compassion, patience, hope, and peace.

NOVEMBER 19

Particular Providence

How abundant are the good things
that you have stored up for those who fear you,
that you bestow in the sight of all,
on those who take refuge in you.

Psalm 31:19 NIV

When all your mercies, O my God,
My waking soul surveys,
Transported with the view, I'm lost
In wonder, love, and praise.

Ten thousand thousand precious gifts
My daily thanks employ,
Nor is the least a cheerful heart
That tastes these gifts with joy.

Through ev'ry passing phase of life
Your goodness I'll pursue
And after death, in distant worlds,
The glorious theme renew.

Through all eternity to you
A joyful song I'll raise,
But, oh, eternity's too short
To utter all your praise.

This morning hymn was written by Joseph Addison in 1712, and it was a thirteen-stanza poem in its first publication. It reminds us to look for moments of joy even on dark days. This was true in ages past, and it remains true today.

As you look ahead to what the rest of the day holds, be sure to look for the mercies of God. A helpful hand, a matter resolved without your intervention, birdsong that lifts your spirits: there are too many mercies to count. Take notice of whatever brings you comfort, relief, joy, peace, and a present mindset today. As you do, offer thanks to your God who provides these things for you to enjoy.

Wonderful One, I see you in the way the stars shine bright on clear nights. I see you in the transition of autumn when leaves turn vibrant and let go of their branches. I trust you with the rhythms of my life just as nature trusts the cycle of the seasons.

King of Heaven

Bless the LORD, my soul,
And all that is within me, bless His holy name.
Who satisfies your years with good things,
So that your youth is renewed like the eagle.
PSALM 103:1, 5 NASB

Praise, my soul, the King of heaven;
To his feet your tribute bring.
Ransomed, healed, restored, forgiven,
Evermore his praises sing.
Alleluia, alleluia!
Praise the everlasting King!

Praise him for his grace and favor
To his people in distress.
Praise him, still the same as ever,
Slow to chide, and swift to bless.
Alleluia, alleluia!
Glorious in his faithfulness!

Fatherlike he tends and spares us;
Well our feeble frame he knows.
In his hand he gently bears us,
Rescues us from all our foes.
Alleluia, alleluia!
Widely yet his mercy flows!

Many hymn writers in the mid-nineteenth century felt the pressure to keep adaptations of the psalms as close to the originals as possible. However, Henry Lyte did not put that pressure on himself. He published paraphrases under the title Spirit of the Psalms that boldly went against the expectation of the day.

God welcomes our genuine responses to his goodness in our lives. His Word does not lose power when we translate it through our lived experiences. Jesus is the living Word, and his Spirit still speaks to us and teaches us. We don't have to be afraid God will not receive our unique worship. He always does.

Lord, I praise you for who you have revealed yourself to be. I want to learn more about you each day through your Word and through fellowship with you.

NOVEMBER 21

Songs of Thankfulness

"God did not send his Son into the world to condemn the world, but in order that the world might be saved through him."
JOHN 3:17 ESV

Songs of thankfulness and praise,
Jesus, Lord, to you we raise,
Manifested by the star
To the Magi from afar,
Branch of royal David's stem,
In your birth at Bethlehem.
Anthems be to you addressed,
God in man made manifest.

Sun and moon shall darkened be,
Stars shall fall, the heav'ns shall flee.
Christ will then like lightning shine;
All will see his glorious sign.
All will then the trumpet hear,
All will see the judge appear.
You by all will be confessed,
God in man made manifest.

Christopher Wordsworth (1897-1885), nephew of the famed poet William Wordsworth, was a prolific author in his own right. He was also a renowned Greek scholar. His hymn, "Songs of Thankfulness and Praise," recounts the ways in which Christ was made manifest. The God who was born of Mary, baptized in the Jordan River, and who performed many miracles throughout his ministry, is the God we worship.

For all Christ did, there is room for personal gratitude. Let's remember the ways Christ made his Father known while we recognize the handiwork of his mercy in our lives. He is worthy to be praised.

Son of God, for who you are, for all you did, and for what you continue to reveal, I am grateful. Be honored in my life as I press in to know you more.

Count Your Blessings

All praise to God, the Father of our Lord Jesus Christ,
who has blessed us with every spiritual blessing
in the heavenly realms because we are united with Christ.

EPHESIANS 1:3 NLT

When upon life's billows you are tempest
tossed,
When you are discouraged, thinking all is lost,
Count your many blessings, name them one
by one,
And it will surprise you what the Lord
hath done.

Count your blessings, name them one by one;
Count your blessings, see what God hath
done;
Count your blessings, name them one by one;
Count your many blessings,
see what God hath done.

When you look at others with their lands
and gold,
Think that Christ has promised you his wealth
untold;
Count your many blessings, money cannot buy
Your reward in heaven, nor your home on high.

So, amid the conflict, whether great or small,
Do not be discouraged, God is over all;
Count your many blessings, angels will attend,
Help and comfort give you to your
journey's end.

Johnson Oatman wrote this text in 1897, and it was then known by the first line: "When Upon Life's Billows You are Tempest Tossed." Commonly known for the refrain today, we can take hope that even in turbulent times, God's goodness is still present in our lives. No one is barren of God's mercy.

This beloved hymn reminds us that when we look for the goodness of God, we will find it. Even during times of great hardship, blessings are present in our lives. None is too small to count. In this season of thanksgiving, take time to count your blessings and name them one by one.

Father, I won't overlook the simple miracles of nourishment, rest, and companionship that fill my life. As I look for the blessings I already have, expand my awareness so I can find them in places I hadn't thought to look.

NOVEMBER 23

In the Garden

On the first day of the week Mary Magdalene
went to the tomb early, while it was still dark,
and saw that the stone had been taken away from the tomb.

JOHN 20:1 NKJV

I come to the garden alone,
While the dew is still on the roses;
And the voice I hear, falling on my ear,
The Son of God discloses.

And he walks with me, and he talks with me,
And he tells me I am his own,
And the joy we share as we tarry there,
None other has ever known.

He speaks, and the sound of his voice
Is so sweet the birds hush their singing;
And the melody that he gave to me
Within my heart is ringing.

I'd stay in the garden with him
Tho' the night around me be falling;
But he bids me go; thro' the voice of woe,
His voice to me is calling.

This hymn speaks of a deeply personal friendship with the Lord. He walks with us in the gardens of our lives: places of sorrow, solitude, or expectation. He takes time with us. Whenever we come to him, he meets us with the power of his presence. His love is not generalized; it is specific to each of us.

Charles Austin Miles (1868-1946) was inspired to write this hymn from Mary Magdalene's perspective after reading John 20. She was the first to encounter the risen Lord, and what a profound experience it must have been. Wherever you are today, know that the Lord meets you when you come looking for him. You are his, and he delights in spending time with you.

Resurrected Lord, thank you for knowing me and loving me as I am. I come to you with an open and expectant heart today. Meet me in the garden of my heart and speak to me.

Come Ye Thankful People

Jesus, the One who says these things are true, says,
"Yes, I am coming soon."
Amen. Come, Lord Jesus!
REVELATION 22:20 NCV

Come, ye thankful people, come,
Raise the song of harvest home;
All is safely gathered in,
Ere the winter storms begin.
God our Maker doth provide
For our wants to be supplied;
Come to God's own temple, come,
Raise the song of harvest home.

For the Lord our God shall come,
And shall take the harvest home;
From the field shall in that day
All offenses purge away,
Giving angels charge at last
In the fire the tares to cast;
But the fruitful ears to store
In the garner evermore.

Jesus said to his followers, "There are many people to harvest but only a few workers to help harvest them. Pray to the Lord, who owns the harvest, that he will send more workers to gather his harvest" (Matthew 9:37-38). God speaks in ways his audience can comprehend. For an agrigucultural culture, describing God's kingdom as fields that are sown and harvested made sense. In the same way, this hymn was written for English village harvest festivals in 1844.

Whether we live in the country, the city, or somewhere in between, we can appreciate the ways God moves through his people. When we partner with him, we do our work and trust God to do what we cannot. Let's not neglect our part in spreading the good news of his love.

God of the harvest, I am your partner and friend. I long to be about my Father's work, so let me not lose sight of what that is.

NOVEMBER 25

Bountiful Cup

He watches over his nest like an eagle
and hovers over his young;
he spreads his wings, catches him,
and carries him on his feathers.
DEUTERONOMY 32:11 CSB

O thou, whose bounty fills my cup
With ev'ry blessing meet!
I give thee thanks for ev'ry drop—
The bitter and the sweet.

I praise thee for the desert road,
And for the river-side;
For all thy goodness hath bestowed,
And all thy grace denied.

I thank thee for both smile and frown,
And for the gain and loss;
I praise thee for the future crown,
And for the present cross.

I bless thee for the glad increase,
And for the waning joy;
And for this strange, this settled peace,
Which nothing can destroy.

Though this hymn may be more obscure than most we've covered, it is filled with good advice about humble thanks to God in the tension of both good and hard times. The hymn's author, Jane Crewdson (1809-1863), knew the hardship of sickness, and even during that time, she found a way to deepen her walk with the Lord.

It is easier to give thanks when we are at peace and happy. However, there are reasons to choose to give thanks in hardship. When we do, we lift our attention from the pain and look for little miracles of blessings around us. We slow down enough to notice the ground beneath our feet, the sunlight playing off the trees, and the feel of our lungs expanding with each breath, and we ground our attention in God's gracious presence with us in those things.

Lord, thank you for your presence with me now. Thank you for the blessing of knowing you and being known by you. I will ground myself in you.

I'll Praise My Maker

I will give thanks to you, LORD,
with all my heart;
I will tell of all your wonderful deeds.
PSALM 9:1 NIV

I'll praise my maker with my breath,
And when my voice is lost in death,
Praise shall employ my nobler powers
My days of praise shall ne'er be past,
While life, and thought, and being last,
Or immortality endures.

Why should I make a man my trust?
Princes must die and turn to dust;
Vain is the help of flesh and blood:
Their breath departs, their pomp and power,
And thoughts all vanish in an hour,
Nor can they make their promise good.

I'll praise him while he lends me breath;
And when my voice is lost in death,
Praise shall employ my nobler powers;
My days of praise shall ne'er be past,
While life and thought and being last,
Or immortality endures.

This hymn was written by Isaac Watts and first published in 1719. Watts is commonly referred to as the father of English hymnody for his prolific and high quality writings. Originally titled "Praise God for His Goodness and Truth," this hymn is a paraphrase of Psalm 146. We too can find reason to praise God for his goodness and truth today.

The very breath filling our lungs is a gift from God. The sun shines down on us in a tender display of God's kindness. The rains that water the earth are showers of blessing. The natural world can encourage us to praise the Lord for all he offers. We are his children, and he delights in us. Let's take delight in our wonderful Father too.

Father, you are ruler above all, and you are worthy of my praise. May my life honor you, and may I know you more today as I lean in to hear your voice.

NOVEMBER 27

Bringing in the Sheaves

Those who sow their tears as seeds
will reap a harvest with joyful shouts of glee.
They may weep as they go out carrying their seed to sow,
but they will return with joyful laughter and shouting with gladness
as they bring back armloads of blessing and a harvest overflowing!

Psalm 126:5-6 TPT

Sowing in the morning, sowing seeds of kindness,
Sowing in the noontide and the dewy eve;
Waiting for the harvest, and the time of reaping,
We shall come rejoicing, bringing in the sheaves.

Bringing in the sheaves,
Bringing in the sheaves,
We shall come rejoicing, bringing in the sheaves;

Sowing in the sunshine, sowing in the shadows,
Fearing neither clouds nor winter's chilling breeze;
By and by the harvest, and the labor ended,
We shall come rejoicing, bringing in the sheaves.

Inspired by Psalm 126:6, Knowles Shaw wrote the lyrics to this hymn in 1874. Sheaves are bundles of ripe grain bundled up and carried by harvesters. The visuals of this hymn are based, as many harvest hymns are, on the communal work and celebratory power of reaping the abundance of what we sow.

2 Corinthians 9:6 says: "The person who sows sparingly will also reap sparingly, and the person who sows generously will also reap generously" (CSB). Let's do the work sowing seeds of kindness, peace, hope, and all the fruit of the Spirit. As we sow, so will we reap. Those abundant fields? They tell of the glory of God in our lives.

King of the harvest, in everything I do, I need your blessing. May you be glorified by my efforts, and may I learn to rest in the off seasons in your abiding peace.

God on High

The next day he saw Jesus coming to him, and said, "Behold, the Lamb of God who takes away the sin of the world!"

John 1:29 NASB

All glory be to God on high,
Who hath our race befriended!
To us no harm shall now come nigh,
The strife at last is ended.
God showeth his good will to men,
And peace shall reign on earth again;
O thank him for his goodness!

We praise, we worship thee, we trust,
And give thee thanks forever,
O Father, that thy rule is just
And wise, and changes never.
Thy boundless pow'r o'er all things reigns,
Done is whate'er thy will ordains:
Well for us that thou rulest.

This song is a series of praises to God. It follows a pattern common in doxologies used in Greek liturgies of the early church. It is a translation of the fourth-century Latin text "Gloria in excelsis Deo." The hymn has been used in many liturgical settings, and it works well as a doxology.

Even if you have never been to a liturgical service, you can learn to appreciate the message in the literature. "All Glory Be to God on High" is filled with Scriptural truth, so spend some time digging through it today. Whether you simply read through it or listen to a sung rendition, allow the words to sink in and worship the Lord your God.

Glorious One, you are worthy of my attention. I give it to you now, and I worship your holy name.

NOVEMBER 29

A Rose E'er Blooming

A shoot will come up from the stump of Jesse;
from his roots a Branch will bear fruit.

ISAIAH 11:1 NIV

Lo, how a rose e'er blooming
From tender stem hath sprung!
Of Jesse's lineage coming
As men of old have sung.
It came, a flower bright,
Amid the cold of winter
When half-gone was the night.

This flower, whose fragrance tender
With sweetness fills the air,
Dispels with glorious splendor
The darkness everywhere.
True man, yet very God,
From sin and death he saves us
And lightens every load.

This Advent hymn dates back several centuries to its original German text. It was translated into English by several people, but the most commonly sung version we find today was translated by Theodore Baker in 1894. The rose is a picture of Jesus Christ as the root of Jesse, the father of King David.

The music accompanying this hymn is beautiful, and it supports the text well. If you have a moment, listen to a recording, and allow it to wash over you. There are many versions; find one you enjoy. Consider how the imagery of Christ as a rose never ceasing to bloom may lead you to his persisting beauty. He is beautiful, and the aroma of his life is fragrant still.

Jesus, as I look on the beauty of nature, I wonder how much more beautiful you must be. May your fragrance permeate my life as I draw near to you.

Glad Men of Old

When they heard the king, they departed;
and behold, the star which they had seen in the East went before them,
till it came and stood over where the young Child was.

MATTHEW 2:9 NKJV

As with gladness men of old
Did the guiding star behold,
As with joy they hailed its light,
Leading onward, beaming bright,
So, most gracious Lord, may we
Evermore be led by thee.

As with joyful steps they sped,
Savior, to thy lowly bed,
There to bend the knee before
Thee, whom heav'n and earth adore,
So may we with willing feet
Ever seek thy mercy seat.

In the heav'nly country bright
Need they no created light;
Thou its light, its joy, its crown,
Thou its sun which goes not down.
There forever may we sing
Alleluias to our King!

William Dix (1837-1898) wrote this hymn while he was ill. He did not even get out of bed to do it! Thankfully, God does not require us to be at our best to offer what we have. We may find ourselves creatively inspired while we are resting or hurting. Take hold of inspiration when it strikes; you never know what may come of it.

This hymn tracks the journey of the wise men as they followed the star to worship Christ, and it echoes our Christian pilgrimage. As we follow Jesus on the narrow path, his presence is as costly as any treasure we could offer him. Even so, we offer him the gifts we have, and he offers us everything he is.

Jesus, I want to be close to you more than I want to wander. As I offer you my small gifts, I know I receive abundantly more from your presence. I'm grateful to be yours.

December

I hear the Savior say,
"Thy strength indeed is small;
Child of weakness, watch and pray,
Find in me thine all in all."

Long Expected Jesus

"Jerusalem, get up and shine,
because your light has come,
and the glory of the LORD shines on you."

ISAIAH 60:1 NCV

Come, thou long expected Jesus,
Born to set thy people free;
From our fears and sins release us,
Let us find our rest in thee.
Israel's strength and consolation,
Hope of all the earth thou art;
Dear desire of every nation,
Joy of every longing heart.

Born thy people to deliver,
Born a child and yet a King,
Born to reign in us forever,
Now thy gracious kingdom bring.
By thine own eternal spirit
Rule in all our hearts alone;
By thine all sufficient merit,
Raise us to thy glorious throne.

Written to be included in Charles Wesley's 1744 book, *Hymns for the Nativity of Our Lord*, this hymn uses imagery that speaks of Christ's first coming while also alluding to his long-awaited return. It is a song we can sing during Advent while calling on him to come again.

Whether this season brings deep joy, great longing, or a lingering sadness (or perhaps a bit of each of those things), the Lord faithfully meets his people. His Spirit comforts our hearts even as we long for Jesus' physical return. We can wait with hope, through every trial and circumstance, for he is with us in his Spirit. He will not fail us.

Jesus, thank you for coming to earth and putting on flesh and bones to meet us where we are. Thank you for your Spirit who ministers to me today. I long for you, but even as I yearn, I know and love you now.

DECEMBER 2

We Adore Thee

Sing to Him, sing praises to Him;
Speak of all His wonders.
1 CHRONICLES 16:9 NASB

Joyful, joyful, we adore thee,
God of glory, Lord of love.
Hearts unfold like flow'rs before thee,
Praising thee their sun above.
Melt the clouds of sin and sadness;
Drive our fear and doubt away.
Giver of immortal gladness,
Fill us with the light of day!

Mortals, join the mighty chorus
Which the morning stars began.
Love divine is reigning o'er us,
Leading us with mercy's hand.
Ever singing, march we onward,
Victors in the midst of strife.
Joyful music lifts us sunward
In the triumph song of life.

A beautiful hymn of praise from all creation, Henry Van Dyke's 1907 hymn was written with inspiration from the mountains surrounding him. He wrote it to be sung to Beethoven's "Ode to Joy," which is fitting for the theme. Have you ever been so in awe of creation that it inspired you in an unexpected way?

Whether you are full of wonder or struggling to find peace, allow the joy of Van Dyke's hymn to permeate your heart as you play, sing, or listen to it. You may find your mood changes when directing your heart to the Lord.

Glorious Lord, you are worthy of praise from every part of creation. I don't want to withhold my worship because of worry. I offer you my heart and praise. Please fill me with your joy as I do.

Realms of Glory

"When the Son of Man comes in His glory,
and all the holy angels with Him,
then He will sit on the throne of His glory."

MATTHEW 25:31 NKJV

Angels from the realms of glory,
Wing your flight o'er all the earth;
Ye who sang creation's story
Now proclaim Messiah's birth.

Come and worship, come and worship,
Worship Christ, the newborn king.

Shepherds, in the field abiding,
Watching o'er your flocks by night,
God with us is now residing;
Yonder shines the infant light.

Sages, leave your contemplations,
Brighter visions beam afar;
Seek the great desire of nations;
Ye have seen his natal star.

James Montgomery was the son of Moravian missionaries. They felt the call to move to Barbados, but they did not take James with them. Instead, they put him in an Irish boarding school. Though he never saw them again, he inherited their religious fervor and passion for foreign missions. He published this hymn based on Luke 2 in 1816.

When we are impressed by a passage of Scripture, it can be both cathartic and powerful to express our paraphrase. Many of the psalms we go to over and over again were expressions of Scriptural meditations mixed with the experience of the writer. Our personal process is seen, known, and accepted by God as we seek to know him more. Offer him your true expression today.

Lord Jesus, thank you for meeting me in this moment. I offer you my heart, adoration, and curiosity. Inspire me with your presence.

DECEMBER 4

The First Noel

When the set time had fully come, God sent his Son,
born of a woman, born under the law,
to redeem those under the law,
that we might receive adoption to sonship.

GALATIANS 4:4-5 NIV

The first noel the angels did say
Was to certain poor shepherds in fields as
they lay,
In fields where they lay keeping their sheep
On a cold winter's night that was so deep.
Noel, noel, noel, noel!
Born is the King of Israel!

They looked up and saw a star
Shining in the east beyond them far;
And to the earth it gave great light,
And so it continued both day and night.
Noel, noel, noel, noel!
Born is the King of Israel!

This star drew nigh to the northwest,
Over Bethlehem it took its rest;
And there it did both stop and stay
Right over the place where Jesus lay.
Noel, noel, noel, noel!
Born is the King of Israel!

First appearing in an 1823 publication, this anonymous carol is an ancient folk song. Although not wholly historically accurate, the pleasant melody and chorus have kept this hymn popular for centuries. Noel, taken from the Latin root natalis, means birthday. In this hymn, we remember the birth of Christ and the celebration it deserves.

In this season of Christmas, may we remember what it is all about. It is not simply about festivities, presents, or gathering together. It is about remembering the birth of Christ and the power of his life, death, and resurrection over our lives today. Let us worship the Lord and remember the reason we rejoice.

Jesus, thank you for coming to earth as a baby, born in the humblest circumstances, so we could know what God is like. I lay aside the pull of consumerism to slow down in your presence. You are worthy of my attention.

Midnight Clear

When he brought his supreme Son into the world,
God said, "Let all of God's angels worship him."

HEBREWS 1:6 NLT

It came upon the midnight clear,
That glorious song of old,
From angels bending near the earth
To touch their harps of gold:
"Peace on the earth, good will to men,
From heaven's all-gracious King."
The world in solemn stillness lay,
To hear the angels sing.

And ye, beneath life's crushing load,
Whose forms are bending low,
Who toil along the climbing way
With painful steps and slow,
Look now! For glad and golden hours
Come swiftly on the wing.
O rest beside the weary road,
And hear the angels sing!

Written shortly before the outbreak of the Civil War, Edmund Hamilton Sears' hymn focuses on the angels' declaration of peace on earth. Whatever societal or political climate we find ourselves in, we can join with the angels and ask for peace on earth as it is in heaven.

Christ remains our hope and Prince of peace. He is the fullness of God in human form. He is our great Savior, and his presence is our close comfort. His peace and mercy stand in direct contrast to the war, oppression, and hostility we experience on earth. As we wait for Christ to return, he is our perfect portion.

Prince of Peace, thank you for the power of your Spirit's presence to calm, subdue, and comfort. May there be peace on earth as in heaven.

Shepherds Watched

An angel of the Lord stood before them,
and the glory of the Lord shone around them,
and they were terrified.

LUKE 2:9 CSB

While shepherds watched their flocks by night,
All seated on the ground,
An angel of the Lord came down,
And glory shone around.

"Fear not," said he for mighty dread
Had seized their troubled mind
"Glad tidings of great joy I bring
To you and all mankind.

"To you, in David's town, this day
Is born of David's line
A Savior, who is Christ the Lord;
and this shall be the sign:

"All glory be to God on high,
And to the earth be peace;
To those on whom his favor rests
Goodwill shall never cease."

Nahum Tate first published this hymn in 1700 and based it on the narrative in Luke 2 where shepherds encountered the God's heavenly host. He was adept at adapting others' works, and that talent shines in his exposition of Luke 2. When we feel creatively stuck, it can be inspiring and refreshing to paraphrase a meaningful passage or story.

The angels in Luke showed up to speak to shepherds and not well-known or wealthy people. God also reveals himself to us no matter who we are. We don't need wealth, status, or a platform to know God. He is revealed to the poor as well as to the rich. Praise God; he does not discriminate or withhold himself from us.

Great God, thank you for your accessible mercy and grace through Christ. I humble myself before you.

The Herald Angels Sing

He is the image of the invisible God,
the firstborn of all creation.

Colossians 1:15 ESV

Hark! The herald angels sing,
"Glory to the newborn King:
Peace on earth, and mercy mild,
God and sinners reconciled!"
Joyful, all ye nations, rise,
Join the triumph of the skies;
With th'angelic hosts proclaim,
"Christ is born in Bethlehem!"

Hark! The herald angels sing,
"Glory to the newborn King"

Hail the heaven-born Prince of Peace!
Hail the sun of righteousness!
Light and life to all he brings,
Risen with healing in his wings.
Mild he lays his glory by,
Born that we no more may die,
Born to raise us from the earth,
Born to give us second birth.

Charles Wesley published this hymn in 1739, and it is full of the theological insight Wesley is known for. He notoriously did not like others taking liberty with his text, but his friend George Whitefield changed the words from "Hark how all the welkin [heavens] rings" to "Hark! The herald angels sing."

When we let go of our need to control the narrative of Christ's story, we allow his mercy to shine. This lets others receive and encounter the love of God in their own way.

Righteous One, your power speaks for itself. I am your child, and you are my God. Be glorified.

Joy to the World

At that time people will say, "Our God is doing this!
We have waited for him, and he has come to save us.
This is the LORD. We waited for him,
so we will rejoice and be happy when he saves us."

ISAIAH 25:9 NCV

Joy to the world, the Lord is come!
Let earth receive her King;
Let ev'ry heart prepare him room
And heav'n and nature sing,
And heav'n and nature sing,
And heav'n, and heav'n and nature sing.

Joy to the earth, the Savior reigns!
Let men their songs employ,
While fields and floods, rocks, hills, and plains,
Repeat the sounding joy,
Repeat the sounding joy,
Repeat, repeat the sounding joy.

He rules the world with truth and grace
And makes the nations prove
The glories of his righteousness
And wonders of his love,
And wonders of his love,
And wonders, wonders of his love.

It may be surprising to know that Isaac Watts did not write this hymn as a Christmas song. It is a paraphrase of Psalm 98, and it was included in the 1719 publication The Psalms of David Imitated in the Language of the New Testament. Watts was impressed by the true, full meaning of shouting joyfully to the Lord.

Many Scriptures speak of the joy of the Lord, and Psalm 98 is one. Christ's coming was a profound gift to all creation the likes of which we have not seen since. He is our Savior and hope. We rejoice in the grace of his coming to earth and in the power of his salvation. Joy to the world, indeed!

Savior, you are the reason I rejoice. In every season and circumstance, you remain true. As I praise you and meditate on your Word, let joy rise within my heart and expand my love for you.

Hallelujah Chorus

The seventh angel sounded;
and there were loud voices in heaven, saying,
"The kingdom of the world has become
the kingdom of our Lord and of His Christ;
and He will reign forever and ever."

REVELATION 11:15 NASB

Hallelujah! Hallelujah!
Hallelujah! Hallelujah! Hallelujah!
For the Lord God omnipotent reigneth.

The kingdom of this world is become
The kingdom of our Lord, and of his Christ,
And he shall reign for ever and ever.

King of kings, and Lord of lords.
King of kings, and Lord of lords.
King of kings, and Lord of lords,
And Lord of lords, and he shall reign,
And he shall reign for ever and ever,
For ever and ever.

Hallelujah! Hallelujah!
And he shall reign for ever and ever, for ever and ever.
King of kings! And Lord of lords!

Taken from Handel's renowned work, Messiah, the Hallelujah Chorus is a triumphant piece celebrating the power of Christ our risen King. During the Christmas and Easter seasons, you can find choirs performing Handel's Messiah all over the world. Its power and relevance has persisted since it was first written in the mid-1700s.

The declaration of Christ's lordship and the chorus of hallelujahs throughout can carry us into a jubilant state of heart and mind. Consider playing this chorus as you reflect on the glory of your God and King today. You might be inspired to add a few hallelujahs of your own.

King of kings, you are worthy of my praise, adoration, and attention. I give you all those things today as I fix the eyes of my heart on you. Hallelujah!

Heard on High

Bless the Lord, all his messengers of power,
for you are his mighty heroes who listen intently
to the voice of his word to do it.

Psalm 103:20 TPT

Angels we have heard on high,
Sweetly singing o'er the plains,
And the mountains in reply
Echoing their joyous strains.

Gloria in excelsis Deo,
Gloria in excelsis Deo.

Shepherds, why this jubilee?
Why your joyous strains prolong?
What the gladsome tidings be
Which inspire your heav'nly song?

Come to Bethlehem and see
Him whose birth the angels sing;
Come, adore on bended knee
Christ the Lord, the newborn King.

This popular carol was originally written in French in the 1700s. In 1862, it was published in English with the words we now associate with the hymn from Henri Hemy's translation. The carol follows the account of the shepherds in Luke 2 as they heard the angels singing "Gloria in excelsis Deo," which is Latin for "Glory to God in the highest."

Have you ever thought about how you would respond if you heard a chorus of angels praising God in the middle of nowhere? The shepherds were in fields with their sheep when suddenly an angel of the Lord appeared. From there, they heard the news of Christ's birth. It is hard to imagine remaining indifferent to such glorious news delivered in such a spectacular way.

Glorious Jesus, you are always worthy of my adoration. I offer you praise today as I think about the shepherds and their experience. Encounter me with your glory.

We Three Kings

After Jesus was born in Bethlehem of Judea in the days of Herod the king, behold, wise men from the East came to Jerusalem, saying, "Where is He who has been born King of the Jews? For we have seen His star in the East and have come to worship Him."

MATTHEW 2:1-2 NKJV

We three kings of Orient are;
Bearing gifts we traverse afar,
Field and fountain, moor and mountain,
Following yonder star.

O star of wonder, star of light,
Star with royal beauty bright,
Westward leading, still proceeding,
Guide us to thy perfect light.

Born a King on Bethlehem's plain,
Gold I bring to crown him again,
King forever, ceasing never,
Over us all to reign.

Glorious now behold him arise;
King and God and sacrifice:
Alleluia, alleluia,
Sounds through the earth and skies.

In its fullness, this hymn presents the journey and gifts of the Magi to Jesus as told in Matthew 2. The three gifts they offered were gold, frankincense and myrrh. As we sing John Henry Hopkins' 1857 hymn at the holidays, we remember the journey of the Magi. Just as they traveled to bring Jesus costly gifts, we too can offer precious gifts to the Lord.

Reflect on what you have to offer the Lord. What do you want to give him? He is the author of creation, and everything you have originated with him. Knowing this is a season of giving, don't neglect to include Christ on your gift list. The wonderful news is that he is pleased with a humble heart and the desire to know him.

Worthy King, I will not offer you the scraps of my heart or life this season. You get access to the most highly prized areas of my life, for they are gifts from your hand. It is my honor to offer back to you what you have freely and kindly given me.

Good King Wenceslas

"When you give a banquet, invite the poor, the crippled, the lame, the blind, and you will be blessed. Although they cannot repay you, you will be repaid at the resurrection of the righteous."

Luke 14:13-14 NIV

Good King Wenceslas looked out on the feast of Stephen,
When the snow lay round about, deep and crisp and even.
Brightly shone the moon that night, though the frost was cruel,
When a poor man came in sight, gath'ring winter fuel.

In his master's steps he trod, where the snow lay dinted;
Heat was in the very sod which the saint had printed.
Therefore, Christian men, be sure, while God's gifts possessing,
You who now will bless the poor shall yourselves find blessing.

If you have ever wondered about the origin of this poetic chronicle, you are not alone. King Wenceslas was an ancient Bohemian duke known for showing concern for the poor and taking steps to reform the judicial system in the land he ruled. John Mason Neale wrote this hymn in 1857 as a poem to honor the godly king and his charitable heart and work.

No matter our station in life or our economic circumstances, we can minister to the poor with what we have. Jesus encouraged us to live generously. We should not turn a blind eye from the vulnerable; we can dignify them with respect, care, and a helping hand.

Generous Lord, I don't want to forget the importance of living generously and helping those who need it. May I become more like you as I consciously take steps to help those around me.

Come Ye Faithful

They hurried to the village and found Mary and Joseph.
And there was the baby, lying in the manger.
LUKE 2:16 NLT

O come, all ye faithful,
Joyful and triumphant!
O come ye, O come ye to Bethlehem!
Come and behold him, born the King of angels.

O come, let us adore him,
O come, let us adore him,
O come, let us adore him,
Christ the Lord!

Sing, choirs of angels,
Sing in exultation,
Sing, all ye citizens of heav'n above!
Glory to God, all glory in the highest:

Yea, Lord, we greet thee,
Born this happy morning;
Jesus, to thee be all glory giv'n!
Word of the Father, now in flesh appearing.

This text was originally written in Latin in the 1700s by John Francis Wade. It is still performed this way in many liturgical services. Translated by an Englishman a century later, we have the version sung every Christmas by millions of people. Its refrain is a beautiful invitation: "O come, let us adore him, Christ the Lord!"

How many of us, rushing through the busyness of the holidays, forget to slow down and sit in the presence of God? Even if we turn our attention to him for a moment, he is near. It can be in a waiting room or during holiday travel. Let us not neglect to take time to adore him, for his presence brings life and light to all who know him.

Lord Jesus, thank you for the gift of your presence. I come to you today with an open heart of adoration.

What Child Is This

The angel replied to her, "The Holy Spirit will come upon you,
and the power of the Most High will overshadow you.
Therefore, the holy one to be born will be called the Son of God."

LUKE 1:35 CSB

What Child is this, who, laid to rest,
On Mary's lap is sleeping?
Whom angels greet with anthems sweet,
While shepherds watch are keeping?

This, this is Christ, the King,
Whom shepherds guard and angels sing:
Haste, haste to bring him laud,
The babe, the Son of Mary!

Why lies he in such mean estate,
Where ox and ass are feeding?
Good Christian, fear: for sinners here
The silent Word is pleading.

So bring him incense, gold, and myrrh,
Come, peasant, king to own him.
The King of kings salvation brings;
Let loving hearts enthrone him.

The famous tune to which this hymn is sung is the old British "Greensleeves." The medieval tune remains iconic, though in modern times, it's mostly through association with this carol. The harmonies present in the tune are beautiful, and it does not need much instrumentation for the song to soar.

As you listen to this tune today, allow the declaration of the chorus to be triumphant as it is meant to be. Jesus is as worthy of our adoration and praise today as he ever was, and we can offer him our pure worship as we sing our surrender to his ways.

King Jesus, thank you for coming to the earth in such a gentle and unassuming way to reveal the kindness of the Father. Continue to reveal the Father's heart to me as I worship you.

Christmas Day Bells

"Glory to God in the highest,
and on earth peace
among those with whom he is pleased!"
LUKE 2:14 ESV

I heard the bells on Christmas day
Their old familiar carols play,
And wild and sweet the words repeat
Of peace of earth, good will to men.

And in despair I bowed my head:
"There is no peace on earth," I said,
"For hate is strong, and mocks the song
Of peace on earth, good will to men."

Then pealed the bells more loud and deep:
"God is not dead, nor doth he sleep;
The wrong shall fail, the right prevail,
With peace on earth, good will to men."

Till, ringing, singing on its way,
The world revolved from night to day
A voice, a chime, a chant sublime,
Of peace on earth, good will to men.

Written during the Civil War while Henry Wadsworth Longfellow was nursing his wounded son back to health, the text of this hymn illustrates the despair he felt as he heard the Christmas bells ringing in 1863. But like the psalmists before him, Longfellow did not end on a depressing note; he chose a hopeful one.

If you are struggling to know the peace of God during this holiday season, know that it is as palpable and near in our struggles as it is in calmer times. Hope is alive, and through Christ, there is "peace on earth, good will to men."

Jesus, you are my hope even when I can't sense the lightness of your load. You are close in chaos and in grief. Bring relief to my soul as I listen for your voice today.

DECEMBER 16

Little Bethlehem

The Lord himself will give you a sign:
The virgin will be pregnant.
She will have a son,
and she will name him Immanuel.

ISAIAH 7:14 NCV

O little town of Bethlehem,
How still we see thee lie!
Above thy deep and dreamless sleep
The silent stars go by;
Yet in thy dark streets shineth
The everlasting light.
The hopes and fears of all the years
Are met in thee tonight.

O holy child of Bethlehem,
Descend to us, we pray,
Cast out our sin and enter in,
Be born in us today.
We hear the Christmas angels
The great glad tidings tell;
O come to us, abide with us,
Our Lord Immanuel!

It was not a literal silent night, but Christ was born in the sleepy little town of Bethlehem without much ado other than the angels' proclamations. God meets us in ordinary places. Phillips Brooks wrote this hymn for the children at his church to sing during their Christmas program in 1867. He recalled the Christmas Eve he spent in Bethlehem on a trip to the Holy Land which was highly impactful for him. From this inspired memory, we have "O Little Town of Bethlehem."

God meets us in our silent nights when those around us are sleeping. Only God and the angels see what we go through. Fortunately, God is always ready to listen, comfort, and advise us.

Immanuel, I am grateful I am never alone. Meet me in the mundane of my life and be glorified in it.

Away in a Manger

She gave birth to her firstborn son;
and she wrapped Him in cloths, and laid Him in a manger,
because there was no room for them in the inn.

Luke 2:7 NASB

Away in a manger, no crib for a bed,
The little Lord Jesus laid down his sweet head.
The stars in the bright sky looked down where he lay,
The little Lord Jesus asleep on the hay.

The cattle are lowing, the baby awakes,
But little Lord Jesus no crying he makes.
I love you, Lord Jesus; look down from the sky,
And stay by my side until morning is nigh.

Be near me, Lord Jesus; I ask you to stay
Close by me forever and love me, I pray.
Bless all the dear children in your tender care,
And take us to heaven to live with you there.

An anonymous children's hymn, "Away in a Manger" first was published with the two original stanzas in 1885. Beneath the hymn was a notation claiming it was also known as "Luther's Cradle Hymn." Supposedly, it was composed by Martin Luther for his children. While we don't know if this was its true origin, the simple children's hymn is a comfort to young and old.

The third stanza encourages us to turn our hearts and attention to the Lord Jesus. It is an invitation for him to be near to us in good times and through the hardships of life. It's an apt prayer for every moment and season for ourselves and also for the vulnerable around us.

Lord Jesus, I ask you to stay close by me throughout the ebbs and flows of life. Please also be near to the children in my life. Watch over them and keep them close to your heart.

DECEMBER 18

O Come Emmanuel

"Behold, the virgin shall be with child, and bear a Son, and they shall call His name Immanuel," which is translated, "God with us."

MATTHEW 1:23 NKJV

O come, O come, Emmanuel,
And ransom captive Israel
That mourns in lonely exile here
Until the Son of God appear.

Rejoice! Rejoice! Emmanuel
Shall come to you, O Israel!

O come, O Root of Jesse,
Free your own from Satan's tyranny;
From depths of hell your people save,
And give them vict'ry o'er the grave.

O come, O Key of David, come,
And open wide our heav'nly home;
Make safe the way that leads on high,
And close the path to misery.

The text for this hymn comes from a Latin poem dating back to the eighth century. The version we now know and use was translated by John Mason Neale in 1851. Emmanuel means "God with us." Each time we sing this phrase, we invite "God with us" to be our comfort, joy, and salvation.

How have you experienced God with you? What has he done that makes your heart rejoice in his presence? Christ has come, and the Holy Spirit is near. You have all you need for fellowship with God, for Christ has made a way for you to come to the Father. He lavishes you in love and wraps around you with grace. Rejoice, for he is God with you.

Emmanuel, I can't fully express my gratitude to you for all you are, all you have done, and all you continue to do. I rejoice in your presence, and I take delight in your nearness.

Silent Night

The shepherds returned, glorifying and praising God
for all the things they had heard and seen,
which were just as they had been told.

LUKE 2:20 NIV

Silent night, holy night!
All is calm, all is bright
Round yon virgin mother and child.
Holy infant, so tender and mild,
Sleep in heavenly peace,
Sleep in heavenly peace.

Silent night, holy night!
Shepherds quake at the sight.
Glories stream from heaven afar,
Heav'nly hosts sing, alleluia!
Christ, the Savior, is born!
Christ, the Savior, is born!

Silent night, holy night!
Son of God, love's pure light
Radiant beams from thy holy face
With the dawn of redeeming grace,
Jesus, Lord, at thy birth,
Jesus, Lord, at thy birth.

Born out of necessity, this hymn was written for voice and guitar for the Christmas Eve service at St. Nicholas' Church in Austria in 1818. The church organ had broken down earlier that day, but the parish priest, Joseph Mohr, along with his organist, Franz Gruber, composed this now-beloved hymn so they would have music that evening.

Necessity, as the saying goes, is the mother of invention. This was true Christmas Eve 1818 in a town in Austria, and it can be true for each of us today. The next time our plans are thwarted, what creative solutions can we find? We may just find a beloved new path or tradition born out of unexpected circumstances.

Faithful One, you are never surprised by the things that surprise us. You are infinitely wise and creative, and I want to walk in faith and innovation when my plans are sidetracked. May I look for creative solutions and find joy as I do.

DECEMBER 20

Royal David's City

Now we see but a faint reflection of riddles and mysteries
as though reflected in a mirror, but one day we will see face-to-face.
My understanding is incomplete now, but one day
I will understand everything,
just as everything about me has been fully understood.

1 Corinthians 13:12 TPT

Once in royal David's city
Stood a lowly cattle shed,
Where a mother laid her baby
In a manger for his bed:
Mary was that mother mild,
Jesus Christ, her little child.

And our eyes at last shall see him,
Through his own redeeming love,
For that child, so dear and gentle,
Is our Lord in heav'n above,
And he leads his children on
To the place where he is gone.

Not in that poor, lowly stable
With the oxen standing by
We shall see him, but in heaven,
Set at God's right hand on high.
Then like stars his children crowned,
All in white, his praise will sound.

The author of this hymn, Cecil Frances Humphrey, published it in Hymns for Little Children in 1848. The collection was a compilation of thirteen hymns written to explain the Apostles' Creed to younger minds. "Once in Royal David's City" expounds on the phrase "who was conceived by the Holy Spirit, born of the Virgin Mary."

Christ's birth was only the beginning of the story. Let's not forget to look beyond his humble beginnings to the power of his life, ministry, and sacrifice. He rose again so we might be free from sin; he could offer us no better gift.

Lord Jesus, I trust one day I will see you fully, as I am fully seen and known now.

God Rest Ye Merry

This is a trustworthy saying, and everyone should accept it:
"Christ Jesus came into the world to save sinners"

1 Timothy 1:15 NLT

God rest you merry, gentlemen,
Let nothing you dismay;
Remember Christ, our Savior
Was born on Christmas Day
To save us all from Satan's pow'r
When we were gone astray.

O tidings of comfort and joy, comfort and joy,
O tidings of comfort and joy.

From God our heav'nly Father
A blessed angel came
And unto certain shepherds
Brought tidings of the same,
How that in Bethlehem was born
The son of God by name.

"Fear not," then said the angel,
"Let nothing you affright;
This day is born a Savior,
The true and radiant light,
To free all those who trust in him
From Satan's pow'r and might."

Perhaps one of the oldest Christmas carols, this hymn's origins are largely unkown. It was written as an English carol in the style of a folk ballad and had to be adapted for church use. The first publication of its verses was in a broadside paper in 1760. Charles Dickens even made mention of the carol in his play A Christmas Carol in 1843.

Wherever this season finds you, may you find "tidings of comfort and joy." Whatever challenges you face or unexpected hopes fill your heart, may you find in each one these tidings of great comfort and incandescent joy.

Savior, thank you for the power of your presence that fills me with joy and comfort in every season of my soul. You are my close confidante and my trustworthy friend and help.

DECEMBER 22

A Child Is Born

A child will be born for us, a son will be given to us,
and the government will be on his shoulders.
He will be named Wonderful Counselor, Mighty God,
Eternal Father, Prince of Peace.

Isaiah 9:6 CSB

For unto us a child is born,
Unto us a Son is given,
Unto us a Son is given:
And his name shall be called
Wonderful, Counselor,
The Mighty God,
The Everlasting Father,
The Prince of Peace,
The Everlasting Father,
The Prince of Peace.

Taken directly from Isaiah 9, the text of this portion of Handel's Messiah is a wonderful addition to any hymn sing of the season. It declares Scripture word for word. This is a practice we can incorporate into our personal devotional times with the Lord any time of the year.

What is one of your favorite Scriptures? Why not try setting it to a melody today, whether it's already a tune you know or one you improvise on the spot. The Lord loves our worship, and our hearts and minds may remember the truth of Scripture more readily when we sing it.

Wonderful Counselor, there is no one like you in all the earth. You are great and worthy to be praised. As I offer you my song, will you allow your truth to sink deeper into my consciousness? I long to worship you in spirit and truth.

Mortal Flesh Keep Silence

"The Lord is in his holy temple;
let all the earth keep silence before him."
Habakkuk 2:20 ESV

Let all mortal flesh keep silence
And with fear and trembling stand;
Ponder nothing earthly-minded,
For with blessing in his hand
Christ, our God, to earth descending,
Comes our homage to command.

King of kings, yet born of Mary,
As of old on earth he stood,
Lord of lords in human likeness,
In the body and the blood
He will give to all the faithful
His own self for heav'nly food.

Rank on rank the host of heaven
Spreads its vanguard on the way
As the light from light, descending
From the realms of endless day,
Comes the pow'rs of hell to vanquish
As the darkness clears away.

Perhaps you find yourself unfamiliar with today's hymn. It is one of the lesser-sung Christmas hymns but no less powerful and evocative. This version came to us in the nineteenth century, but the words are based on an ancient text, the Liturgy of St. James, specifically the "Prayer of the Cherubic Hymn" within it.

Our worship does not always need to take on a loud, outward form. It can be reverent and quiet, silently taking in the awe of who God is, what he has done, and his continued presence. In moments throughout your day, take time to silently acknowledge your King and Savior.

Jesus, I worship you in reverence. I am thankful I can do this quietly in my heart. Be honored in my life and receive the honor my heart and attention offer you.

O Holy Night

"The second command is this:
'Love your neighbor as you love yourself.'
There are no commands more important than these."

MARK 12:31 NCV

O holy night! The stars are brightly shining;
It is the night of the dear Savior's birth.
Long lay the world in sin and error pining,
Till he appeared and the soul felt its worth.
A thrill of hope—the weary world rejoices,
For yonder breaks a new and glorious morn!
Fall on your knees! O hear the angel voices!
O night divine, O night when Christ was born!
O night, O holy night, O night divine!

Truly he taught us to love one another;
His law is love and his gospel is peace.
Chains shall he break, for the slave is our brother,
And in his name all oppression shall cease.
Sweet hymns of joy in grateful chorus raise we;
Let all within us praise his holy name.
Christ is the Lord! O praise his name forever!
His pow'r and glory evermore proclaim!

This beloved Christmas hymn originated as a French carol. Its words were written by the French poet, Placide Cappeau, and its music was composed by Adolphe Charles Adam. An American, John Dwight, translated it into English in the nineteenth century. Through each of these unique and humble men, we have a hymn that evokes the holiness of God in a deeply moving way.

Not only does this hymn remind us of the baby Jesus, it also reminds us of powerful teachings of Christ. "He taught us to love one another; his law is love and his gospel is peace." When we show love to one another and offer peace, we reflect the power of Christ at work in our hearts. Honor the Lord and the holiness of his coming by choosing to love in word and deed today.

Holy One, this evening I celebrate your birth. You are the liberator of the oppressed and vulnerable. Help me display your law of love and gospel of peace.

Tell It on the Mountain

Go up on a high mountain, Zion, messenger of good news,
Raise your voice forcefully, Jerusalem, messenger of good news;
Raise it up, do not fear. Say to the cities of Judah, "Here is your God!"

ISAIAH 40:9 NASB

Go tell it on the mountain,
Over the hills, and ev'rywhere;
Go, tell it on the mountain
That Jesus Christ is born.

While shepherds kept their watching
O'er silent flocks by night,
Behold, throughout the heavens
There shone a holy light.

The shepherds feared and trembled
When lo, above the earth
Rang out the angel chorus
That hailed our Savior's birth.

Down in a lowly manger
The humble Christ was born,
And God sent us salvation
That blessed Christmas morn.

An African American contribution to the Christmas canon, "Go, Tell it on the Mountain," is a beloved spiritual whose text was first printed in 1907 by John Wesley Work Jr. Work, and his two sons after him, made it their mission to study, collect, and publish the extraordinary spirituals of African Americans created as an oral tradition under slavery. The refrain of this hymn was and remains a declaraction of God's deliverance for his people.

Christ is our hope, deliverer, and Savior. He is the fulfillment of every promise, and in him we find our peace, joy, and liberty. May we join with those who in oppression sang the good news that stands the test of time: "Jesus Christ is born."

Mighty Deliverer, what good news awaits us all as we realize the power of your coming. You have not gone into hiding; the freedom of your love is available now.

DECEMBER 26

All People on Earth

They sang responsively, praising and giving thanks to the Lord: "For He is good, For His mercy endures forever toward Israel."

Ezra 3:11 NKJV

All people that on earth do dwell,
Sing to the Lord with cheerful voice.
Serve him with joy, his praises tell,
Come now before him and rejoice!

Know that the Lord is God indeed;
He formed us all without our aid.
We are the flock he comes to feed,
The sheep who by his hand were made.

O enter then his gates with joy,
Within his courts his praise proclaim.
Let thankful songs your tongues employ.
O bless and magnify his name.

Trust that the Lord our God is good,
His mercy is forever sure.
His faithfulness at all times stood
And shall from age to age endure.

Written during the Reformation when many British protestants were driven from their homeland to seek safety, William Kethe penned this hymn in Geneva. Learning from and inspired by the French disciples around him, he and others worked to paraphrase psalms into metrical verse. "All People" is a paraphrase of Psalm 100.

Compare Psalm 100 with the musical paraphrase before you now. What stands out to you the most? The Lord often uses fresh revelation and language to awaken our hearts to the depths of his truth.

Lord, thank you for the power of your Word that stands the test of time. Speak to me in new ways as I revisit familiar themes and verses. Bring revelation to alight my heart and mind with the profound beauty of your truth.

Worship the King

"Thrones were set in place, and the Ancient of Days took his seat.
His clothing was as white as snow; the hair of his head was white like wool.
His throne was flaming with fire, and its wheels were all ablaze."

DANIEL 7:9 NIV

O worship the King all-glorious above,
O gratefully sing his power and his love:
Our shield and defender, the Ancient of Days,
Pavilioned in splendor and girded with praise.

O tell of his might and sing of his grace,
Whose robe is the light, whose canopy space.
His chariots of wrath the deep
thunderclouds form,
And dark is his path on the wings of the storm.

Your bountiful care, what tongue can recite?
It breathes in the air, it shines in the light;
It streams from the hills, it descends to the
plain,
And sweetly distills in the dew and the rain.

O measureless might, unchangeable love,
Whom angels delight to worship above!
Your ransomed creation, with glory ablaze,
In true adoration shall sing to your praise!

Written as a meditation on the theme of creation presented in Psalm 104, Robert Grant's 1833 hymn encourages us to see the power of God through creation's story as well as through the redemptive power of Christ's love. Does a specific part of creation fill you with awe? Perhaps you sense it when you are standing by open water stretching as far as the eye can see. Maybe you feel it most among majestic mountains or through images from the depths of space.

Whatever leads you to sense the greatness of God, take time to connect to it today and allow it to lead you in praise to the throne of your God. You may not be able to transport yourself to your favorite place today, but the Spirit of God ushers you to the throne of the King of kings no matter where you are.

Majestic One, thank you for the power of your wisdom paired with your love. I am in awe of you.

God Is Working

Go ahead—let everyone know it!
Tell the world how he broke through and delivered you
from the power of darkness
and has gathered us together from all over the world.
He has set us free to be his very own!

Psalm 107:2-3 TPT

God is working this purpose out,
As year succeeds to year;
God is working this purpose out,
And the time is drawing near;
Nearer and nearer draws the time,
the time that shall surely be:
When the earth shall be filled with the glory
of God
As the waters cover the sea.

Let us go forth in the strength of God,
With the banner of Christ unfurled,
That the light of the glorious gospel of truth
May shine throughout the world.
Let us all fight with sorrow and sin
To set the captives free,
That the earth may be filled with the glory
of God
As the waters cover the sea.

God is infinitely wise and works together threads that seem completely out of place. He weaves them together into the tapestry of his great mercy. Nothing is wasted in his kingdom, and he will continue to faithfully work out his promises in the earth. With the confidence of God's strength and sovereignty, we can join with his purposes in our lives.

As you think through the last year, what areas are you proud of? In which areas do you want to grow in the coming year? Even as you recognize God's faithful thread of mercy through your life, decide how you want to partner with him and promote his purposes.

Mighty God, I see your hand on my life. Help me continue to follow your ways.

Thy Mercy and Grace

As for me, I will sing about your power.
Each morning I will sing with joy about your unfailing love.
For you have been my refuge,
a place of safety when I am in distress.

Psalm 59:16 NLT

For thy mercy and thy grace,
Faithful through another year,
Hear our song of thankfulness;,
Jesus, our Redeemer, hear.

In our weakness and distress,
Rock of Strength, be thou our stay;
In the pathless wilderness
Be our true and living way.

Keep us faithful, keep us pure,
Keep us evermore thine own.
Help, O help us to endure,
Fit us for thy promised crown.

So within thy palace gate
We shall praise on golden strings
Thee, the only potentate,
Lord of lords and King of kings.

Written specifically for the New Year by Henry Downton in 1841, this hymn gives us opportunity to give thanks for the passing year and ask for God's grace and help in the coming one. When we take time to remember the victories, reliefs, and challenges we have waded through, our remembrance may turn to grateful joy.

The God who faithfully walked us through this year will faithfully go with us into the next. There is no challenge he cannot help us overcome. No circumstance surprises him. We can throw the anchor of our hope into the great sea of his mercy and trust him to do what we cannot on our own.

Faithful Father, your presence makes my life lighter. You are my close comfort, overwhelming joy, and present help in times of trouble. I can't begin to thank you for all the ways you have kept me. Give me peace as I cling to you.

Founded on God

May the God of hope fill you with all joy and peace as you believe so that you may overflow with hope by the power of the Holy Spirit.

ROMANS 15:13 CSB

All my hope on God is founded;
He doth still my trust renew.
Me through change and chance he guideth,
Only good and only true.
God unknown, he alone
Calls my heart to be his own.

God's great goodness aye endureth,
Deep his wisdom, passing thought:
Splendor, light, and life attend him,
Beauty springeth out of naught.
Evermore, from his store
New-born worlds rise and adore.

Daily doth th' Almighty giver
Bounteous gifts on us bestow;
His desire our soul delighteth,
Pleasure leads us where we go.
Love doth stand, at his hand;
Joy doth wait on his command.

Originally written in German by Joachim Neander in the seventeenth century, this hymn was translated into English by Robert Bridges in the early twentieth century. Bridges was an English poet who started out as a doctor. He became a poet laureate when he was sixty-nine. It is never too late to discover a new passion in life or to pursue it.

If you feel as if your best days are behind you, perhaps today is a good day to research the many people who achieved success in new fields late in life. As long as you are living, there is hope, purpose, and joy to uncover. Don't disqualify yourself from a new adventure. May all your hope be founded on God.

Almighty One, in your kingdom, there are always fresh chances and new opportunities. Breathe hope on the desires of my heart and bless the work of my hands.

DECEMBER 31

Blessings of the Year

Praise the Lord, God our Savior,
who helps us every day.
PSALM 68:19 NCV

For all the blessings of the year,
For all the friends we hold so dear,
For peace on earth, both far and near,
We give you thanks, O Lord.

For life and health, those common things,
Which ev'ry day and hour brings,
For home, where our affection clings,
We give you thanks, O Lord.

For your great love which never tires,
Which all our better thought inspires,
And warms our lives with heav'nly fires,
We give you thanks, O Lord.

Although there isn't much information about this 1909 hymn's author, Albert Hutchinson, it is a great hymn to offer praise and thanks to God specifically for the last year. It is simple in its construction and theme, and that simplicity may appeal to those who don't love to spend too much time thinking about the past.

Instead of focusing on every detail you can from the last year, use this hymn as a simple prayer to close it out. You can give thanks to God for the generosity of his goodness without specific examples. You can release the bad, the good, and all that is past with a simple prayer of thanks. Let go of what you no longer need to hold.

Lord, thank you for the understanding you show, the faithfulness of your presence, and the promise of your comfort, peace, and joy in the days to come. For all this and more, I give you thanks, O Lord.